Higher Education Management

SRHE and Open University Press Imprint
General Editor: Heather Eggins

Current titles include:

Higher Education Management

The Key Elements

Edited by
David Warner and
David Palfreyman

The Society for Research into Higher Education
& Open University Press

Dedicated to my Parents

David Palfreyman

Published by SRHE and
Open University Press
Celtic Court
22 Ballmoor
Buckingham
MK18 1XM

email: enquiries@openup.co.uk
world wide web: http://www.openup.co.uk

and 325 Chestnut Street
Philadelphia, PA 19106, USA

First Published 1996
Reprinted 2000

A catalogue record of this book is available from the British Library

ISBN 0 335 19569 5 (pb)   0 335 19570 9 (hb)

Library of Congress Cataloging-in-Publication Data
Higher education management : the key elements / edited by David
  Warner and David Palfreyman.
      p.   cm.
    Includes bibliographical references and index.
    ISBN 0–335–19570–9 (hardcover). — ISBN 0–335–19569–5 (pbk.)
    1. Education, Higher—Great Britain—Administration.   I. Warner,
  David, 1947– .   II. Palfreyman, David, 1954–
  LB2341.8.G7H55   1996   96–3296
  378.1'01—dc20   CIP

Typeset by Graphicraft Limited, Hong Kong

Printed and bound in Great Britain by
Marston Lindsay Ross International Ltd,
Oxfordshire

Contents

Notes on Contributors

The views expressed in this book are those of each contributor and are not necessarily those of his or her employer.

David Adamson is Bursar of the University of Bristol, with a very wide range of responsibilities, including the management of an estate comprising 360 buildings and a recurrent budget in excess of £12 million. Until 1987, he worked around the world as an engineer and manager with the army, the United Nations and various construction companies.

Frank Albrighton has been Director of Public Affairs at the University of Birmingham since 1981. Before that he held a similar post at the University of East Anglia. He is author of two 'good practice guides' published by the then Conference of University Administrators: *Can I Quote You on That?*, a guide to working with the media, and *Open Daze*. With Julia Thomas, he was joint editor of the magazine *Development in Education*, which existed from 1991 to 1993.

Barry Benjamin is Head of Management Accounting at the University of the West of England, Bristol. He was responsible for the financial preparation of the institution for incorporation during the period 1987–9, while in the post-incorporation phase he has been actively involved in developing devolved budgeting and the supporting financial reporting infrastructure within the institution. Previously, he worked primarily within the private sector with a number of UK multinational companies in a senior finance role.

Mark Clark worked in the private sector before starting a career in university management at the University of Warwick, where he has held posts in research management and management of earned-income programmes, and currently works in industrial development.

Sue Dopson is a Lecturer in Management Studies at the University of Oxford and Fellow of Templeton College. Prior to these appointments, she was a

Research Fellow at Templeton and a personnel manager in the National Health Service. Sue's research interests include the nature of managerial work, changes in the role of the middle manager, career issues for managers, management in the public sector and managing with professionals.

Diana Eastcott joined the Learning Methods Unit at the University of Central England in Birmingham in 1983, where her main focus is to work with academic staff to develop and sustain the quality of teaching and learning across the University. She has published on many aspects of improving student learning, active learning and independent learning, and has run a wide range of workshops, courses and consultancies.

Bob Farmer is Head of the Learning Methods Unit at the University of Central England in Birmingham, a position he has held since 1989. He came into higher education from the Royal Air Force and, following a period in teacher education, has had 14 years' experience as a teacher and consultant in staff development.

John Gledhill is the Academic Registrar at Coventry University. After completing his PhD at the University of London in 1973, he worked for two years at the then Hatfield Polytechnic (now the University of Hertfordshire) before joining the University of Warwick and then moving to Coventry.

Alison Hall joined the Personnel Office of Loughborough University of Technology in 1989, having previously carried out research in virology and molecular biology. She has a generalist personnel role, concerned principally with academic and related staff. Alison was seconded to the Universities and Colleges Employers Association in 1994, where her responsibilities included industrial relations policy development and the renegotiation of a major national collective agreement.

Colin Harrison is Professor of Educational Technology, Dean of the Faculty of Educational Services and Pro-Vice-Chancellor at Anglia Polytechnic University. He has published widely on many aspects of academic support services and his books include the widely read *Basics of Librarianship*, which is now in its third edition.

John Hogan is Academic Registrar at the University of Durham. He gained a doctorate at the University of Sussex before starting his managerial career at the University of Warwick, where he specialized in postgraduate matters. John is General Secretary of the Council for Graduate Education.

Ian McNay is a professor at Anglia Polytechnic University. He heads the Centre for Higher Education Management, which offers bespoke courses, consultancy, organization development and research services in the UK and overseas. Ian has worked as an academic and manager on both sides of the former binary line, and in Belgium and Spain.

David Palfreyman is the Bursar of and a Fellow of New College, Oxford, having previously worked at the Universities of Liverpool and Warwick. He is heavily involved in management development programmes, being the joint director of the annual CVCP/UCoSDA course for UK higher education managers and a director of the annual Warwick/Oxford course for managers of overseas HE institutions. David has written extensively on the management of universities and is a member of the editorial boards of the magazine *Managing Higher Education* and of the new AUA journal *Perspectives.*

Derek Phillips is Director of Domestic Services at the University of Exeter, a post he has held since 1972. Prior to that, he worked in local government and for the Southern Universities Management Services Unit. Derek is also Managing Director of Exeter Enterprises Ltd (the consultancy company of the university) and Secretary of the Conference of University Business Officers.

Russell Rowley is Director of Student Services at the University of Central England in Birmingham. Over a number of years he has been responsible for the development of a range of coordinated student support services. Russell is currently Chair of the Association of Managers of Student Services in Higher Education.

John Sandbach is Director of Finance at the University of Liverpool, having previously held appointments at the Universities of Durham and Reading. He is a member of the Chartered Institute of Public Finance and Accountancy and chairman of that Institute's Higher and Further Education Panel. He is a Fellow of the Royal Society of Arts, Industry and Commerce and a contributor to many publications.

Paddy Stephenson has been the Secretary and Registrar of UMIST since 1986. Prior to that, he worked at the Universities of Warwick, Sussex and Nottingham. He has taken a particular interest in administrative staff career development matters, and at various times has been chairman of the CUA Staff Development Committee, a member of the UCoSDA Activities Review Committee and chairman of the CUA Corporate Planning Forum, and has contributed to a variety of staff development courses.

Harold Thomas is an education consultant with over 25 years' experience as a university manager. After commencing his career at the University of Wales registry he moved first to the University of Bristol, where he became Deputy Registrar and then Financial Planning Manager, and subsequently to the University of Essex as Academic Registrar. Harold is a Fellow of the Institute of Chartered Secretaries and Administrators and was recently awarded a PhD for a study on the implementation of devolved, formula-based systems of resource allocation.

Julia Thomas is Deputy Director of Public Affairs at the University of Birmingham, where she is responsible for publications, media relations and alumni relations. She entered university public relations from a background in publishing. She has acted as consultant editor to the United Nations High Commission for Refugees in Geneva and was, with Frank Albrighton, joint editor of *Development in Education*. Publications that Julia edits at Birmingham have won nine prizes in the Heist annual awards competition, four of them gaining first prizes.

David Warner is a professor and Pro-Vice-Chancellor at the University of Central England in Birmingham, having previously worked in a school, an FE college and the Universities of East Anglia and Warwick. He has published extensively on many aspects of educational management and is the co-editor of *Visual and Corporate Identity, Managing Educational Property* and *Human Resource Management in Higher and Further Education* (Open University Press), co-author of *The Income Generation Handbook* and editor of the journal *International Education*.

Selected Abbreviations

ABRC	Advisory Board for the Research Councils
APU	Anglia Polytechnic University
AUA	Association of University Administrators (previously the Conference of University Administrators)
AUCF	average unit of council funding
AUDE	Association of University Directors of Estates
AUT	Association of University Teachers
BES	business expansion scheme
BMS	building management services
BUAC	British Universities Accommodation Consortium
CCTV	closed circuit television
CHE	college of higher education
CHEEP	Consortium for Higher Education Energy Purchasing
CIPFA	Chartered Institute of Public Finance and Accounting
CNAA	Council for National Academic Awards
CONNECT	the marketing brand name of the Higher Education Accommodation Consortium
CSNs	contract student numbers
CSUP	Committee of Scottish University Principals
CUA	Conference of University Administrators (now the Association of University Administrators)
CVCP	Committee of Vice-Chancellors and Principals
DES	Department of Education and Science (renamed Department for Education and now Department for Education and Employment)
DfE	Department for Education
DevR	development research
DR	dual support
EC	European Community
EEA	European Economic Area
EP(C)A	Employment Protection (Consolidation) Act

ERA	Education Reform Act (1988)
ERDF	European Regional Development Fund
ESF	European Social Fund
ESRC	Economic and Social Research Council
ETAP	effective teaching and assessment programme
EU	European Union
FE	further education
FT	full-time
FTE	full-time equivalent
GALA	guidance and learner autonomy
GR	generic research
HE	higher education
HEBE	Higher Education Business Enterprises
HEFCE	Higher Education Funding Council for England
HEI	higher education institution
HEIST	Higher Education Information Services Trust
HEQC	Higher Education Quality Council
HESA	Higher Education Statistics Agency
HMOs	houses in multiple occupation
IP	intellectual property
IPD	Institute of Personnel and Development
IRLR	Industrial Relations Law Reports
ISDX–PABX	integrated services digital exchange–private automatic branch exchange
IT	information technology
JANET	Joint Academic Network (to be upgraded to SUPERJANET)
JCT	Joint Contracts Tribunal
LBC	listed building consent
MAC	management and administrative computing
MASNs	maximum aggregate student numbers
MCI	management charter initiative
NALGO	National Association of Local Government Officers
NATFHE	National Association of Teachers in Further and Higher Education
NEC	new engineering contract
NPC	National Postgraduate Committee
NVQ	National Vocational Qualification
OECD	Organisation for Economic Co-operation and Development
PCE	post-compulsory education
PCFC	Polytechnics and Colleges Funding Council
PGCE	postgraduate certificate in education
PGR	postgraduate research
PGT	postgraduate taught
PIs	performance indicators
PSI	Policy Studies Institute
PT	part-time

PVC	pro-vice-chancellor
QR	quality-related research
RAE	research assessment exercise
RBL	resource-based learning
SCAMAD	Standing Conference on the Accreditation of Management and Administrative Development Programmes
SEDA	Staff and Educational Development Association
SSS	student support services
SWOT	strengths, weaknesses, opportunities and threats
TEED	Training, Enterprise and Education Directorate
TQM	total quality management
TUCO	The University Catering Officers
TURERA	Trade Union Reform and Employment Rights Act
UCAS	Universities and Colleges Admissions Service
UCoSDA	Universities and Colleges Staff Development Agency (previously USDTU)
UFC	Universities Funding Council (replaced by the national Higher Education Funding Councils)
UG	undergraduate
UGC	Universities Grants Committee (replaced by the Universities Funding Council)
USDTU	Universities Staff Development and Training Unit (now UCoSDA)
UKCGE	UK Council for Graduate Education
USR	Universities Statistical Record
USS	universities superannuation scheme

1

Setting the Scene

David Palfreyman and David Warner

The use and scope of the book

Everyone who works in higher education (HE hereafter) quickly becomes aware that our institutions contain two different types of managers: those who run academic departments or units (i.e. primarily for teaching, research or a combination of both), and those who run service departments or units, whether they be essentially academic in nature, such as the registry or the library, or more obviously of a physical support character, such as portering, residential accommodation or estates. Many of the former have accepted the title of 'manager' only with some reluctance, and many of the latter have been traditionally, and still are, called by the former (and sometimes by themselves) 'administrators'. *Higher Education Management* provides comprehensive coverage of the key functions of these 'administrators', although the editors believe that it will also be of considerable value to academic managers, who should become more aware of the way in which their institutions are run outside of their relatively narrow domains.

Higher Education Management has been written by a mixed team of senior managers and academics in such a way that it can be read straight through to gain a full picture. The editors firmly believe that, whatever specialist area one is working in, it is essential to know about related areas of management. This holistic approach is becoming essential for all managers now that there is such a strong emphasis on strategic planning. Moreover, as managers move up the hierarchy, then such 'helicopter vision' becomes a *sine qua non* of success.

At the same time, each chapter has been constructed to be free-standing and to provide a fairly in-depth treatment of the topic it covers. Readers are invited to reflect upon the tasks they currently perform and to compare their approach with the best practice described herein from other related areas. The editors have, therefore, added a brief comment at the head of each chapter and removed inconsistencies, but have not attempted to homogenize individual styles, or to eliminate repetition that is necessary to understand a chapter read in isolation.

The remainder of this chapter will explore the administration–management debate: the relative roles of 'pure administrators' and academics as managers, and the differing roles of each in the chartered universities and in the former polytechnics and institutes of higher education. Throughout this book we have used the terms 'chartered' and 'statutory' universities to distinguish between those institutions which were universities before the Education Reform Act (ERA) of 1988 and the Further and Higher Education Act of 1992 ('chartered') and those which were created by these statutes ('statutory'). This avoids the confusion inherent in the terms 'traditional' or 'old' university and 'new' university, because the former category comprises a very wide range of universities established over a period of some six centuries and includes at least two groups which have previously been called 'new' (for example, New College, Oxford, founded in the late fourteenth century, and the 'new' or 'plate glass' universities founded in the mid-1960s). We will then briefly consider the history of higher education (primarily university) 'administration' as a profession, or at least a career, before, finally, examining the evolving function of the 'administrator' or manager in educational institutions of ever-increasing size, complexity and variety of activity.

Administrator or manager?

The Concise Oxford Dictionary (1982) defines 'administration' as: 'management (of business); management of public affairs, government; the ministry; the Government . . .'; an 'administrator' is a 'manager (of business or public affairs); one capable of organising; one who performs official duties . . .' A 'manager' is defined as: 'person conducting a business, institution, etc.', while 'the management' is 'governing body, board of directors', and 'to manage' is to 'organize, regulate, be manager of, (household, institution, State) . . . gain one's ends with (person, etc.) by tact, flattery, dictation, etc.' It is perhaps this implication in the last phrase that being a manager suggests *manipulating* others ('gain one's ends'), as well as impersonal resources, that makes it, in some HE cultures, 'a dirty word'.

Thus, catering might be in the control of the 'catering manager' or the 'catering officer' and, even in the most conservative institution, the price of chips is no longer set by a committee: the officer or manager really does manage. One is, however, much less likely to encounter a 'departmental manager' or a 'faculty manager' rather than a 'departmental administrator' or a 'faculty secretary', lest this implies that academics, like humble catering employees, or 'inputs' such as chips, are in need of, and susceptible to, management; least of all by a non-academic as opposed to, say, a 'dean' or a 'head (chair) of department' (who is still unlikely to be styled 'academic staff manager' or similar).

It is the contention of the editors that discussion and conflict over the use of the terms 'administrator' or 'manager', 'administration' or 'management', is a sterile division in the context of this book. The function being carried out is something that 'the real world' would readily recognize as running an operation with certain limited resources and within set parameters in the most economical and efficient way compatible with being effective in achieving agreed objectives. In the private sector one might find this function being performed by a 'chief executive', 'general manager' or 'managing director' for a whole company, while the 'production manager', the 'marketing manager' or (interestingly) the 'company secretary' looks after a specific area. In the HE institutions we will find 'vice-chancellor', 'director', 'principal', 'dean', 'head/chair of department', 'directors of finance, personnel and estates', 'faculty secretary' and 'print room manager'. This is a confusing mix of terminology, which is exacerbated when one remembers that the formal title of a head of an HE corporation created by the ERA is 'chief executive'.

Whether our national representative body is the Association of University Administrators (AUA) or the Association of University Managers is of little consequence in terms of the daily routine working lives of its members. Whether universities are administered by government or managed like a biscuit factory might be of relevance in the collegiality–managerialism debate discussed at length in Chapter 2, but it is not a *major* issue of concern to this book, with its emphasis on practice and its likely readership. From now on, the terms 'manager' and 'management' (except in quotations and in historical contexts) will be used, rather than 'administrator' and 'administration' – which at least means the volume will be fractionally shorter!

A confusion of titles, grades, terms and conditions, and job descriptions

Until the mid-1970s chartered university manager posts were spread over many and varied short grades, differing from institution to institution. Then came a national system of grades largely mirroring the academic salary scales and involving membership of the same pension scheme (Universities' Superannuation Scheme) and of the same union (Association of University Teachers, AUT) as 'academic-related senior administrative staff'. More recently the grades have been rearranged slightly, but the principle remains the same: managers, as opposed to clerical officers or secretaries, in the chartered universities are roughly on a par with similar professionally qualified staff in HE libraries and with their academic colleagues in departments and faculties. The only key differences are that they usually did not have tenure even before its abolition by the ERA in 1988 (although the registrar probably did, and many senior managers at Oxford did), that they tend to work fixed (minimum) hours and have specified leave, and that they more obviously work within an hierarchy. Apart from those with a specific professional background – accountants, surveyors – and a few who have worked their way through from clerical posts, almost all such staff are graduates, and at some HE institutions those entering the registry often have similar academic qualifications to those taking up arts or social sciences academic posts. Very recently, however, there has been talk of uncoupling 'senior administrative staff' posts from the academic pay negotiations and national scales – back to the 1960s position!

Before the ERA the statutory universities were at the apex of the local government system of education. As a result, their managers were graded as local government officers (and therefore considerably lower than their academic colleagues) and there were very few senior professional posts because these functions were undertaken by staff in the appropriate departments of the relevant local authority. Since independence, the situation has begun to alter and more, better paid, managers have been injected into the institutions. However, gradings and terms and conditions of service are much more local than in the chartered universities; those managers who are members of a union (and many senior managers are not) do not belong to the 'academic' union (NATFHE) but to Unison (previously NALGO), and the managers contribute to a different pension scheme (the Local Government Pension Scheme) from their academic colleagues, who participate in the Teachers' Superannuation Scheme. Moreover, the same titled post in a statutory university may well have a somewhat different job description and expectation of the qualifications and experience of the post-holder from apparently the same job in a chartered university.

The permanent pro-vice-chancellor (PVC) phenomenon

The reason for this variation in the roles and powers of some senior managers in statutory universities when compared with chartered universities stems partially from the history of the appointments as described above and partially from what we call 'the permanent pro-vice-chancellor phenomenon'. In chartered universities the position of PVC (there are commonly three) is usually filled by a senior academic for a period of three or four years. However, there is an expectation that each PVC will return in due course to his or her substantive academic post and that very few staff will be appointed directly to support these PVCs.

In the statutory universities, the PVCs are appointed to permanent posts and adopt clearly defined areas of responsibility, both executive and strategic, with staff reporting directly to them. These two factors of permanence and support staff mean that PVCs are likely to be far more powerful in the statutory than in the chartered universities and that the senior posts in the non-academic management team (and especially its head) are correspondingly weaker. This clear-cut distinction between the position of PVCs in the statutory and chartered universities is, of course, blurred in many institutions and change is undoubtedly in the air. However, the principle holds and is at the centre of the collegiality–managerialism debate dealt with later in the book.

Them and us

In almost all HE institutions, there is a 'them' and 'us' aspect to the manager–academic relationship, which will vary from nothing more sinister than staff club banter – the registry table with its more formally dressed occupants standing out among the tables of 'jeans and jumpers' academics (at least in 1960s institutions) – to real conflict and tension, especially at a time of cuts, when perhaps the one topic that academic departments can agree on is the need to prune the 'management'. Such a 'them and us' mentality can be found in other organizations where there is a bureaucracy that must interact with professionals, such as the National Health Service (NHS), and it is not necessarily unhealthy, providing the 'management' earns the respect of the academics it supports, not by being servile but by being competent, economical and effective, and by being a vital part of the extensive team of talents needed to make a modern HE institution function properly.

Some degree of 'them and us' is virtually unavoidable, since it often falls to the 'management' to enforce institutional rules and regulations that appear at times to some rank-and-file academics as irksome, or to point at harsh and unpalatable facts of financial life that are unwelcome to faculty boards or similar. It is perhaps easier if such officialdom comes in a form that has a similar academic pedigree, from colleagues with whom the academics may well socialize, who are neither paid as inferior underlings nor elevated well above their academic colleagues in superior offices on special 'remuneration packages'. Mintzberg (1983: 199) looks at the role of 'administrators' within 'the professional bureaucracy', and his comments will strike a chord with most HE institutional managers:

> The professional administrator spends much time handling disturbances in the structure . . . the professional administrators – especially those at higher levels – serve key roles at the boundary of the organisation, between the professionals inside and interested parties – governments, client associations, and so on – on the outside . . . the professional becomes dependent on the *effective* [our emphasis] administrator.

Raelin (1985: 270) speaks on the same subject:

> The inherent conflict between managers and professionals results basically from a clash of cultures: the corporate culture, which captures the commitment of managers, and the professional culture, which socializes professionals . . . Since professionals are by nature individualistic and resent conformity to regulations imposed upon them from

outside the profession, it is no wonder that they tend to disregard procedures used to standardize some decision-making in their organisations ... The ideal is that one day professional accomplishment will become consonant with managerial proficiency.

Jarratt (1985: 33) noted, in criticizing the collegial model of chartered university governance, the existence of 'large and powerful academic departments together with individual academics who sometimes see their academic discipline as more important than the long-term well-being of the university which houses them'.

A little history

Moodie and Eustace (1974: 11) began their text by noting how little had been written about university government since, in 1213, the Chancellor of the University of Paris lamented: 'In the old days when ... the name of Universities was unknown, lectures ... were more frequent and there was more zeal for study. But now that you are invited into a University, lectures are rare, things are hurried and little is learned, the time taken for lectures being spent in Meetings and discussions.' No doubt 1990s UK hospital doctors would say much the same about the recent NHS 'reforms'. Meetings, however, need agendas first and minutes later, and agendas and minutes give rise, sooner or later, to full-time professional bureaucrats, and hence the 'ancient', or rather medieval, universities of Oxford and Cambridge had their registrars to record decisions, to enter student names on rolls, to maintain the list of graduates. Gradually the registrar got a deputy, and the deputy needed an assistant and so on.

Hence Moodie and Eustace devote Chapter 7 to 'The bureaucracy', the 'officials', people then barely tolerated at Oxbridge, where the cult of the gentleman academic amateur remained strong well into the 1970s, and even today is still seen in the way that busy academics take on a stint as 'senior tutor' or 'tutor for admissions' within their colleges, performing administrative duties undertaken by assistant registrars at other universities. As Moodie and Eustace (1974: 156) comment,

The strong anarchic element in the outlook of academics in this country has always tended to the view, as Merton College, Oxford, has put it [in evidence to the Franks Commission of Enquiry (1966) on the running of the University of Oxford in the mid-1960s] that 'education in general and university education par excellence are worlds in which the administrator should be kept in his place' ... This view has largely prevailed ... The bureaucracy in fact was not professionalised until quite recently and the Register typically was a former lecturer of limited academic distinction ... His few assistants, even if graduates, were usually of much lower calibre ... No longer, however, is it remotely possible to run a university with 'three men and a boy' helped by two typists and the Vice-Chancellor's Secretary. There has therefore grown up since the mid-fifties, a large new career in university administration.

One is reminded of 1950s *Carry on Doctor* films, where the hospital was run by the consultant (the domineering black-jacketed and pin-stripe trousered James Robertson Justice) and the matron (the formidable and starched Hattie Jacques), and the concept of 'unit managers', 'management accountants' or, even worse, 'management consultants' in shiny well-cut suits lay in the distant future.

Moodie and Eustace (1974: 161–2) saw the key job of the university administrator as

> to make it possible for decisions to be taken at the right time, by the right people, and on the basis of proper information [and] once decisions are taken, the officials are expected to ensure that they are carried out. [They are also] the guardians of established procedures [with the result that] friction is unavoidable, it being in the nature of bureaucracies to stress rules and of professionals [academics, social workers, doctors] to stress their own exceptional cases.

The officials, however, are not just facilitators, but also initiators, their initiatives often arising from the fact that they are the institution's eyes, ears, conscience and memory, in contrast to committee members who serve and go. Increasingly they are also collators and analysts of information concerning the measurement of performance and the spread of 'best practice' as institutions compare themselves (sometimes against selected comparators–'benchmarking') or are compared against national norms by external agencies. On the whole, the authors did not see university administrators as a threat to academic decision- and policy-making: 'In general, the vast majority of university officials regard their duty as seeing to it only that the essential decisions are taken, and taken on the most reasonable grounds possible. They do not believe that they should themselves take these decisions; but if no one else comes forward to take them the bureaucrats may have to' (Moodie and Eustace, 1974: 169). Halsey and Trow (1971: 124) at a similar time noted: 'The administrative staff of British universities appears . . . small in numbers and strongly conditioned to subservience to the academic will.'

The history of the growth of the role and number of university officials is told in Bosworth's (1986) *Beyond the Limelight: Essays on the Occasion of the Silver Jubilee of the Conference of University Administrators.* The volume tells the story of how certain young administrators (Currie, Lockwood, Bosworth and Walsh) at the University of Manchester set up regular annual meetings of university managers, which now involve gatherings of 1500 or more, and of how gradually the Manchester registrar's (Vincent Knowles) model of appointing 'bright, young things' as assistants caught on (even if, at times, they were given rather boring tasks): 'His administrative assistants were able, sociable, enjoyed discussions, could hold their own with academic colleagues, knew a lot about the place and wanted to find out more... something of an elite' (Bosworth, 1986: 4). The attitude of their seniors to the idea of the juniors meeting up in this way 'ranged from ambiguous support to outright hostility'. The gang, thankfully, pressed on; the meetings, like Topsy, grew and grew, moving steadily around the country, with sessions from the 1960s which sound remarkably familiar in the 1990s: 'The changing pattern of the British university system', 'The universities and government – the latest developments', 'The training of university administrators', 'The public image of the universities', 'Universities and society' and 'The management of universities'. One young Turk, Mike Shattock, now registrar at the University of Warwick, is quoted as calling for enhanced administrative training (Bosworth, 1986: 15–16):

> The fact remains that whole areas of university administration now depend upon them ['professional techniques'] and will, I fear, do so increasingly in the future... We are taking on an ever increasing number of academically well-qualified young graduates and progressively rendering them quite unfit for return to the outside world... If we do not discuss this this year a further year will have elapsed and we may be left commenting on something worked out by our not noticeably progressive masters.

But things did eventually progress, involving not only the Conference of University Administrators (CUA) but also the Committee of Vice-Chancellors and Principals (CVCP), via its Administrative Staff Training Committee, and the AUT, although whether the 'profession' will yet get a marketable and portable qualification which might assist its members to return to 'the outside world' remains to be seen, as the Universities' and Colleges' Staff Development Agency (see UCoSDA, 1995) sets up a standing conference to explore the possibility of a Master in Business Administration (Higher Education Management), or similar, offered in a network of centres across the country. Chapter 3 of the Bosworth volume (1986: 67) discusses the history of training and staff development for university administrative staff 'from the training desert of the mid-1960s to the position today which, if still not a lush forest, has at least a healthy growth of shrubbery'. Also of relevance are the more recent UCoSDA (1992) review and prescriptions by Guildford, Palfreyman and Thomas, and UCoSDA Briefing Paper 16 (1995), *Training and Development for University Administrators: a Position/Discussion Paper*, which discusses the wide variety of roles and expectations in relation to university managers across the range of chartered and statutory institutions.

The (draft) remit of the UCoSDA Standing Conference (SCAMAD), at the time of writing, is:

> The work of UCoSDA's Standing Conference on Accreditation of Management/Administration Development shall be:

1. to formulate, support and promote a framework for qualifications relevant to higher education management and administration;
2. to act as a co-ordinating body for regional and distance-learning providers which have credibility and authority;
3. to support credit equivalences on a consistent basis;
4. to advise on recognised curricula which form the basis of credits;
5. to promote systematic accredited development for administrators and managers; and
6. to promote, in conjunction with other initiatives within and outwith UCoSDA, the broader development of management/administration.

The standing conference will, for example, explore the possibility of the management development course for university managers, directed each year at Oxford University by the editors, being used for accreditation towards a range of degree and NVQ qualifications offered by a network of regional HE centres and by distance-learning. Hence one of the directors/editors (Palfreyman) is a member of the UCoSDA standing conference.

In so far as the Bosworth volume is one of the very few books dedicated to the HE manager (apart from the one now being read), it is appropriate to quote from its definitions of the role of the HE manager at length:

> Universities have become very complex institutions requiring of their administrative staff professional commitment, the exercise of sophisticated skills and the shouldering of responsibilities at levels scarcely imagined by their predecessors of twenty-five years ago. But their role nevertheless remains the same. They do and should continue to work quietly, unobtrusively and effectively beyond the limelight of the academic staff . . .
>
> The British University administrator is, in the tradition of Bentham, Haldane and Beveridge, an institutional person dedicated to maintaining and improving that institution through good administration regardless of his or her personal allegiances . . .
>
> In many institutions career administrators have made up for weak academic leadership . . .
>
> The quality of the talent recruited into university administration since the 1950s must have been well above the average for all professional occupations and higher than for all but a very few . . . If so, should not more care have been taken to either increase the low ceilings of responsibility and reward compared with the professions and industry or to ensure that individuals would obtain credentials which gave them external transferability? . . .
>
> It is doubtful if the universities could have expanded so rapidly and smoothly without the new class of administrators.
>
> (Bosworth, 1986: xi, 81, 82, 83, 84)

This last point refers to the expansion of the 1960s, but is equally applicable to the late 1980s and early 1990s.

The 1990s HE institution and its ever-greater need for effective managers

Even twenty years ago, before the hectic 1980s (another) decade of change for UK higher education, Fielden and Lockwood (1973: 186) declared: 'Universities require administrations of high calibre . . . to provide an efficient service to support the operations and developments of the university . . . which in turn depends upon the motivation and quality of its members.' This was in the context of universities then recently having 'managed the vast expansion, in size and complexity, which has occurred in the past decade, conscientiously and with considerable skill'. The processes called for an ever-greater range of expertise and flexibility on the part of higher education managers.

By the late 1980s an Organisation for Economic Co-operation and Development (OECD) survey could comment on administration:

> Whilst the culture of the full-time administrative class in universities is more likely than that of other groups in academia to display the classical features of bureaucracy, this tendency is limited by some significant characteristics of the academic enterprise [compared with, say, central or local government] . . . Most full-time university administrators are open to approaches from any member of the academic staff . . . [and interact] with *all* the individuals and groups that constitute the academic body . . . Administration is a facilitating activity. In high-status universities, the academic reputation . . . of professors create[s] relations of dependency that limit the acquisition of power by administrators. At the other end of the academic pecking order, however, as accommodation and furnishings [and contracts of employment] sometimes testify, there are fewer breaks on opportunities for administrative self-aggrandizement!
>
> (OECD, 1987: 86–7)

Yet increasing complexity, including greater external intervention and regulation, creates circumstances in which the central management has 'to exercise judgement, to arbitrate even-handedly between interested parties, and even to accept responsibility for decisions that may not be theirs to make, in order that other individuals and groups can avoid having to bear the consequence of their action' (OECD, 1987: 88). At times of crisis especially, senior managers can very much be pushed to the fore, as is instanced by Walford (1987), writing on the management of change at Aston University in the early to mid-1980s.

So the role of, at least, senior higher education managers is changing by becoming more explicitly political and high-profile: 'As more and more of the future success of the institution depends on effective planning and the efficient execution of the plans, whose interpreters the secretariat must normally be (since they drafted it), the secretarial staff (and especially their boss) become more powerful' (Bland, 1990: 68). In addition, for all managers the pace has quickened, the range of skills required has widened and the need for 'the strategic view' has increased as an antidote to the risk of over-specialization.

These points are powerfully made by Lockwood and Davies (1985: 314, 325, 327):

> the Administration should be in a position to comprehend the whole university and ... to assist greatly both in the avoidance of conflicts and discontinuities and in the promotion of innovation ... a university needs an efficient and comprehensive Administration which contains a wide range of specialist skills and the flexibility to respond to the changing wishes and situation of the university. The Administration is party to almost all of the activities of the institution ... and in certain areas the well-being of the university is reliant upon the quality of the skills and the levels of motivation within the Administration ... administrators acting sometimes as clerks and sometimes as consultants, sometimes as policemen and sometimes as entrepreneurs.

Lockwood and Davies (1985: 327) argue that a range of changes is shaping the need for new methods and expertise within, and for ever-increasing imagination and flexibility on the part of HE managers:

> Individuals whose work used to consist mainly of the writing of formal documents and the maintenance of records might well need to be able to negotiate across the table, to possess the political skills to deal in different styles in various arenas (e.g. the Students' Union bar, the Senior Common Room lounge, the Town Hall, etc.) with interest groups of great variety; to possess detailed knowledge of the law and its applications over a very broad field; to possess the ability to write promotional literature, handle the media, give oral presentations about the university, etc.; to understand investment appraisals and costing techniques; and to conduct commercial bargaining.

The administration clearly seeks to serve the interests of the institution, which as Lockwood and Davies stress are *not* necessarily *exactly* the same as those of the academic community. There are other groups to consider, ranging from the lay-member majority that is formally and legally in control of the institution at meetings of the council or governing Board, to students and domestic and manual staff. There may be friction, as friendly 'them and us' banter becomes biting and loaded:

> If institutional manageability and responsiveness are to be increased, Administrations should be more assertive that the distinctive competence of the academic professional lies in matters academic; it does not endow the individuals with superior knowledge or wisdom in all matters, neither does it necessarily provide the individual with skills of leadership or management, and nor does it elevate academic faculty as

a class into an aristocratic situation *vis-à-vis* the servant classes or other
employees.

(Lockwood and Davies, 1985: 315)

The UCoSDA *Handbook for University Administrators and Managers* (1994b)
contains an excellent article by George Kiloh (Deputy Registrar at the University of Sussex), which points out that the growth of part-time and mature,
self-financing students as consumers, the widening range of activities in
which HE institutions are involved, curricular change and vocationalism,
external audit of teaching, research and finance, the diversity of institutions within the expanded system and the premium on maximizing space
utilization all point to efficient *and effective* management as critical. Kiloh
(UCoSDA, 1994b: 5) writes, 'The administrator is a manager who must
marshal resources, interpret to colleagues the demands and pressures on
them, solve problems and obtain commitment to change. He or she must
do this with objectivity, within the corporate culture of the institution and
with a knowledge of outside pressures.' Kiloh labels the many roles to be
played by the HE manager: the foot soldier (the boring routines of any job
or organization); the messenger (the window-on-the-world, the listening
post); the prophet (foresight, 'the dispassionate examination of facts with
the intention of discerning trends, threats and opportunities'); the junction
box (making 'connections between unlikely subjects in the interests of producing desirable and acceptable change'); Houdini (finding solutions); the
priest (interpreting regulations); the politician ('identify possibilities and
sell them to colleagues; networking is vital'); the auditor ('detached analysis'); the champion (ensuring that 'the individual does not get lost in the
machine'); Stakhanov (long hours and hard work, no room for 'gentlemen's'
hours). He concludes: 'No-one suggests honestly that the administrator has
an easy task. It requires intellect, awareness, tact, organisation and imagination. It will require more as the years pass' (UCoSDA, 1994b: 10). Readers
may well concur.

Finally, a series of interviews for an MBA dissertation, published as an
article (Palfreyman, 1989), and, more accessibly, partly reproduced in
Universities in the Marketplace (CUA, 1992), found academics at the University of Warwick, despite some banter along 'them and us' lines, echoing the
Kiloh and Lockwood and Davies analysis. One interviewee from the School
of Industrial and Business Studies carefully and most helpfully analysed the
role of the non-academic management into the following constituent parts:

1. *Encouragement.* Others used terms such as 'empathy', 'us not them', 'pool
   of ideas', 'sounding-board', 'approachability', 'flexibility', 'helpful and
   imaginative', 'natural and equal respect', 'responsiveness'.
2. *Diagnostic skill as to what resources and assistance are needed,* which others
   expressed as 'smoothing the way', 'not stopping and blocking', 'an expertise in getting things done', 'not sticklers but enablers', 'a guide
   through the problem areas', 'problem-solving', 'pointing to resources',
   'interpret rules to achieve an end and not to obstruct it', 'not stoppers'.

3. *Plug into support services.*
4. *Linkages,* a concept referred to by virtually all the interviewees: 'a clearing-house', 'able to spot opportunities', 'alert academics', 'set up meetings', 'marriage-broker', 'a window on the world', 'a linking mechanism'.
5. *Flavour of the commercial world.*
6. *Technical skills,* in such aspects as publicity, promotion, marketing, mailing lists, environmental monitoring.

Thus, in short, the role was seen as *facilitation,* as assisting the academic to bring to fruition an innovative or entrepreneurial idea by the use of specialized technical skills and the centralized control of information channels; but with a degree of initiation, of being the catalyst and making linkages among academics and between academics and the outside world (yet, as one academic expressed it, '*not* forcing the issue').

To sum up, university managers, and, of course, academics, have increasingly to be entrepreneurial within 'the entrepreneurial and adaptive university' (Davies, 1984). In fact, rather than like entrepreneurs risking their own cash in business ventures, they are *intrapreneurs,* utilizing the institution's resources to move it in new directions (Perlman, 1988: 18–19):

> In intrapreneurship, employees of a college or university are a prime source of ideas and their analysis and implementation . . . Intrapreneurs pay attention to vision, to newness; stewards [and they too are needed in a successful HE institution] pay attention to balance, organisation, efficiency, and stable growth . . . management in colleges and universities is overbalanced towards the steward end of the continuum.

So, administrator or manager? Facilitator or initiator? Humbler minute-writer or *éminence grise,* a power behind the throne? Rigid purveyor and quoter of statutes and regulations or imaginative finder of ways around such constraints against doing new and exciting things? Bureaucrat or intrapreneur? Stick-in-the-mud or 'change-master'? The chances are that during a career in higher education the reader will be all of these, and possibly several of them even in the same job over a fairly short period of time. For example, the person in charge of examinations will need carefully to apply precise rules and regulations to keep students (and academics!) in line, to ensure that matters are fair and seen to be fair. But he or she may well need to be ingenious, flexible and a clever negotiator to get the best deal for printing examination papers or hiring extra examination halls. Your personality may make you more comfortable with one role rather than another – some folk are more adaptable than others, some old dogs continue to learn new tricks. The culture of the institution, and of the part of it within which you currently work, may force you to adopt a different role from that which you instinctively prefer. But you can change jobs and institutions, and the institution may well change around you.

Final thoughts

The world of the 1990s UK higher education manager, as described in the past few pages, is of necessity, and happily, very different from that portrayed in Dundonald's *Letters to a Vice-Chancellor* (1962: 34–7)

> The really lifeless thing is administration as it is understood and practised . . . You will find yourself entangled in a babu system, where thirty per cent error is accepted and anything less becomes matter for modest self-congratulations . . . In all British universities, of whatever kind, the tradition of the amateur is unfailingly strong; and in British universities the tradition is that of the gentleman amateur . . . The jolly amateurism.

We have come a long way since Vincent Knowles appointed his cadre of bright young things in the early 1960s, but as two members of that elite band of pioneer higher education managers, Stewart Bosworth (later Registrar of the University of Salford) and Geoffrey Lockwood (later Registrar of the University of Sussex), warned,

> A primary task, therefore, is for administrators to be more positive in explaining their value to the University . . . Unless administrators can get that message across, and live up to its meaning, they cannot expect to obtain the internal understanding of their roles, and the resources necessary to fulfil them . . . administrators must increasingly accept responsibility . . . In the circumstances likely to prevail in future years administrators cannot simply sit behind their desks and react to others; they are part of management and not just administration . . . If they don't they will rightly disappear. Moreover, administrators will need to exercise competence over broader ranges of skills and with a deeper knowledge of the academic heartland of their university . . . These assertions about administrators exercising more responsibility more widely do not require any change to University governance, they require administrators to accept the institutional responsibility for which they are paid . . .
>
> (Bosworth, 1986: 85–7)

We, the editors, can hope only that this book will help our colleagues, existing and potential, to live up to the ever-more demanding roles mapped out for them in the increasingly complex and diverse institutions of HE within which they will be working in the next century (as neatly summed up by Barzun, 1991: 110):

> The universities are expected, among other things, to turn out scientists and engineers, foster international understanding, provide a home for the arts, satisfy divergent tastes in culture and sexual morals, recast the penal code and train equally for the professions and for a life of cultural contentment in the coming Era of Leisure.

We trust that a better understanding of the specialisms of their colleagues will go far towards creating the management team which is so essential for future success – a success upon which British society and the British economy may yet come to depend as never before in a world of 'knowledge industries' where the 'value added' by a sophisticated workforce is crucial to survival amidst intense competition within 'the global village'.

2

Organizational Culture

Sue Dopson and Ian McNay

Editors' introduction

What is a university or college? Can it be managed like other corporate enterprises? Is it effectively an organization like any other, or is it *sui generis?*

The *Oxford English Dictionary* defines 'university' as: 'educational institution designed for instruction or examination or both of students in all or many of the more important branches of learning, conferring degrees in various faculties and often embodying colleges and similar institutions.' Jocular definitions go something along the lines of: 'a university is a collection of academics united only by a common grievance over the lack of car parking,' or 'a university is a combination of academic departments linked together only by a central heating system.' In times of financial retrenchment perhaps a university is a set of academic departments unified only by a shared assumption that the management is over-sized and over-expensive!

The debate over what is a university is a fairly long-standing and extensive one, and still ongoing. Relevant works include Newman (1852), Whitehead (1929), Flexner (1930), Truscot (1943, 1945), Jaspers (1946), Moberley (1949), Proctor (1957), Niblett (1962), Kerr (1963), Sparrow (1967), Robinson (1968), Minogue (1973), Cameron (1978), Bok (1982), Clark (1983, 1984), Scott (1984, 1990, 1995b), Bloom (1987), OECD (1987, 1991), Giamatti (1988), Warnock (1989), Barnett (1990), Carter (1990), Rosovsky (1990), Barzun (1991), Hague (1991, 1993), Duke (1992), Getman (1992), Pelikan (1992), Clark (1993), Oakeshott (1993), Oakley (1993), Russell (1993), Clark (1996).

The discussion of how universities are best managed is also a full one. For instance, see Cornford (1908), Dundonald (1962), Rourke and Brooks (1968), Cohen and March (1974), Cyert (1975), Piper and Glatter (1977), Keller (1983), Walford (1987), Birnbaum (1988), Perlman (1988), Becher (1989), Becher and Kogan (1992), Berquist (1992), Middlehurst (1993), Trow (1994), Dearlove (1995a,b). Miller (1994) especially has a good review of management models for universities: 'organized anarchy', 'garbage can', 'loose-coupled', 'bureaucracy', 'rational', 'collegiality', 'political systems', 'interactionist', 'the liberal university', 'the research university', 'the multiuniversity', 'the people's university', 'complete mess up'.

Moreover, the conflict between university autonomy (and within that academic freedom) and the state, and the debate as to whether universities should serve the economy as factories for vocational qualifications, are age-old. Relevant works here include Thompson (1971), Daalder and Shils (1982), Kogan (1983), Carswell (1985), Middleton (1985), Wiener (1985), Barnett (1986, 1995), Shinn (1986), Stankiewicz (1986), Kedourie (1989), Palfreyman (1989), Sheffield (1990), Smith (1991), Anderson (1992), IPPR (1992), Tapper and Salter (1992), Rubenstein (1993), Butterworth and Tarling (1994), Ellis (1994), Salter and Tapper (1994), Shattock (1994), Somer (1995), Keep and Mayhew (1996).

There is space here only for a few brief comments on the collegiality–managerialism debate, drawing upon a fraction of the literature mentioned above. (An exhaustive list has been provided for those of a philosophical turn of mind who may wish to explore these interesting questions, but note the dominance of US thinking. British vice-chancellors in recent decades have *not* put pen to paper on the meaning of and management of universities in the way that US retiring presidents of Harvard, Yale etc. have, although they did set out some thoughts in *slim* volumes in the immediate post-war period (for example, Moberley, 1949).)

Collegiality is to be found in its most undiluted form in the academic *demos* of Oxford and Cambridge, institutions which have no lay-member dominated council or board of governors, being universities where the academics are self-governing and, at least in the constituent colleges, unhierarchical. The other end of the spectrum (the statutory universities) is the most *dirigiste*, where the vice-chancellor is very much a Jarratt chief executive.

Tapper and Salter comment:

What in future Oxford and Cambridge cannot expect to be (and there is no evidence that they consciously sought this) are models for the rest of the British university system. Their exceptionalism will be there to be admired, envied or despised, but it will not be for replication. Although in the past British universities had different characteristics, they also shared a common idea of what it meant to be a university. We are moving rapidly towards an even more differentiated system in which the universities – including Oxbridge – are not in control of their values and purposes . . . [But, sadly, what] has been lacking in the recent crisis has been any serious attempt to formulate a new model of the English university. It may now be too late for this and the best that the universities can hope to do is to travel down [the] route of competent leadership and managerial efficiency. Even so, one would have hoped for a concerted attempt to escape the confines of nostalgia and damage limitation. *Surely the most profound criticism of the universities has been their failure to create their own vision of the future?* [italics added.] One that, because it was based upon a political reality combining the best of the past with the recognition that universities were going to be very different kinds of institutions in the future, could be sold to the public at large. The age needed a Newman, or even a Moberley.

(Tapper and Salter, 1992: 243, 245–6)

What we got is managerialism, as discussed in Weil (1994) and UCoSDA (1994a); the latter refers to the 'greater concentration of power at the centre of institutions, less consultation, fewer committees'.

Other collegial organizations, to varying degrees (and in some cases also struggling to come to terms with accountability and managerialism), include the national museums (such as the Victoria & Albert), Sotheby's, Lloyds of London, accountancy firms and partnerships of management consultants and solicitors, barristers' chambers, and the deans and chapters of cathedrals. Perhaps there is scope to argue that the idea, indeed ideal, is the university as an organization model in itself, *not* one beholden to a corporate business model, and even as a model which may yet have something to offer other organizations. Charles Handy (1983) saw the consensual, participative and, dare one say, collegial organizational model, based on the university, as becoming of increasing relevance in the twenty-first century, as employing organizations seek to minimize the contribution of an ever-more articulate and well-educated workforce, as they need to add value in developed Western countries by way of product innovation in order to compete with the many developing countries, which have got the edge in the economical production of basic goods.

More recently, Handy (1994) talks of the federal model for effective organization, especially if a large organization is to be able to cope with rapid external change:

> Federalism is, therefore, fraught with difficulties because it is trying to combine those two opposites, to manage the paradox. Twin citizenship makes it possible. Sovereignty is not ceded but shared. The large institution is not 'them' but 'us' . . . Federalism is an old idea, but its time may have come again, because it has been designed to create a balance of power within an institution . . . There is room in federalism for the small to influence the mighty, and for individuals to flex their muscles . . . federalism is an exercise in the balancing of power . . . it is messy, untidy and always a little out of control [recognize the characteristics?] . . . [But] there is no real alternative in a complicated world.

(Handy, 1994: 102, 98–9)

All this, of course, relates to the relevant cybernetic law: a system must be as internally complex as is appropriate to reflect the degree of external complexity it has to face. Similarly, one may be hearing the swish of the pendulum swinging from 1980s public sector managerialism. John Gray, in

Beyond the New Right (1993: 61–2), points out that: 'in higher education, the danger is that universities come to be regarded by government as little more than auxiliaries of economic policy . . . it ought to be a central maxim of Conservative government that autonomous institutions have their own internal ends and purposes and are not mere instruments of the ephemeral goals of the government of the day.' He goes on:

> Conservatism is not, like socialism or liberalism, a one-generation philosophy . . . it is necessary to repudiate firmly the neo-liberal metaphor of society as a contract, in which market exchange is primordial. If society is a contract, it is only in Edmund Burke's sense – a contract between the living, the dead and those that are yet unborn . . . the danger of the neo-liberalism that has lately come to dominate Conservative thinking is the danger of utopianism . . . above all, Conservatives must recall the dangers of ideology, and the limits of theory . . . it is the sceptical spirit which should inform the policies devised by Conservatives.
>
> (Gray, 1993: 64–5)

Finally, one might mention Warren's article (1994: 30) calling for new university managerialism to be tempered with a dose of collegiality:

> when the polytechnics were made into the 'new' universities they started to dismantle the key elements of collegiality which are the main source of their stability and vitality. Consequently, the new universities are starting to exhibit the traits of bureaucratic anomic life: increased conflict, staff dissatisfaction and alienation which can be redeemed only by a restoration of elements of collegiate life which will help to renew their moral authority, shared academic values and service of community . . . [Otherwise] dysfunctional results of the machine bureaucracy will inhibit their future flourishing.

Ryder (1996) compares 'authoritarian management' in some UK universities with the former centrally planned economies of the old USSR and its eastern European satellites: he comments that 'University Senates or Councils have been dispensed with in the name of efficiency, and replaced by a kind of University Politburo which operates behind closed doors'.

This is the longest introduction the editors offer because we regard this chapter as crucial in covering the key determinant (the fit between its culture and its management style) in whether an HEI is successful or not, and whether the individual within the organization is fully committed and his or her skills are fully utilized. We hope you will enjoy reading it from the perspectives of both managing *and being managed.*

Introduction

In the past ten years the public sector has faced a number of complex pressures to change the way in which it manages and provides services.

Efficiency, economy and effectiveness are the espoused objectives of change; the managerialism of the private sector the means to achieve them. Research done in a number of public sector settings demonstrates that simply to transfer managerialist approaches from the private sector and expect improvements in service is dangerously seductive. Such logic underestimates the complexity of achieving organizational change in settings where there exist many interest groups, intense public and media interest and strong organizational cultures. In some companies, approaches are being imported the other way: Rover Group has guaranteed security of tenure and given local decision-making power to shopfloor project groups that are not dissimilar to higher education course teams. Despite this, the evangelism continues. Ranson and Stewart (1994) suggest that the debate is ideological as much as organizational. For example, the administrative costs of state pension schemes are lower than those of comparable private schemes. None the less, the pressures to privatize continue and, as Ranson and Stewart note,

> The language appropriate to one kind of organization has now become the currency for all. Underlying most approaches to management are values that thrive in the domain of the private. The values of the public domain are, seemingly, not perceived as relevant to management theories. Organization models assume the values of the private even when their focus is public.
>
> (Ranson and Stewart, 1994: 4)

The purpose of this chapter is to reflect on the term 'organizational culture' in the particular context of higher education management, itself subject to the pressures Ranson and Stewart highlight in their quotation. We aim to stimulate you to reflect on the nature of the organization in which you work, as well as your role in that organization and the opportunities that exist to shape your organization's culture. The chapter begins by considering the meaning of 'organizational culture', and first draws on a model, developed by Charles Handy (1993), for exploring the different cultures that might exist within an organization. This model is discussed at some length because it offers a framework for you to consider the culture in which you work, and it also links to a second framework that we use to discuss the changing culture of higher education.

What is organizational culture?

'Culture' is a word often used in organizations to mean 'the way we do things around here'. Although this definition may feel intuitively correct, it underestimates the complexity of the concept. Figure 2.1 attempts to tease out this complexity.

An organization's culture is made up of a combination of rituals, routines,

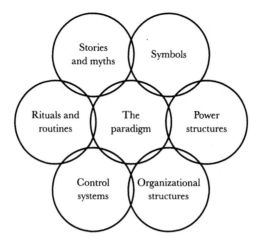

Figure 2.1 The cultural web of an organization
Source: Johnson (1990)

stories, myths and symbols that give very clear messages about what is seen as acceptable and unacceptable behaviour. However, an organization's culture is also influenced by the way in which power is distributed in the organization, and how work is structured and controlled. Culture is therefore a combination of values, structure and power that has implications for every aspect of an organization's operations and external relationships.

We also know from research in this area that there are other important influences on cultures, including the history, traditions and 'ownership' of the organization, its size, goals and objectives, the technology it operates with, the nature of the workforce and the environment in which it is situated.

What organizational culture do you work in?

To help to address this question we draw on a framework offered by Charles Handy (1993), and represented in Figure 2.2.

The first of the cultures is the *power culture*, represented by Zeus, the god of power. Often found in small entrepreneurial organizations, it is pictured as a web because it depends on a central power source (a central figure or a coalition). It is a very political organization and decisions are taken largely on the outcome of a balance of influence rather than on procedural grounds. A lot of deal-making goes on. Decisions are usually made that will satisfy the central power source.

A power culture operates largely on the basis of anticipating the wishes of those seen to hold power. Control is often exercised by the centre through the selection of individuals and close control over resources. Individuals

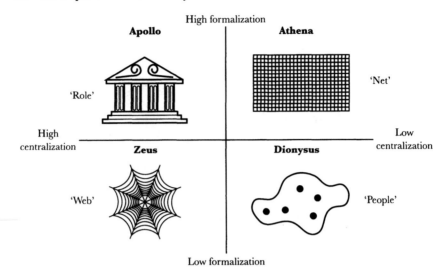

Figure 2.2 Culture quadrant, following Handy

operating in a power culture will prosper if they are power-oriented and, politically minded, enjoy risk-taking and can live with low security. People higher up the organization are often motivated by the drive for personal power and endeavour to build up close relationships with key figures. The lower ranks of the organization are often motivated by fear and dependency, although such fear can be mitigated by the benevolent paternalism of the 'boss'. Individuals working in this type of organization will be judged by results rather than by the way in which they achieve their goals. Often these cultures are tough and abrasive: they lead to high turnover, particularly among middle managers as they either fail or leave the hyper-competitive atmosphere.

The claimed strength of this culture is that it can move very quickly if threatened, although this is clearly dependent on the individual or coalition at the centre. A major problem for this culture is growth. The web can break if it seeks to link too many activities, and struggles for dominance may result. The quality of the individual in the centre is crucial, and this raises the question of succession. The sudden loss of the central power source can be a disaster. Generally, in this culture the employee resource is underused and the boss resource overused. We see it in some HEIs with powerful vice-chancellors or with power concentrated in a small senior management team. It may not fit the size of the institution or its traditional culture, and so creates conflict.

The second of Handy's cultural types is the *role culture*. This culture is often stereotyped as a bureaucracy. Its logo is a temple, signifying its reliance on its pillars – the functions of the organization. Its patron god is Apollo, the god of reason. Where decisions are made depends on the amount of money involved and the extent to which the decision is not clear from the existing policies or procedures, usually defined or approved by committees. The work that goes on in the organization is controlled by procedures or rules, so this culture relies on job descriptions, procedures for communications or rules for the settlement of disputes. The functions (pillars) are coordinated by a narrow band of senior managers, who represent the only personal coordination needed, since rules and guidelines guide the functions. Hierarchy is important, and people know their place. Position power is the major source of power, and personal power is frowned upon. In this culture the role or the job description is often more important than the individual who fills it. Performance over and above the role is not usually required and, indeed, can be disruptive.

A well-managed role culture offers security and predictability to the individual. The organization values and rewards consistency, order and predictability. Those who stay within the rules feel sale from the exercise of arbitrary power. This may even give a certain freedom of action, which would be constrained by uncertainty – the individual fear of capriciousness in the power culture.

The strength of this culture, argues Handy, lies where economy of scale is more important than flexibility. Role cultures are, however, slow to perceive the need to change, and slow to change when they do see the need, because very often they have relied on building up procedures and not people. This culture can be very frustrating for individuals who want to control their own work or who are power-oriented.

This type of organization is likely to succeed as long as it can operate in a stable environment: if it can control its environment by monopoly, the market is stable or its product life is a long one. Generally the role culture overuses the talents and energies of the designers of systems and underuses those of the 'doers'. A great deal of management ingenuity goes into the design and development of structures and systems which then limit and frustrate the ingenuity and initiative of the people who are charged with performing the work.

The third of Handy's cultural types is the *task culture*. Represented by a net, this culture is linked to taskforce and project team environments. A key characteristic is that it has some clearly articulated mission statement that is oriented to making a difference. Decisions are often made on the basis of expert knowledge and are geared towards advancing the mission. It is the mission statement that acts as the control and coordination mechanism.

Individuals know that they are unlikely to 'go wrong' if they pursue tasks associated with the mission. Influence and power are more widely dispersed. It is a team culture where outcomes should obliterate individual differences of status or style differences. The task culture assumes that people enjoy working at tasks that are rewarding and advance the shared purpose. The emphasis is on people being internally motivated: that is, the organization should provide opportunities for its members to use their talents and abilities in ways that are intrinsically satisfying and advance a purpose to which the individual is personally committed. There may be some room for individual professional interpretation of mission at a devolved level. A strength of the task culture is that it can evoke a sense of passion and commitment to work. The organization can empower people to learn and create new ways to achieve the mission ideals by making the appropriate resources available. However, a weakness of this culture is that in one's pursuit of the noble goals of the mission one can lose one's sense of balance, such that people exploit themselves in the service of the organization's purpose. Furthermore, this culture can be under-organized, relying on high motivation to overcome its deficiencies in structure, systems and managing change. There may also be 'mission drift' if there is loose control of activity, or individuals' commitment is not congruent with the institution's.

The last of Handy's cultures is the *people culture*. It is unusual, in that the individual is the starting point. If there is a structure or an organization, it is there to serve and assist the individuals within it. Dionysus is the patron god, the god of the self-oriented individual. Not many organizations can exist in this kind of culture, since most have objectives over and above the collective objectives of those who comprise them. Furthermore, control mechanisms are impossible in these cultures except by mutual consent.

Decisions are made on the basis of consensus. Coordination and control are achieved mainly through the selection of people who fit in with the existing individualistic culture. Influence is dispersed in this culture but power often lies with those who have relevant expertise. The ability to control one's work is the major source of motivation. At its best, the people culture can evoke high commitment and can be supportive. However, its strength can be a major weakness in that people tend to avoid useful conflict in order to practise harmony, and decisions can be taken covertly.

Organizations are rarely pure examples of these cultures. Instead, a mixture exists, although Handy claims that there is usually a dominant cultural orientation. He and other commentators in this area argue that one culture should not swamp an organization; however, differentiation can lead to fragmentation. Therefore, a crucial task is to ensure integration. The question is who takes on this task and how.

The literature on organizational behaviour offers some insights into the mechanisms available to people for embedding a particular way of working in an organization. There are a number of individual actions that are important in sending signals about a particular culture. These include: what 'leaders' pay attention to, seek to measure and control; reactions to critical incidents and organization crisis; deliberate role modelling, teaching and coaching; the criteria used for the allocation of rewards and status and the criteria used for recruitment, selection, promotion, retirement and excommunication. Any individual action occurs in a context, and in order to be able to consider the culture of the organization you work in and your desire to see. changes to it, it is necessary to appreciate the complexity of the context and how it has changed over time. The next section seeks to explore these issues.

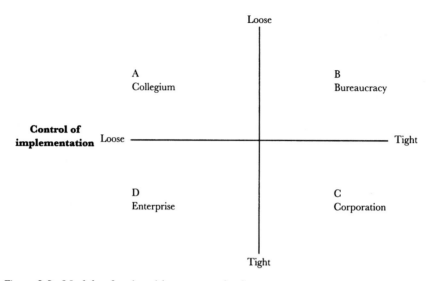

Figure 2.3 Models of universities as organizations

The changing culture of universities

One of the authors, on the basis of empirical work in universities, has developed a model of four cultures which have substantial congruence with Handy's (McNay, 1995c). Building on Weick's (1976) concept of education institutions as 'loosely coupled organizations', the model (see Figure 2.3) plots the degree of collective tightness or looseness in definition of policy and in the control of practice – the implementation of policy. The four quadrants are then labelled collegial academy (loose, loose), bureaucracy (loose definition, tight control of implementation), corporation (tight, tight) and enterprise (tight policy frame, loose control of activity).

None of the cultures is exclusive. Each is conditioned by its neighbours, or should be: one of the findings of the work is the danger of corruption by an introverted preoccupation with one of them. In this section the styles and tactics of leaders in each of the four are examined against a general sketch of the characteristics of each.

The collegial academy is the ideal of a past golden age of self-regulating academics working in the same place but independently and autonomously, indulged as elite intellectuals by the state, somewhat akin to state patronage of arts activities as an essential civilizing influence in a civilized society. There was a 'common culture', as Robbins recognized (Committee on Higher Education, 1963), shared with their establishment sponsors. In England, the domination of Oxbridge was key to this coexistence (Ellis, 1994). Indeed, there are still some in the Campaign for Academic Autonomy who believe that the state should have no part in regulating what happens to the £6 billion spent annually in universities (Russell, 1993). The chartered universities had little academic 'inspection' before 1988 and many resent what there now is. This echoes the claims of police forces to be able to regulate themselves, yet, to take one example, one researcher (Shilling, 1995) has demonstrated that internal systems for student appeals vary considerably and some disregard principles of natural justice. There is corruption, too, in academic conservatism and cliquishness, with certain views which challenge received orthodoxy being sidelined. Where one school of thought has captured a dominant position, others may be excluded from grant awards. The defence of autonomy, verging at times on paranoia, has meant that poor work has gone unregulated. Similarly, courses may have lacked coherence, continuity, consistency and quality because of the *noli me tangere* ('don't interfere') philosophy. In the then polytechnics and colleges, CNAA put a stop to that, and encouraged a professionalism in teaching which did not exist elsewhere, as any training for teachers, supervisors, managers was resisted.

Any leader here has to tread carefully. Handy (1983), in another publication, labels them 'organizations of consent'. People want a right to be consulted, and are content without a regular vote, provided they can operate a veto when 'management' steps out of line: a non-participative democracy. The rejection by the London School of Economics of top-up fees and Oxford University's veto vote on Margaret Thatcher's honorary degree are cases in point. So the leader is 'transactional', working with and building on traditions as a 'white hat' change agent. His or her personal academic status gives professional power and the style of 'management by walking about' (MBWA) applies personal power to sensing views and generating consensus and compromise. The leader gains legitimacy by bottom-up according of authority. The elected status of many heads of department in chartered universities codifies this, and their short term in office prevents reversion to some of the autocratic *ex officio* professorial heads of single chair departments of the pre-Robbins period. (Editor's note: see Amis *Lucky Jim* (1954) and compare Bradbury *The History Man* (1975), followed by Bradbury *Cuts* (1987), for the fictional image of academic life.)

In the bureaucracy the consent processes are formalized in committees – representative democracy – and procedural power becomes dominant. There may be no clear policy framework but there are precedents against which to judge proposals and regulatory frames of 'general principles' of operation to condition behaviour. This system is good at saying 'no', but may stop when the noes stop and not progress to the quality decision of a committed 'yes'. It rarely generates innovation from within itself: its forte is regulation, no bad thing in itself and a necessary but not sufficient condition for good management. The leader needs a command of the rule and of case law, and control of agendas, minutes and information flow. So the image is of a nominal leader or leaders in the chair, but behind that throne a Wolsey, Mazarin or Rasputin. Machiavellian leaders then negotiate for delegated authority from formal meetings and take decision-making into a less visible arena, where they have more positional or personal power and can subordinate the opposition. This may break the 'corruption' in this quadrant, which equates standards to standardization and where systems serve themselves, not others. Decisiveness may replace democracy, but it is also corruptible.

In the corporation, the academics recapture the control that they may have lost in a plethora of committees. The working group, the team (so much more flexible and dynamic) replaces the committee. Remaining committees are rationalized, slimmed down and dominated by the senior management. This is a crisis mode, with positional power and the purse strings being used to promote conformity to corporate objectives. Image counts for a lot, internally and externally, so money is spent on power suites, not student support. Key people scan the environment and position the institution in relation to perceived policy imperatives. Internal patronage and personal sanctions become commonplace: in the current exposures of corruption the whistle blowers are often condemned, not rewarded, while the offenders are bought out. Leaders are transformational, bringing new values (note our opening remarks) and new visions for which they evangelize with charismatic zeal. Yet in the long run they do not resolve the crises they may have inherited, or created (Bensimon, 1993). Attempts to subordinate the academics identifying with collegial modes may result in insubordination: the University of Huddersfield has seen the most recent revolt, but there have been other coups in former polytechnics, where aspirant leaders, often members of the inner cabinet senior management team, have used community members to exert pressure on the chair of governors. The chair is somewhat akin to the governor-general (remember Sir John Kerr and Gough Whitlam?); this can be a very political culture. The danger is that leaders relate to a small, self-selecting, external group. At Derby College, Wilmorton, there was no strong bureaucracy to regulate the conduct of the principal and chair of governors: the clerk to governors was on a casual contract. Thus decisions were taken oblivious to wider perceptions. In the chartered university sector the case of University College Cardiff might be cited (Shattock, 1994). Here the dominance of the principal in resisting the realities of the external corporate state, and its controls, brought the college close to formal bankruptcy.

The enterprise culture may keep awareness of the market to the fore and re-emphasize the tasks of the university: to serve its clients and communities. It relies on a clear mission statement with established priorities and plans that link policy to practice; this is often missing or ill-managed (McNay, 1995a). It relies on good market intelligence and good internal data systems, which are also often missing or ill-managed (Thomas, 1995). Its appeal is often commercial, based on extrinsic motivation and rewards, which do not attract many academics (Morrell, 1992) or will detach them from the core of the university (Schuller, 1992). The culture may be good for innovation and bring team members together from different enclaves of the collegial academy: that is its strength. But, as Handy underlines, teams can be ephemeral: they form, storm, norm and perform, but do not transform easily when the task changes. In the Open University, course teams are vibrant in the creative stages, but, once a course is 'on stream', few members want to be involved in maintenance, however essential, or even creative, it may be. It is worthy, but invisible, work, left to others.

That is one danger here – that novelty is more important than quality. The diversity contrasts with the equity and normality of the diametric bureaucracy. A second danger is of mission drift. If markets, their demands and abilities to pay determine what is done, this distorts the profile of any institution because some markets are stronger, more strident, more sexy, than others. The leader, then, has to manage with a range of levers in a bargaining process to maintain a balance between core activities and an expanding margin of more temporary products. This is a completely different discourse from any that universities have been accustomed to. It is one that is increasingly necessary as the state moves from its corporate bureaucracy to a corporate enterprise culture and expects universities to follow. Of course, the funding councils are still the major customers and still operate as controllers or steerers, despite denials. The bureaucracy of maximum aggregate student numbers (MASNs) and the perceived standardization pressures from quality assessment processes and the research assessment exercise keep a major pressure on universities still in the corporate bureaucracy culture. The reduction in core resourcing from the state is pushing them to the corporate enterprise quadrants. Pressures from students, long accorded less status than desirable by the collegial academy academics, may bring an enterprising collegial model to the fore, with a student-centred curriculum, which mixes the best of approaches based on competences and outcomes for the market with the rigour generated by the knowledge innovators in the mission university, with its mature values (Leavis, 1943; Adelman, 1973).

These trends towards corporate enterprise mean that non-academic managers in universities need to change too. In the collegium they were liberal generalists in an amateur way. Growth, specialization and economic pressures have made this an outmoded form. The menagers have come from dominance in the bureaucracy to subordination in the corporation; there is now a need for a new balanced partnership. Studies at Bristol and Essex (Thomas, 1995) show that delegation and devolution to departments (a collegial structure) may encourage neither efficient use of present resources nor better generation of new resources. Many academic heads are still resistant to training (Middlehurst, 1993). They may be more *aware* now of the issues, their *attitudes* may have changed, even their *aptitudes*, but many still are suspicious about management. This is understandable: they were not born managers, they have had it thrust upon them without training. Furthermore, can academics be *assisted* in their management role? Service support is best located close to the client; there is preference for a 'one-stop shop' at faculty or departmental level. Students may prefer this, too.

In the enterprise culture anyone and everyone is a point of access to the whole, unlike in the fragmented fissiparous collegium. Already some central services (finance) have staff with an identified portfolio of client departments (somewhat like an advertising agency) where they develop knowledge of the local culture. As other central services merge or grow (marketing, external funding, international offices), a similar approach could develop. At some point, then, there will be a switch from 'located centrally, acting locally', to 'based locally, thinking corporately'. They will also, then, link laterally to other service area representatives to develop a collective, sensitive, proactive partnership with academic colleagues. Internal cultures reflect external contexts and pressures and, perhaps, vice versa, with permeable system boundaries. So the time for internal change should be soon, to show that universities should not to be subject to even more external controls on their policies, their operations and their cultures as simply agencies of the state with no autonomy.

Discussion

What we have had, in recent years, is a lack of debate about what *should be*, though the National Commission on Education (1994) provoked some strategic commentaries to set alongside Ron Barnett's philosophical treatises (Barnett, 1990). What we have had instead is a lament for the past and a romantic reminiscing over a lost era based mainly on two higher education institutions, not nearly 150. Halsey (1992) leads the way in noting the move from collegiality, based on elite institutions, to corporate hierarchy based on elite decision-makers *within* institutions:

> The British senior common room today presents a spectacle more interesting than joyful . . . the collegiate university still commands wide and powerful affections and interests. But the world is now more competitive and more threatening. The collegiate idea is challenged . . . Will commensality survive and, if so, with what further modifications? And, finally if *not*, what kind of effective university could be envisaged for the twenty-first century? . . . The age of 'faculty' domination in colleges, universities, and schools had to end with the rise of mass systems of higher education . . . the prestige of academic people in the eyes of both the politician and the populace has plummeted . . . The outlook for British higher education is bleak . . . The attack on academic autonomy, or . . . the demand from the state that intellectual labour be proletarianized, has been conspicuously aggressive in the past decade.
> (Halsey, 1992: 1, 174, 266, 268–70)

Salter and Tapper (1994: 70) relate this to state corporatism:

> We have argued that the corporate autonomy of universities has always been exercised within externally imposed boundaries. At one time those boundaries were imposed by a powerful segment of university opinion

and led to a university system that was élitist (both in terms of its pedagogical values and those whom it was prepared to admit), high in cost, and lacking in diversity. In recent years the state has reclaimed the control of those boundaries, and has insisted upon managerial strategies which will result in a system which is more diverse in character, has lower unit costs and is overall far less élitist. In the process of this change, university autonomy has evolved markedly: from the idea of development initiated from below, to the idea that once granted their resources the universities were responsible for spending them, to the idea that universities need to make choices within boundaries that discriminate against some decisions while encouraging others . . . The state may demand greater financial accountability, and the universities to demonstrate that it has received value-for-money, but it is also keen to encourage diversity. Such a strategy has increased the range of choices available to universities, while decreasing the job security of academics. In the process it has redistributed power within the universities, reversing the seemingly ever-expanding authority of the dons. What may bother many dons is the apparent decline in their influence upon institutional decision-making, that in its current form autonomy appears to be more dependant on the judgement of university officials than on the wisdom of university academics. Thus university autonomy has been reconstituted while donnish domination has declined. In the process, the link between institutional and individual autonomy . . . has been broken.

We would argue that whereas with the bureaucracy a case could be argued (with Fielden, 1975) for 'the decline of the professor and the rise of the registrar', in the corporate hierarchy senior academics have recaptured control: it is from the ranks of the collegium that leaders have been recruited. They should then have a sensitivity to the cultural particularity of higher education that Livingstone (1974: 54–5) touched upon in commentary on the consultancy report on Warwick University, which believed that the committee system of government was in danger of running riot and that more, not less, hierarchy was needed:

> What the Tyzack consultants failed to understand is the difference between the concepts of efficiency and effectiveness . . . There is no known case in the history of organizations where bureaucratically organized institutions, for that is what Tyzack, and those others who urge universities to be more 'businesslike' imply, have been successful in discovering new knowledge. Nor, in education, have such institutions been known to instil a sense of responsible critical enquiry in their charges. Either they produce technicians, which is entirely appropriate in some cases, or nihilists.

Thus, collegiality may not be *efficient* by the norms of other organizations, but it may well be more *effective* in achieving the outcome of a 'good university' than rampant managerialism. What may emerge is an internal binary system. On the one hand the committees of the collegial bureaucracy can provide an arena for an open, deliberative, iterative process to reconcile the concerns of senior managers of a corporate disposition and of academic staff with collegial yearnings. The latter need to recognize the benefits of and legitimacy of collectivity; the former need to accept the benefits of consultation, to achieve consensus and commitment, and to abjure the autocratic authority vested in them, at least in modern universities, by legislation. So there will emerge an agreed mission, widely owned, and a framework for strategic development.

This takes time, and the united collective needs to resist external pressures from representatives of the corporate state, with its stop–go short-termism. There cannot be a good response to major policy initiatives in a matter of weeks. Equally, there should be resistance to the constant thirst for data by regulatory bodies and to routinization of inspection. There should, for quality control, be management by exception in a climate of trust; not universal inspection in a climate of suspicion which generates game-playing ploys and wastes time better spent on improving quality than constantly proving it.

On the other hand, the enterprise culture can provide a base for tactical adjustment and adaptation within the agreed mission and strategic framework. This will allow variations to cope with the different discipline cultures (Becher, 1989), something the standardized norms of the bureaucracy find difficult. It also allows for flexible regroupings to overcome the sometimes rigid disciplinary redoubts in the collegium. It can provide feedback from the customers to inform both parties to reviews of policy and strategy. It links two key aspects of professionalism: service and standards. These, then, provide characteristics distinctive from the cultures of privatization: a participative, representative democracy where managers and workers are not in opposition; a tolerance of diversity, not a company conformity to corporate images; and the legitimate representation of interests to continue to pursue activities of value, which add value (like research, external examining for nominal fees, service on advisory public bodies) but do not generate profit.

Conclusion

We have sought to explore the changing context of higher education and the implications for leaders and administrators. Clearly, significant role changes have occurred, but such changes are by no means unique. Managers in both public and private sectors have to cope with the requirement to become more generalist, to extend the range of their managerial skills and competences, to manage complex change at a time when their performance is under constant scrutiny, the resources they have to manage are constantly questioned and traditional career paths are crumbling. The upshot of all this change is that those charged with managing have to consider what they are doing and why, if they are to survive and thrive in the more demanding contexts in which they work. The concept of organizational culture is useful in helping to address such issues and to encourage staff to be assertive in defence of their values, developed and proven over years of professional practice.

We have highlighted one framework taken from Charles Handy as a means for the reader to ponder on some important questions. McNay's model has related this to higher education. These questions include: what organizational culture do you work in; what are its strengths and weaknesses; should it be changed in some way; and what role can you play in doing so? Ducking these questions will inevitably lead only to disjointed incremental change and missed opportunities to play an effective role for both institutions and individuals within them. Other chapters in this book may help you reflect on operational issues: these need to be set in a context of clear values. These underpin institutional mission and individual motivation. If they are congruent, that harmonization should be reflected in a clear equilibrium among the four cultures we have described and their application, with concomitant styles and processes, to appropriate situations where they are 'fit for the purpose'.

3

Strategic Planning

Harold Thomas

Editors' introduction

The title of this chapter describes its contents exactly. The author has clearly set out the processes involved in strategic planning, and above all has 'demystified' them, emphasizing the informal aspects ('discussions in corridors and over coffee') as well as the rational. He focuses on the concept of *integration* and alerts readers to the somewhat neglected area of estates strategy, which is dealt with in more depth in Chapter 10.

Introduction

Organizations 'face reasonably predictable short-term futures but totally unknowable long-term ones' (Stacey, 1993: 246). Such views, which are based on an assessment of the turbulent external environment in which organizations operate, increasingly question the feasibility of detailed long-range planning. Those involved in the management of universities will readily recognize the existence of the turbulent environment, but they will also recognize the time and effort that goes into providing planning documents. If the future is so uncertain then is much of this effort wasted? The answer to that question will lie in the nature of the planning process and the skill with which it is carried out. It will also depend upon what is meant by planning. (See Mintzberg (1994) for a critical assessment of the strategic planning concept.)

There is a danger of believing that planning in HE institutions commenced in the 1980s. Such a view underplays the role of planning in previous decades. The process may have developed over time and in response to changing external circumstances, but it is a fallacy to suppose that it is an invention of the 1980s. It is certainly true, however, that during the past decade the concept of planning has pervaded the consciousness of institutions. Planning officers and planning and resources committees now form key elements in most organizational charts, while analyses of the planning process have become a favourite topic for academic debate. This development was stimulated by the Jarratt Report (1985), which stressed the need to establish strategic plans 'which bring planning, resource allocation and accountability together into one corporate process linking academic, financial and physical aspects' (para. 5.5a). However, there is more to planning than the formal document that emerges after long hours of drafting and discussion. It is arguable that the document itself is not even the most significant element in what is a complex process.

I hope that within this short introduction certain questions are already beginning to form: 'Why plan?' 'Who wants a plan?' 'Who needs a plan?' 'Is planning possible?' 'What goes into a plan?' 'Who plans?' 'Can a plan be brought to fruition?' The purpose of the remainder of this chapter is to address these issues by looking at the influences on institutional strategy and the importance of integration. To place this discussion in context it will be useful first to explore the historic development of the planning process and then to consider the meaning of planning in an institutional setting.

Historical context

Those with long memories of the HE system will recall that until the mid-1970s planning within universities had been based on the quinquennial system. Every five years universities would submit to the University Grants Committee (UGC) a substantial document outlining their needs for the next planning period. The UGC was seen as a buffer between the universities and the government, responsible for both advice to the government on the universities' needs and the disbursement of funds from the government to individual institutions. On the basis of its assessment of institutional plans and the funds made available by the government, the UGC would provide a planning horizon for a five-year period, which allowed institutions some stability in their internal planning. This system broke down in 1975 under the pressure to restrain public spending in the context of the oil-led inflation boom of the period. The late 1970s became a period of drift, with institutions hoping for an eventual return to quinquennial planning while in the immediate future being either unable or unwilling to plan for more than a year at a time, although the returned Labour government of 1977 offered a rolling triennium with a fixed budget for one year, followed by provisional totals for the next two years. Institutions in the public sector were similarly subject to annual funding channelled through the local authorities.

The return of a Conservative government in 1979 was to have a dramatic impact on attitudes towards institutional planning. Although it has been argued (Allen, 1988) that the government did not have a policy on the universities as such until the publication of its Green Paper on HE in 1985 (DES, 1985), it did have a firm commitment to reduce public spending.

This was applied to universities first by increasing fees for overseas students, and removing institutional grants for such students, and second by stringent cuts in grants in 1981, 'a year of drastic policy change' (Becher and Kogan, 1992: 42). The impact in terms of institutional planning was to force on universities an awareness that they would have to adopt a more proactive stance in determining the nature of their own futures. Consequently mission statements began to appear outlining the aims and objectives of the institution. Institutions began to recognize the need to respond to the external environment and to identify their own niche markets.

This period also hastened a change in the relationship between the UGC and universities on the one hand and the UGC and the government on the other. The cuts of 1981 were implemented by the UGC, thereby undermining 'the old idea that the UGC was the universities' friend' (Scott, 1995a: 11), while the tone of the Secretary of State's letters to the Chairman of the UGC was that of master to servant (Joseph, 1982, 1983). By 1985 'the UGC had become a full-blooded planning organisation which required universities to respond in the same mode' (Becher and Kogan, 1992: 45). That response developed into the need to submit planning documents. First required in 1987 to accompany claims for funds set aside by the UGC to encourage early retirement and other costs associated with rationalization, such institutional planning documents have now become an accepted part of the annual management cycle. The funding councils expect institutions to produce strategic plans as a matter of course for their own institutional purposes, but also see those plans, together with institutions' financial forecasts, as assisting the councils' understanding of developments, trends and pressures, both within individual institutions and across the sector as a whole.

While these documents are intended to be set within the context of individual institutions' mission statements, the framework in which institutions operate has arguably been marked by a decline in national planning. The replacement of the UGC by the Universities Funding Council (UFC), with the subsequent establishment of the Higher Education Funding Councils in place of the UFC and PCFC (Polytechnics and Colleges Funding Council), has seen a shift away from a planning body towards funding agencies. Of course, funding mechanisms such as the setting of MASNs and the selective distribution of research funds has an effect on institutional planning. But the Further and Higher Education Act 1992, which abolished the binary line, raises planning issues of inter-institutional and regional collaboration that funding agencies rather than planning bodies are ill-equipped to tackle. In the absence of such central direction it is to market forces that institutions have increasingly turned to influence their planning strategies.

Definition

The most often quoted definition of institutional planning is that given by Lockwood and Davies (1985: 167): 'the continuous and collective exercise of foresight in the integrated process of taking informed decisions affecting the future.' Although it was formulated some ten years ago, there has been no major challenge to this definition. It has been suggested (Whitchurch, 1992) that it might be extended to include the institution's relationship with its environment, expressed in its mission statement or corporate aim, but this is more a reflection of current practice than an undermining of the basic definition. It is worth pausing over the key words in this definition, as each contributes to an understanding of the process.

Continuous emphasizes that the process should not be a one-off exercise in response to periodic demands from the funding council. Nor should plans be regarded as static. With a rapidly shifting environment, the planning process has to be flexible and dynamic, operating at different levels of the organization. The longer the time horizon, the more danger there is in being too prescriptive. Mission statements can set the tone and general direction of the institution for the next few years, but an entrepreneurial HE institution will need the capacity to react quickly to a changing environment.

Collective might at first sight seem an obvious component, but in some ways it strikes at the heart of academic culture. The Jarratt Report (1985: para. 3.41) contended that 'universities are first and foremost corporate enterprises to which subsidiary units and individual academics are responsible and accountable', but it is a fact of academic life that universities tend to be departmental institutions (Becher, 1989). They are loosely coupled organizations (Weick, 1976) where different cultures and criteria for success operate in different parts of the organization. Academics' loyalties tend to be first to their discipline, second to their department and only third to the university. The planning process has to be sensitive to the different aspirations emanating from the institution's constituent parts, but at the same time there has to be critical assessment of strengths and weaknesses in the light of prevailing conditions.

Foresight is a reminder that management in a turbulent environment cannot be a solely bureaucratic process. There has to be encouragement of an entrepreneurial approach at central, departmental and sub-departmental levels. There has to be a combination of what Stacey (1993) has called 'ordinary management' and 'extraordinary management'. The blending of these different but necessary approaches into a strategic plan implies an increasing emphasis on judgement about the future. Heads of department will have a feel for their particular areas. Central managements may be the first to detect the latest government or funding council pronouncement. Their collective foresight should inform the planning process.

Integrated is a concept that is so fundamental and multidimensional that it will form the basis of the next section of this chapter. Suffice it to say at this stage that it was the cuts imposed in 1981 and the subsequent decline in the funding base that forced institutions away from what was previously an academically led planning process and towards a more complex integrated process. The quinquennial statements of the 1960s and 1970s tended to be a shopping list of academic requirements, to which a price in terms of cash and space was subsequently added. At a time of government funded expansion such an approach was adequate, but in times of declining resources the search for efficient and effective management of resources calls for integration of academic, financial, staffing and physical planning within a committee and officer structure that can provide the necessary support and staff work.

Informed implies that there needs to be a sound basis for the planning process. In the first instance that means that consistent, timely and easily understood management information must be available to both the senior management team and departments. That implies a well-run management information system which has the confidence of both the centre and departments. It also implies the availability of performance indicators, which, together with judgement, can provide a basis for decision-making. These performance indicators need to be wide-ranging and brought together in a meaningful way.

Decisions is a reminder that the planning process is not an end in itself. It is a management tool contributing to the decision-making process, a process which should be geared to the objective of excellence in teaching and research. There is no point in having wonderful management information and planning mechanisms if, at the end of the day, an institution as a whole fails to take the key decisions necessary to achieve the goals of the institution. [Editors' note: one of the editors, David Palfreyman, was involved in the University College Cardiff financial debacle in the mid-1980s, being a member of the team from the University of Warwick called in by the college's council to assist in assessing the financial position and in providing an emergency plan to bring the institution back under control (Shattock, 1994, Chapter 6). In some respects the University College Cardiff information systems were more advanced than those in place at the University of Warwick, but the management was incapable of using the data to good effect. A decade later the college has 'merged' with the well-managed University of Wales Institute of Science and Technology next door, and the University of Warwick is generally seen as one of the most effective survivors of the 1980s government funding cuts.]

Planning strategy

While the above definition gives an insight into the various components of the planning process, it is necessary to explore in rather more depth what contributes to a planning strategy. The various components are represented diagrammatically in Figure 3.1. It will be seen that the model recognizes both internal and external influences and is reliant on an institutional analysis of strengths, weaknesses, opportunities and threats (SWOT analysis).

The first internal 'box' is a reminder that no two institutions are identical. Each institution has its own history, which will have affected its culture

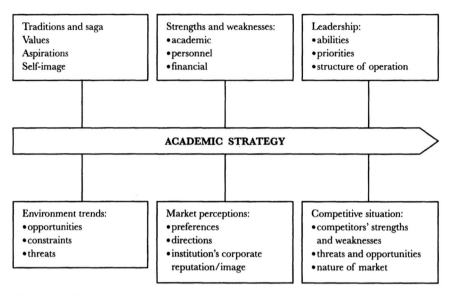

Figure 3.1 Components of a planning system
Source: Keller (1983)

and traditions. In the determination of an institutional strategy the nature of the institution cannot be ignored. This will lead to certain key questions in the planning process, which will link the past with the aspirations and future direction of the institution: 'Where are we now?' 'What do we want to be?' 'Where do we want to go?' 'How do we get there?' 'What do we do next?' 'Who is going to check progress?' 'What performance measures do we set?'

To address these questions one needs a dispassionate assessment of strengths and weaknesses. This will need to be conducted at both departmental and institutional levels and may well be associated with an institution's quality assurance mechanisms. Some institutions, for instance, have instituted periodic reviews of departments and/or courses incorporating not only members external to the department, but also those external to the institution. Such assessments need to range widely. The strength of teaching and research will be an obvious component, but financial strength and space requirements must play their part in the overall assessment.

There is a danger when describing the planning process of falling into the trap of giving the impression of a rational process, which proceeds from a critical analysis through logical debate to the final polished document. Do not be fooled; this is not so. Weiss (1982), for instance, has identified undirected strategies, including reliance on custom and implicit rules, improvisation, mutual adjustment, accretion, negotiation and move and counter-move. More will be said about this in the concluding remarks, but at this stage it is important to realize that coherence and direction in the planning process rely on the quality and priorities of the leadership. The aspirations of the institution as expressed through its mission statement are likely to have been formulated by a few key individuals. The acceptance of those aspirations by the institution as a whole, and the degree of success in achieving them, will depend upon the communication skills of those same key individuals. Leadership qualities at both a central institutional level and within departments are a critical component of a successful strategic plan.

If we turn now to the external dimension, it should be evident that no institution can exist in isolation. There will be environmental trends of both national and regional dimensions. These will indicate opportunities and threats to which each institution will need to respond in the knowledge of its own strengths and weaknesses and in the light of its aspirations. Of course, a perceived threat to one institution may be seen as an opportunity for another. Greater selectivity in research funding, for instance, might suit the strong research institutions but not those with a weaker research profile. Increasingly institutions have adopted a more market orientation. With a decline in government funding the search for additional resources has led to a diversity of income streams. In planning terms, an evaluation of the institution's position in relation, for instance, to its geographical position, the local economy and its industrial orientation will influence its strategic direction.

Similarly, an assessment of the current and future competitive environment will highlight further opportunities and threats. Following the abolition by the Further and Higher Education Act 1992 of the binary divide, there are now an increased number of institutions with the status of universities and an increased number of such institutions within close proximity to each other. In these circumstances the opportunities and threats associated with competition and collaboration are likely to increase. Such trends serve to underline the importance of a rigorous evaluation of an institution's positioning, followed by the will to take consequential decisions on the basis of that evaluation.

This section has stressed both the internal and external dimensions to the planning process and has highlighted the value of undertaking a SWOT analysis. In that context a useful analytical tool is a directional policy matrix. Such a matrix, as adapted by Sizer (1982) is shown in Figure 3.2. This compares a university's strengths in various subject areas relative to other institutions with the future attractiveness of subject areas, so as to identify priority areas for future growth, consolidation and rationalization.

Such a matrix, however, can only be a tool to inform the management process. What may appear to be a weak area may, for instance, make a valuable and indispensable contribution to another area of activity. A science department, for example, might have a weak research record and have difficulty in recruiting honours degree students, but it might form an integral part of the academically more successful faculty of medicine. Such an example merely confirms the complexity of the planning process and emphasizes the need for subjective judgement to be applied to the wealth of factual and analytical information that might be available.

SUBJECT AREA ATTRACTIVENESS

- Market size
- Market growth rate
- Market diversity
- Competitive structure
- Cost structure
- Optimal department size
- Demographic trends
- Scientific importance
- Technological trends
- Social/political and economic trends
- Environmental trends
- Government attitudes
- Employment prospects
- Cultural importance
- Etc.

UNIVERSITY STRENGTHS IN THE SUBJECT AREA

- Size of department
- Market share
- Market position
- Number of applications
- Quality of student intake
- Graduate employment
- Cost per FTE student
- Reputation
- Quality and age of staff
- Research record
- Research capabillity
- Image
- Publications record
- Resources: availability and mobility
- Etc.

	High	Medium	Low
High	Growth	Selective growth or consolidation	Consolidation
Medium	Selective growth or consolidation	Consolidation	Planned withdrawal and redeployment
Low	Consolidation or planned withdrawal and redeployment	Planned withdrawal and redeployment	Planned withdrawal and redeployment

Figure 3.2 Directional policy matrix
Source: Sizer (1982)

Integration

It was seen above that a critical component of the planning process was the concept of integration. It will be obvious from what has been said already that any planning strategy has to take into account academic, financial, staffing and space considerations. During a period of expansion when government funds followed approval of academic plans, issues of integration tended to be of less significance. Conditioned to the primacy of academic planning, many institutions approached the 1981 cuts by converting a financial crisis into an academic crisis, by concentrating on staff losses. The experience of that time led to a future shift of emphasis away from concentration merely on reducing expenditure and towards a more balanced approach of reducing expenditure and encouraging income-generating schemes. As the 1980s progressed and government policy turned towards expansion of student numbers but without matching funds, institutions had to balance their academic aspirations with their ability to raise sufficient funds to sustain these aspirations. Within such a framework some institutions concentrated on an expansion of student numbers, financing additional accommodation out of projected additional fee income; some institutions looked towards more industrial links; and others adopted a more cautious approach to expansion, preferring to build upon their research strengths. The need for a more integrated approach to the planning process therefore began to lead to more diffusion in institutional missions.

Increasingly institutional planning has incorporated not only academic and financial considerations but also the establishment of an estates strategy. The use and costing of space has increased in profile, reflecting the general pressure for more efficient and effective management of resources, of which space forms an important element. An increase in the number and size of classes has led to the need to make more effective use of teaching accommodation, with more elaborate, often computer-based, timetable and room booking systems. Additional residences have often been built to a standard which will attract conference trade during vacation periods, reflecting the need to use the estate to raise income throughout the year. This consideration has also underlined some of the debate about the length of the academic year. Could space be more effectively used by such an extension, or would it adversely affect income from the conference trade or short-course activities generated during the summer and Easter vacations? The balance of argument will vary depending upon the circumstances of each institution, but considerations of this nature are at the heart of the planning process.

Those developments have been reflected within the committee structure. Traditionally, chartered universities have had both a council (court in Scotland) and a senate. The former has been the executive body with responsibility for the business affairs of the institution, including financial and estate matters. Senate, while technically reporting to council, has had primacy in academic matters, in which council would not interfere. Clearly, if planning is to be an integrated process, the responsibilities of these two bodies need to be brought together in some way. This issue received the attention of the Jarratt Committee (1985), which urged 'Councils to assert their responsibilities in governing their institutions notably in respect of strategic plans' (para. 5.5a) and recommended the establishment of 'planning and resources committees of strictly limited size reporting to Senate and Council' (para. 5.5e). Such committees are now a well-established feature of the committee structure of most HE institutions. The composition of such committees raises interesting issues within the decision-making process. The Jarratt Committee believed that they should be composed of 'both lay and academic members all of whom should recognise that they are there to pursue the corporate interest of the university and not to represent sectional interests', under the chairmanship of the vice-chancellor (para. 3.43b). Committee membership may vary between institutions, but their focus is likely to be the coordination of planning strategy and the internal resource allocation methodology and distribution that supports that strategy. A typical committee may be composed of the vice-chancellor (in the chair), chair of council, treasurer, deputy vice-chancellor, one or two pro-vice-chancellors and members appointed by senate and council, perhaps between two and four from each body. This formal structure, however, may well hide much informal interaction. In particular, the influence of the registrar and the planning officer will be significant. They will almost certainly attend meetings of the committee, will have provided much of the documentation and will have a thorough understanding of the issues. Moreover, in recent years the role of deans has become more managerial and in some institutions they are significant budget holders. It is likely that they will be kept fully informed of the committee's deliberations and will have an input into them. In cases where deans are formally members of such committees, however, it is difficult to avoid a tension between their managerial and representational roles. The nature and form of the interaction between different parties in this process will depend heavily on the culture of the institution, but, as mentioned elsewhere in this chapter, it is necessary to understand that the planning process is not merely a rational process. It is also a political process influenced by the priorities and preferences of powerful individuals and interest groups.

The reference to non-academic managers raises the issue of administrative support for the planning process and the degree of integration of the management as a whole. The general pattern in the chartered universities, although there are exceptions, has been for the non-academic management to be headed by a single senior officer with the title of 'registrar' or 'registrar and secretary'. Since the mid-1980s the appointment of planning officers heading a group reporting to the registrar has been a common development. Some institutions have adopted a dual-headed structure, with the registrar responsible for academic administration and perhaps a bursar responsible for financial and estates matters. The advantage of the former model has been the easier integration of the different elements in the

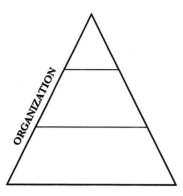

Strategic planning: 3–5-year plans

Tactical planning: annually

Operational planning: daily

Figure 3.3 The planning process within an organization
Source: Simon (1961)

planning process at a level below that of the vice-chancellor. The statutory universities have, in the main, a tradition of a directorate model adopting a team approach. A member of the directorate would be responsible for strategic planning. The evidence of recent years suggests that there has been a shift in the structures of some chartered universities towards the appointment of executive deputy or pro-vice-chancellors, one of whom will have a specific brief for planning and resource allocation issues. Planning officers increasingly interact with this member of the senior management team, sometimes to the detriment of the registrar's influence.

Although the person designated as planning officer will have an overall coordinating role, there will be many members of the non-academic management and academic departments who will be involved in the planning process in some form. A further issue within the concept of integration is therefore the need for interaction between academic departments and the central authorities. This need has increased in recent years, with the adoption in many institutions of enhanced devolution of budgetary responsibility to a school or departmental level.

The need for such interaction is a reminder that the planning process takes place at different levels within an organization. Figure 3.3 differentiates between strategic, tactical and operational planning. It has been suggested in this chapter that strategic planning should indicate in broad terms how the university intends to develop. It will form the basis of mission statements and will be the focus of the formal planning documents submitted to the funding council. While the groundwork for that plan will inevitably be in the hands of a few key individuals, there needs to be a constant interaction between the central management team and the academic departments. There needs to be a 'top-down, bottom-up' process to ensure that the ownership of the strategic plan lies with the institution as a whole. If this is not achieved there will be constant tension between the centre and departments, and inconsistency between institutional policy and departmental practice.

Strategic planning needs to be supported by the necessary funds to convert aspirations into reality. A separate chapter of this book deals with the resource allocation process, but that process cannot be conducted in isolation. It is an integral part of the planning process. Institutions will conduct an annual budgetary exercise. In the context of the model in Figure 3.3 that exercise may be regarded as the tactical planning layer, in which financial allocations give medium-term expression to longer-term strategic plans. That allocation process and the subsequent monitoring of performance will be most effective if there is mutual understanding between managerial and academic staff as to the objectives and operational constraints affecting the process.

This mutual involvement is equally important at the operational level. A heavy burden falls upon heads of department, but it is not only heads of department who are involved in operational planning. Admissions tutors need to recognize the importance of recruitment decisions, research grant applications need to be successful and the distribution of teaching, research and administrative duties between different members of staff is crucial to the management of the department. These operational decisions need to be consistent with both the strategic direction of the institution and the supporting budgetary policy. Again, these decisions will be more effective if there is integration between the academic department and the central institutional authorities. Much of that integration will be informal. Planning and the successful implementation of strategy is as much about discussions in corridors and over coffee as it is about formal committee resolutions and planning statements.

The above emphasis on interaction between academic departments and the central management, and between different branches of the central management, leads to the issue of integration of information. Whether the objective be forward planning, the monitoring of performance or routine daily decisions, the information base must be consistent, reliable, timely and in a form that is easily understood by all users. This is not the place to explore technical requirements, but the quality of the planning process at a strategic, tactical and operational level can be influenced by the quality of an institution's management information system.

Conclusion

As indicated earlier, there is a danger in a chapter such as this that the impression might be given that strategic planning is a rational exercise conducted at specified times and in specified committees by senior members of the institution, who take a dispassionate, analytical view of internal strengths and weaknesses in the light of external opportunities and threats.

I hope that at various points in the above text there has been sufficient indication that institutional planning can be a highly political process. Managerial staff involved in the process need to adopt an objective, professional

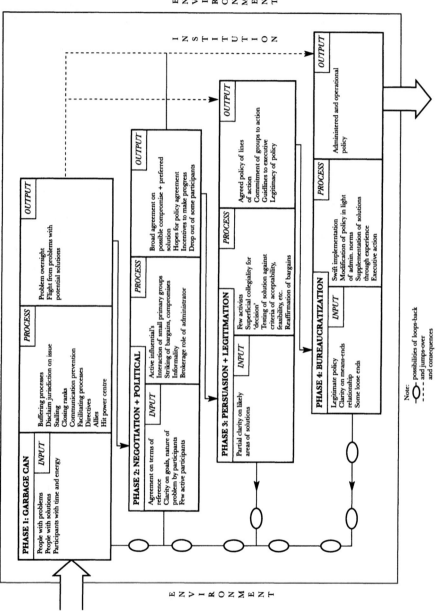

Figure 3.4 Four-phase political model of policy formation

approach, but they also need to be aware of all the undertones and micro-political activity that is taking place. This political element in the planning process has been seen to grow in importance in times of financial restraint (Davies, 1985). As Bruton (1987: 382) has observed, 'the production of an academic plan and allocations to cost centres is unlikely to be reached with full agreement of all parties. Rather it will more than likely be adopted after prolonged bargaining sessions amongst the leading protagonists, and arbitration through majority decisions of senate and council.'

Given this environment, it is useful to see the formation of policy as a sequence of events evolving through different phases. The omission of any one of these phases may lead to problems in implementation. Moreover, there will be times in the process when it will be advantageous to loop back to an earlier phase to check or review progress. A four-phase model is shown in Figure 3.4, and this can provide a useful framework for monitoring the policy formation process. It is a reminder that between initial discussion of issues and final agreement on policy there will be complex phases of negotiation and persuasion.

The observation and knowledge of these processes, combined with the opportunity to contribute to the future of the institution through professional skill and understanding, make involvement in strategic planning such an interesting, complex, fascinating and at times highly satisfying, amusing and frustrating activity.

4

Sources of Funds and Resource Allocation

John Sandbach and Harold Thomas

Editors' introduction

This chapter is in two separate sections: the first deals with the sources of funds for HEIs, and the second examines how these funds are allocated within institutions – resource capture and resource allocation.

John Sandbach provides a valuable analysis of income from the funding councils, explaining in some detail the complexity of both teaching- and research-related funds. (However, the reader is reminded that there are three national HE funding councils and that their practices could, and on some points do, differ. Moreover, funding from government sources seems to be subject to constant change and the reader should *always* check that he or she has in hand the latest arrangements.) Income generation in HE is a vast subject, and the first author has only been able to sketch in a few areas. Readers who wish to go further might consult with benefit *The Income Generation Handbook* (Warner and Leonard, 1992). See also Palfreyman (1989 and 1992b).

Harold Thomas guides us clearly through the key issues in resource allocation. (He does so with brevity, although, as someone who has just completed a doctorate on the topic, he must have been sorely tempted to write at much greater length!)

1 SOURCES OF FUNDS

Introduction

In Dickens' *David Copperfield*, Mr Micawber expounded his first principle of financial management thus: 'Annual income twenty pounds, annual expenditure nineteen and six, result happiness. Annual income twenty pounds, annual expenditure twenty pounds nought and six, result misery.' Unfortunately, Micawber did not seek to accompany his financial principles with any financial planning, preferring to wait for things to 'turn up'. The higher education funding councils have demonstrated an empathy with the Micawber principles, and as a condition of grant they require each institution they fund to 'plan and conduct its financial and academic affairs so as to ensure that its total income is at least sufficient taking one financial year with another to meet its total expenditure and that its financial solvency is maintained.' Waiting for things to turn up is not an option, and therefore maintaining the right relationship between income and expenditure is of paramount importance to an HEI. Indeed, its continued existence relies upon it.

Income

Income is the life-blood of any enterprise. It is particularly advantageous if such income is relatively certain and largely received in cash rather than on credit, this being the case for HEIs. A further feature of successful enterprise is an ability to increase turnover and, while most HEIs strive to do this, they are working under certain constraints.

In 1993–4 the total income of HEIs in Great Britain funded by the former University Funding Council amounted to £5598 million, from the sources shown in Table 4.1.

Funding council grants

The various higher education funding councils are the single main source of public funding for HEIs. While all institutions jealously guard their independence, which is extremely important to them, the annual grant announcement from the funding council is probably the most eagerly awaited letter of the year, as it forms the foundation for the next year's financial plans.

Each year funding councils advise their respective secretaries of state on the funding needs of higher education in their country. The global sum to be made available for higher education in each province is decided by the government and approved by Parliament. These sums are announced by the appropriate secretary of state at the time of the budget statement at the end of November for the year beginning the following April.

From these announcements each funding council converts the global sums into allocations to individual institutions. It does so within policy guidelines provided by the secretary of state and expresses them as sums for the following August to July academic year. Institutions are notified of their allocations in February or March. Through its financial memorandum with its funding council, each institution is accountable to the council, and ultimately to Parliament, for the use of these funds. Indeed, the published accounts of every HEI are required to contain an audit certificate confirming (or otherwise) that funds from the funding council have been applied only for the purposes for which they were received.

Table 4.1 Sources of funding for HEIs

	£ million	£ million	%
Funding council grants			
Recurrent – block	1569		
Recurrent – other	124		
Equipment and furniture	157		
Other	2	1852	33.1
Academic fees			
Full-time home and EU	821		
Overseas students	299		
Part-time degree and diplomas	52		
Other	169	1341	24.0
Endowments, donations and subventions			
Income from endowments	70		
Health and hospital authorities	86		
Other	77	233	4.2
Computer board grants		14	0.2
Residences and catering			
Residences	301		
Catering	92	393	7.0
Other general income			
Investment of other general funds	66		
Other	206	272	4.9
Research grants and contracts			
Research councils	433		
UK charities	290		
Other bodies	494	1217	21.7
Other services		276	4.9
Total income		5598	100

Source: Form 3, 1993–4.

Nature of grant

Although funding councils use a number of elements and formulae in deciding how to allocate grant to institutions, and although it is built up on teaching- and research-related criteria, the basic grant is generally regarded as being a block grant, which institutions are free to distribute internally at their own discretion, as long as it is used for proper academic and academic-related purposes. However, there is increasing pressure being brought to bear on institutions for them to be more accountable for the teaching and research elements of grant.

Funding councils have made it clear that grants are in exchange for teaching and research and are conditional on their delivery. The basis on which funding has been provided is included in the 'funding agreement', which forms part 2 of the financial memorandum between the council and each institution.

The main elements that make up recurrent grant are:

- teaching funds;
- research funds;
- non-formula funds;
- transitional funds.

A feature of council funding since the new combined higher education sector was formed in 1993–4 has been the objective of managing transition to an integrated sector so that no institution has had to cope with unreasonable rates of change in grant from the previous year. Councils have therefore moderated the outcomes from the formula funding methodologies through capping the rate of growth in funds and introducing a safety net to the rate of reduction in funds.

Teaching-related funds

About January each year councils decide the sum to be distributed for teaching from the total sum announced by the secretary of state. This sum is then divided into core funding and margin funding. Core funding is the part of an institution's grant for teaching that is carried forward from one year to the next. It forms a very high percentage of teaching funds, thus providing financial stability, in return for which the institution is required to maintain the number of home/EU student enrolments. Margin funds are distributed on a competitive basis to provide for additional student numbers, the development of infrastructure and support for specific initiatives in teaching.

Core funding for teaching is calculated through a formula using funding cells (see Figure 4.1). These cells are defined by: 11 academic subject categories; two modes of study (full-time and sandwich, and part-time); two levels of study (undergraduate and postgraduate taught, and postgraduate research). The number of funding cells in which any institution receives funding is determined by the number of subjects and courses offered, the types of students taking those courses and the different levels of study. Larger universities will be active in most of the funding cells, with smaller, more specialist, colleges active in only a few. Certified student numbers are returned to the funding council in December as a basis for grant calculation.

The price to be applied to each cell will be influenced by three factors:

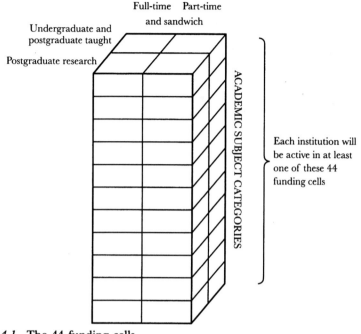

Figure 4.1 The 44 funding cells
Source: HEFCE (1995b)

inflation, efficiency gains and tuition fee compensation. Unit prices are uplifted from year to year to take account of the government's estimate for inflation. However, the government's requirement of recent years that institutions become more efficient has been effected by applying an efficiency gain to the unit of resource. Such efficiency gains have been applied to institutions differentially, based on their average unit of council funding (AUCF). The AUCF is calculated by dividing the amount of council funding in each funding cell by the number of students in that cell. This allows comparisons in the levels of funding to be made between institutions for each funding cell. Institutions with lower AUCFs will be expected to achieve lower percentage efficiency gains. In 1994–5 the government reduced the level of tuition fees by some 45 per cent, but provided funding councils with tuition fee compensation to be distributed through teaching grant. The total amount of core funding for each institution is calculated by adding together the adjusted amounts in each funding cell.

Margin funding aims to secure growth in student numbers and support specific developments in teaching. It is allocated competitively, usually having received bids from institutions in response to initiatives announced by the funding council.

Formula-based margin funds are used to allocate additional funds for student growth, and in the present period of consolidation are rewarding growth in part-time provision. A feature of this methodology is that institutions with the lowest AUCFs will receive the highest proportionate increase. Margin funds may also be distributed through core proposals, where the council invites institutions to make proposals for additional students in response to specific programmes. Funding allocated to institutions whose bids are successful is incorporated into core funding in the following year.

Funding councils notify institutions of the *contract student numbers* (CSNs) that they are expected to teach for available grant, and failure to enrol numbers to this level will lead to a clawback of grant linked to the shortfall. Additionally, institutions are advised of a maximum aggregate student number (MASN) up to which tuition fee compensation is payable. This relates only to students in respect of whom publicly funded fees are payable, but such compensation is held back to the extent that MASN is not met or a penalty imposed where MASN is exceeded by 1.5 per cent (1995–6).

Research-related funds

Research-related grant is distributed selectively to those institutions which have demonstrated strength in research according to national and international standards. Public funds for research are provided under the dual support system, whereby funding council grant contributes to the salaries of permanent academic staff, premises and central computing costs, while research councils meet direct project costs and contribute to indirect project costs.

The general funds provided to institutions by funding councils support basic research and contribute to the cost of research training. This basic research forms the foundation for strategic and applied work, which may be supported later by research councils, charities and industry. Research funding is formula-based, with three elements to the formula:

- quality-related research (QR) reflects quality and volume;
- development research (DevR) to encourage research development;
- generic research (GR) to reward generic research.

QR accounts for some 94 per cent of total research funding. It is built up from individual allocations made for each of 72 units of assessment, which correspond to those used in the research assessment exercise (RAE). The amount allocated to each institution within each subject is proportional to a volume measure multiplied by a quality measure.

$$\text{amount} = \text{quality} \times \text{volume}$$

The quality of research is assessed by peer review in an RAE. The last RAE, conducted in 1992, will inform funding decisions until 1996–7. The latest RAE in 1996 will inform funding from 1997–8. Institutions have been awarded a rating on a scale of 1 to 5 for the quality of research in each unit of assessment in which they made a submission in 1992. This is adjusted to a scale of 0 to 4, where a rating of 1 attracts no funding and the best grade of 5 attracts four times as much rating as a rating of 2. The funding council can vary the relationship between the RAE and the funding scale to make research funding more or less selective.

Volume measures and weightings within each unit of assessment are:

Research active academic staff	1.0
Research assistants and research fellows	0.1
Postgraduate research students	0.15
Research income from charities	0.2 × (charities research income (2-year average)/25,000)

Data are updated annually. The total QR funding for each institution is the sum of individual allocations calculated for each unit of assessment. Increases in funding for 1995–6 have been restricted to 15 per cent.

A small element in the research formula is *DevR*, aimed at fostering the selective development of research potential in institutions in receipt of only limited research funding. Currently DevR is restricted to institutions in the former PCFC sector and, therein, only to those units which scored 2 or above in the 1992 RAE.

A *GR* element was introduced in 1994–5 in response to the theme of wealth creation in the Science and Technology White Paper, *Realising Our Potential*, published in 1993. GR funding seeks to reward collaborative research that does not have a single beneficiary. Allocations are made in proportion to each institution's GR qualifying income, this being defined as the total received from users of research for collaborative projects where the institution retains the intellectual property and publication rights to the related research.

Non-formula grant

Funding councils recognize that not all teaching and research can be adequately supported through formula funding. Therefore non-formula allocations are made for purposes that include London allowances, inherited liabilities and loan charges, copyright libraries, museums, galleries and collections, and minority subjects. These grants are reviewed regularly and, wherever appropriate, phased out or incorporated into formula-based allocations.

There are occasions when funding councils wish to stimulate special initiatives or provide assistance for specific purposes. In such cases an earmarked grant is made, which requires an institution to spend such grant solely on the purpose for which it was awarded. Failure to comply with this requirement will invariably result in clawback of grant.

Capital grants

Capital grants are provided by funding councils to help institutions to maintain and develop their land, buildings and equipment. Estates and equipment funds are distributed by formula, while project grants are bid related.

Some 70 per cent of capital funding is distributed by formula. It is paid as a single grant to meet the costs of estates improvements and equipment purchase. Following the announcement of the government's private finance initiative, it may also be used to service loans for new capital projects. The total grant for each institution consists of a minimum amount plus a sum calculated to reflect the level of teaching and research activity.

In recent years, funding councils have become concerned about the problem of backlog maintenance. Having commissioned independent surveys of each institution, they are providing funding for a fixed number of years to supplement institutions' own efforts to deal with this problem.

Capital project grants are now provided only to help institutions with major projects, whereas such grants used to meet the whole cost. Recent bids for grant have been invited from institutions on the basis that funding councils will only fund a proportion of approved cost (usually 25 per cent). Submission must demonstrate that the project is consistent with the institution's estate strategy and that funding the balance will not adversely effect its financial health.

Tuition fees

Tuition fees are charges levied by an institution in respect of every student it educates in return for education provided. It is usual for the governing body to approve fee levels for all students, though they are likely to be cognizant of various external factors. By far the majority of students fit into the full-time category. Most undergraduate courses are for a three-year period and the vast majority of students on such courses will be in receipt of a mandatory award from their local education authority, if UK based, or will be paid for under EU regulations if within the EU area. Fees are divided into three bands: band 1 relates to classroom-based courses (mainly in arts and humanities); band 2 relates to courses with a significant laboratory or workshop component (primarily in science and engineering); and band 3 covers the clinical elements of medical, dental and veterinary courses.

While there are certain postgraduate courses (for example, postgraduate certificate of education) that qualify for mandatory awards and thus attract an appropriate standard tuition fee, the fees for most postgraduate courses are determined by individual institutions, though the Department for Education and Employment specifies a maximum level it will pay through postgraduate award schemes. The calculation of such fees may be influenced by the level of funding council support, the marginal costs of providing courses and, possibly, market forces, although this last influence has not yet made a significant or obvious impact in the HE sector other than for MBA courses.

Fees for part-time courses are entirely at the discretion of individual institutions and are subject to the same influences as full-time postgraduate courses. The modularization of university degrees (i.e. the ability to put together a degree programme comprising several self-contained course modules, as in the Open University model) may lead to changes in tuition fee funding nationally, as the existing model relating to full-time undergraduate courses becomes more and more inappropriate. However, there is marked variation between part-time course fee levels at different institutions.

Special courses are usually provided at the request of individual companies or for specific industries, and are often the opportunity to forge links between the institution and industry/commerce in its area. Students on such courses will be sponsored by the promoting companies, and the course fees will be a matter of negotiation between the institution and the company, or group of companies, involved. Clearly, in determining fees the institution must have regard to its costs, but will also need to take account of what companies may be prepared to pay and the beneficial impact of having local industry involved in the institution's activities.

Tuition fees for overseas students are a matter for each individual institution. Such fees are usually well in excess of those charged to home students because since 1980 the government has required that overseas fees should cover the full economic cost of tuition. Students from the Channel Islands and the Isle of Man are regarded as Island students, and are charged special fees that include an element for research. These fee levels are set by the Department for Education and Employment.

Distance and open learning courses were for many years seen as the prerogative of the Open University. Many institutions have, however, realized that the development of distance learning materials can lead to significant benefits in recruitment without, necessarily, significant direct cost increases other than the initial preparation of such materials. There are now many courses which have a distance learning component and, although they are not yet particularly significant in overall terms, there will undoubtedly be growth in this area, for which, again, individual institutions determine their own tuition fees.

European funds

The EU provides a significant amount of funding in support of education and training. Generally, EU funding is provided in the form of grants that must be matched by the institution receiving them. Such funding often includes a number of complexities that make this funding, while welcome, often uncertain as to the sum to be received and the timing of receipts.

Under present arrangements there are two principal structural funds.

The European Regional Development Fund (ERDF) provides capital grants, while the European Social Fund (ESF) provides revenue funds. Both funds are designed to support particular policy objectives of the European Union. The European Union also supports various transnational training programmes aimed at improving employment prospects through the exchange of experience and ideas between EU member states. A plethora of different grants have now been consolidated into the LEONARDO and SOCRATES programmes.

Endowments and donations

Endowments and donations form a small part of the total income of higher education institutions, but they can still be a significant factor in the establishment of specific projects in respect of which general appeals for contributions are made. Endowments usually take the form of a gift of a capital sum, the interest and dividends arising from the related investment being used to support a specific activity on a continuing basis; for example, a professorship, a scholarship or a prize fund.

Annual donations from local education authorities are largely historic and now form a small and declining part of institutions' recurrent income.

Other investment income

Higher education institutions are multi-million pound organizations, and often have considerable cash balances available for investment. Finance directors will usually seek to maximize interest earned on such sums while not putting the capital at undue risk. Through effective treasury management institutions can earn significant income.

Research grants and contracts

Institutions are continually striving to increase income from research grants and contracts. These monies are applied for by academics, or groups of academics, for the pursuit of particular lines of research. The most prestigious grants are provided by the research councils, of which there are six.

- The Biotechnology and Biological Sciences Research Council (BBSRC) has responsibility for agriculture, food, plant sciences, animal science and psychology, genetics, microbiology, developmental biology, pollution biology and evolution, invertebrate neuroscience, biotechnology and biomolecular sciences.
- The Engineering and Physical Sciences Research Council (EPSRC) has responsibilities for chemistry, mathematics, some physics, information technology and the various branches of engineering.

- The Economic and Social Research Council (ESRC) covers a very wide range of subjects, including economics, political sciences, social anthropology, sociology, psychology, education, statistics, management and industrial studies.
- The Medical Research Council (MRC) is the main government agency for the promotion of medical research.
- The Natural Environment Research Council (NERC) supports research in the area of geological sciences, oceanography, marine and other life sciences, science-based archaeology, atmospheric sciences and environmental pollution.
- The Particle Physics and Astronomy Research Council (PPARC) looks after particle physics, solar system science, astronomy and astrophysics.

Research Council grants are intended to cover direct costs and some of the related indirect costs. The amount contributed to an institution's indirect costs is calculated as 40 per cent of the gross salary costs met through each grant. The balance of indirect cost is deemed to be met from the research element of funding council grant under the dual support principle.

Research contract work is provided to government, local authorities, industry and commerce. For such work the funding councils expect that in determining the price to be charged institutions should cover the full cost, including all indirect costs, unless the institution considers that there are circumstances in which this would not be appropriate or in the best interests of the institution. This area is dealt with more fully in the second section of Chapter 9.

Consultancies

Institutions, as part of their quest to find new income sources, are increasingly undertaking consultancies for, and providing other services to, external bodies on a commercial basis. Examples of such consultancies are advice on business development and the testing of products. Much will depend on an institution's subject mix and special expertise of staff. Many institutions operate such services through wholly owned trading companies.

Services rendered

HEIs, by their very nature, contain a wide variety of expertise, which provides opportunities to supply a market. It is not possible to detail a comprehensive list of the services institutions provide, but some of the more common ones are outlined in succeeding paragraphs.

Not all services provide an opportunity to make an economic charge. Many universities validate courses in institutions that do not have the power to award their own degrees. The fee, which is charged for each student registered, is now negotiated between institutions. It is intended to cover the costs incurred by the university in course approval and the examination of students.

A more commercial approach can be taken where an institution is required to tender for courses. This is currently occurring in areas such as nursing and professions allied to medicine, where institutions are being invited to provide courses of a prescribed quality at competitive prices. Institutions with medical schools have developed special arrangements to provide a range of services to hospitals. Quite complex relationships exist between medical faculties and the health service but in the laboratory disciplines there are opportunities to provide a wide range of diagnostic services to local hospitals at agreed charges.

In the provision of any service to an outside party, institutions are under the same obligations from the financial memorandum with the funding council to cost adequately the service being provided as a basis for deciding on a proper charge.

Catering and residences

The provision of catering services and residential accommodation to its students is regarded as being ancillary to the primary purpose of an HEI. The general principle to be applied is that users should meet the cost of providing such services through the charge levied. There is a long-standing principle that catering and residence accounts should operate on a self-financing basis and not be subsidized from funds awarded for academic purposes.

There has always been scope for charging students less than a full economic charge. Institutions have sought to balance catering and residence accounts by making more economic charges to non-student users, such as conferences, holiday lettings and catering functions. This policy helps to maximize income and spread fixed costs over the largest possible customer base.

The use of HE residential and teaching facilities by conferences, particularly during vacation periods, is well established and is often the way in which the catering and residence account is kept in balance. The value and volume of conference activities on an institution's premises should not be underestimated, and is one of the important factors that needs to be taken into account when changes to an institution's academic pattern are being considered. This topic is dealt with more fully in Chapter 11.

2 RESOURCE ALLOCATION

Introduction

The previous section of this chapter has reviewed the sources of funding available to institutions. The purpose of this section is to consider how those funds are allocated within institutions. Although the emphasis here will be on the principles of allocation to academic departments, it is important to remember that the same standards of financial management apply to heads of budget centres in the non-academic areas.

Expenditure

HE institutions are regarded as 'not for profit' organizations and therefore, while they are required to operate within available income, expenditure is likely to be closely related to income. In 1993–4 total expenditure by HEIs in Great Britain funded by the former Universities Funding Council was as shown in Table 4.2.

Table 4.2   Expenditure by HEIs, 1993–4

	£ million	£ million	%
Academic departments			
Academic and related staff	1384		
Technical staff	198		
Clerical and secretarial staff	130		
Other staff	14		
Departmental expenditure	362	2088	38.6
Academic services			
Libraries	157		
Computer facilities	75		
Other	65	297	5.5
General educational expenditure		104	1.9
Premises		533	9.9
Administration		287	5.3
Student and staff facilities		89	1.6
Equipment and furniture		201	3.7
Residences and catering			
Residences	294		
Catering	93	387	7.2
Miscellaneous expenditure		145	2.7
Research grants and contracts		1048	19.4
Other services		227	4.2
Total expenditure		5406	100
Employee costs		3206	59.3
Other costs		2200	40.7
		5406	100

Source: Form 3, 1993–4.

Allocation and control

The essential element of financial management is the annual budget. This is an income and expenditure plan that seeks to identify and quantify the revenue resources available to an institution and to relate expenditure to strategic plans and available income.

Once budgets have been approved it is important that those responsible for incurring and controlling expenditure, heads of budgetary units, are provided with regular financial information to enable them to manage the expenditure for which they are accountable. Regular information reports should include details of expenditure to date and commitments made but not yet paid, comparing these with approved budgets and expenditure plans.

Current trends are for a lessening of detailed central control by the allowance of a greater devolution of resources to budget units and the allotment to them of flexible management and virement within prescribed parameters. The devolution of budgets is enhanced when it is accompanied by a transparent and flexible resource allocation model to reflect strategic plans.

As explained in Chapter 3, the resource allocation process should be seen within the wider context of institutional planning, and many of the issues that emerged in the course of that chapter are equally applicable in the context of the allocation of resources. As such, this process of resource allocation should be regarded as the annual movement towards meeting the institution's long-term objectives. Mention of the annual budget also looks towards Chapter 5, which incorporates comments on such issues as devolution. This section can, therefore, be seen as a link between strategic planning, the attraction of funds and the management of those funds.

Earlier in this chapter, sources of income were seen to fall into two broad categories: funding council income for teaching and research and non funding council income. The latter used to be referred to as 'soft money', but it is indicative of today's climate with its emphasis on entrepreneurial activity that several HEIs now refer to their market generated funds as 'hard', whereas money from government is regarded as 'soft', subject to political whim and the vagaries of national economies (McNay, 1995a). Whatever terms are used, however, it is evident that volume in terms of student numbers, quality of research output and entrepreneurial activity all contribute to the total resources available to an institution. An appreciation of these various elements is significant, not only in understanding income streams, but also in appreciating internal allocation methodologies that are directed at maintaining an element of stability to core activities, supporting areas of excellence and new initiatives and providing incentives for income-generating activity. It is the balance between these different objectives that is influenced by the strategic direction of the institution and is a key element in the management process.

Recent trends

Since the mid-1980s, the resource allocation process has been subject to two particular influences. First, consistent with the Jarratt Report (1985), which recommended 'budget delegation to appropriate centres which are held responsible to the planning and resources committee for what they have achieved against their budgets' (para. 5.5f), there has been an emphasis on greater devolution to a budget centre level. It should not be thought, however, that the concept of devolution is something new. Historically, institutions have experienced an element of devolution, in that heads of department have been accountable for consumables and equipment expenditure, but devolution tends to become more meaningful to budget managers when they are also given responsibility for managing staffing resources. More sophisticated models charge budgetary units with utilities, such as telephones, postage, stationery, reprographics and in some cases energy. There is increasing interest in charging for space in an attempt to make units aware of the cost of space, and in some cases to encourage maximizing usage by giving refunds where space is surrendered. In a full cost allocation model, central services are also charged to budget units, and this tends to encourage efficiency by keeping the costs of central units under continuous scrutiny. Whatever costs are devolved to budget managers to control, an essential feature is that these should be costs that a manager can directly influence and control; otherwise management becomes artificial and accountability more difficult to promote.

The critical issue, therefore, is not the principle of devolution, but the degree and level of devolution that enhances efficient and effective management of resources, particularly during times of financial stringency (Pratt and Silverman, 1988). Alongside this thrust, the Jarratt Report (1985) commended the practice of developing departmental profit and loss statements (para. 3.35d). Such a practice has gained in popularity now that it is known how much each basic unit attracts from the funding council.

This leads to the second relatively recent influence: the move towards more formulaic approaches in the form of profit and loss accounts for budget centres. Again, the use of formulae is nothing new to institutions, which have adopted a range of approaches over many years (Shattock and Rigby, 1983), but the increase in transparency of the funding council methodology has increased pressure to adopt formulaic approaches at an institutional level, and in particular raises the issue of the extent to which the coefficients in any internal model should reflect those adopted by the funding council. This change was begun in 1986, when the UGC announced that its allocations would in future be based on teaching and research components (UGC, 1986). The former would be determined by student numbers and a unit of resource that differed between disciplines but not between universities, while the latter would be determined according to the outcome of the newly established research assessment exercise. The previous historic pattern of funding was thereby broken, although the UGC emphasized that its allocation represented a block grant as before, and that it was the responsibility of individual institutions to allocate this grant internally. The UGC did not divulge the coefficients in its formula, and many institutions spent time in unravelling the UGC's methodology so that their internal processes could be informed by knowledge of the income attracted by each of their academic departments. Although there is still some opaqueness in aspects of the allocation procedure (Johnston, 1993), the UGC's successor bodies have been more open about the details of their formula approach. The current methodology is described earlier in this chapter.

Devolution

Despite these twin pressures of devolution and formula-based systems, there has been a range of responses from institutions (Williams, 1992). As a consequence, both devolution and formula-based approaches may be regarded as continuums, the place of any institution along those continuums reflecting a range of factors. It has been recognized that stability in any organization is dependent upon the maintenance of a balance between the interrelated variables of task, technology, structure and people (Leavitt, 1965). These variables need to be kept in 'dynamic equilibrium', while being subjected to influences from the external environment (Scott Morton, 1992), as otherwise a period of mismatch will follow (Donaldson, 1987). The introduction of devolution will undoubtedly change the tasks and responsibilities of members of staff: heads of department will have more financial responsibility and non-academic management staff will need to adopt a more facilitating, interactive role in their relationships with academic departments. Prerequisites for a successful system of devolution therefore include: appropriate training and staff development; management information systems, which can provide accurate, timely, consistent and easily understood information; and support structures that are appropriate for the institution. In particular, the level and extent of devolution will need to recognize the culture of the institution and the historic power bases within it. To devolve to a faculty level when the traditional power lies at the level of the department might be expected to give rise to considerable micropolitical activity, while devolving to a departmental level may have the effect of creating management units that, while being viable academic units, are too small to exercise effective flexibility in the management of resources. As well as the various prerequisites outlined above, therefore, there will be certain determinants that will influence the nature and extent of devolution in any particular institution. These will include the priorities and preferences of the senior management team, more specifically: the management style of the vice-chancellor; organizational structure and culture; availability of staff with appropriate skills at a department level; subject mix and financial health of departments; and the micro-political forces that will be brought to bear on any change process.

Of course, the implication of what has been said above implies that stability is what is required. It may be that circumstances will dictate a need to shift the institution in a particular direction. For instance, the rationale of devolution is that it brings the pressures of the external environment to bear at a budget centre level, and by empowerment to managers at that level creates the opportunity for greater flexibility and speed of response. With a move away from collegiality and bureaucratic norms towards a more entrepreneurial culture (McNay, 1995a), the concept of devolution is an attractive proposition to senior managers who see a need to change the culture of the institution. Devolution is, therefore, as much concerned with cultural change as with financial management. If resource allocation methodologies are to be used in this way, however, there has to be a recognition that the groundwork will need to be set, particularly in terms of staff training, management information systems and the establishment of clear guidelines, if sound principles of financial management are to be maintained. More on this will be said in the next chapter.

Formulaic approaches

Irrespective of the level of devolution within an institution, there has to be some mechanism for allocating resources. The following comments address in particular allocations to academic areas. Allocations to central services are likely to be subject to a range of approaches and performance indicators depending upon the degree of centralization or decentralization adopted. While some areas, such as catering and residences, will be expected to generate market income, other areas will be judged on a needs basis in the light of prevailing financial pressures.

As indicated earlier in this chapter, the various methods for allocating income to budget centres may be regarded as a continuum. At one end, institutions may use a historic basis adjusted according to the sum available in any given year. At the other end, allocation may be governed by a predetermined formula. Between these extremes will lie a range of methodologies incorporating a balance between managerial judgement and the use of formulae. The formulaic approach may take the form of either a single profit and loss account for each unit or a number of indicators to allocate, for instance, equipment grant or the number of staff in different categories. The trend in recent years, consistent with the rationale of devolution, has been towards producing profit and loss accounts for budget centres, but the extent to which those budget centres are expected to live within the income they earn is a policy issue for each institution. It is possible, for instance, to use a profit and loss account as an evaluative tool, which informs rather than determines the process of allocation. As higher education has expanded and the allocation process has become more transparent, however, 'the link between the allocation of resources and evaluation became stronger and more explicit' (Becher and Kogan, 1992: 157).

Such considerations lead to the concept of a three-stage approach to the allocation of resources. The first stage will involve an appreciation of how the funding council's formula affects the institution. This is essential information required by senior managers and should reflect, through raw data, the funding council's model at an institutional level as an aid to managerial judgement. To this model should be added information on income from non funding council sources. Anything beyond this first stage of management information begins to involve internal decisions. The second stage may, for instance, involve a decision on the level of central overheads or the amount of earned income to be allocated to departments. The extent of these 'policy prompts or funding levers' (Fielden, 1993: para. 3) might change over time depending upon circumstances: the more anxious the central authorities to increase the number of overseas students, for example, the higher might be the percentage of fee income allocated to the academic department. It is obviously desirable for incentives to academic departments to be consistent: to install a system of incentives which is then withdrawn can create disillusionment and be counterproductive. Against these income figures will be set anticipated expenditure.

Both stage 1 and stage 2 provide valuable management information to senior staff. At an institutional level it is likely that such information will influence the planning process and will provide an opportunity for integration between strategic, tactical and operational planning. It should also be expected that the figures will be used by heads of department as part of the micro-political debate. Neither of these first two stages, however, is likely to be sufficiently refined to act as a determinant of allocations to a budget centre level.

It is at the third stage that institutions will have to decide their method of allocating resources to budget centres and the degree to which this will be influenced by a formulaic methodology. It is at this stage in particular that institutional history and culture and the personal preferences and priorities of key figures, particularly the vice-chancellor, will be significant. Where the HEI, or some of its budget centres, are in deficit, managerial intervention will be inevitable if realistic budgets are to be established. Even in healthy surplus situations, it may be desirable to 'top-slice' funds for allocation outside the model in order to pump prime new initiatives. A critical strategic issue is likely to be the balance between supporting highly rated research departments and trying to improve those with lower ratings. If all QR income is allocated to those departments attracting such funds, then the opportunities for improvement elsewhere or for supporting new initiatives are diminished. On the other hand, failure to support income-generating departments can lead to loss of morale and create disincentive. It is also possible that a sudden change from a historic basis to formula funding may shift the shape of the university. This will give rise to considerable micro-political activity and needs to be supported by sound managerial reasoning if it is to be successfully implemented. Moreover, a model that is heavily dependent on the influence of the funding council's coefficients will be subject to oscillation as those coefficients change; for instance, after each new research assessment exercise. Any internal model needs to take into account that shifts in institutional funding may be too great to pass to a budget centre level without some period of transition.

Conclusion

This chapter has reviewed the various sources of funds available to institutions and recent trends in resource allocation methodology. It has drawn particular attention to the shift towards income-generating activities and the trend towards budget centre accounting and reflecting at an institutional level the methodologies adopted by the funding councils. While these trends may be designed to bring an element of rationality and transparency into the resource allocation process, that process is still influenced by subjective judgement and the priorities and preferences of key individuals. Whatever institutional methodology is adopted, however, it is critical that the process is consistent with providing support for the teaching and research objectives of the institution. That support will need to incorporate sound financial management, which is the focus of the next chapter.

5

Financial Management

Barry Benjamin

Editors' introduction

Financial management affects all HE managers – academic and non-academic alike. In this chapter the author has covered the key financial parameters that are necessary for HE institutions as public bodies and highlighted some of the major elements of financial and management accounting. It is always difficult to assign certain functions to a clear management section, and the editors would like to alert readers to the fact that many HE 'finance offices' also have responsibility for insurance and the wider area of risk management. This topic is covered in depth in Chapter 12 of the Open University Press publication *Managing Educational Property* (Warner and Kelly, 1994).

Finally, the editors would like to draw the attention of readers to the financial policy that determines the *modus operandi* of one large statutory university:

- expenditure will not exceed income;
- no short-term borrowing to cover recurrent expenditure shortfalls;
- establish a reserve fund;
- staff costs not to exceed 66 per cent of annual turnover.

Introduction

In the eyes of the majority of managers and academic staff within higher education, the importance of their institution relates to the impact of the academic process of teaching and/or research. This is an understandable and natural consequence of their understanding of the *raison d'être* of higher education. However, in the matter of finance, a large number of staff employed within HE remain in total ignorance of the budgetary breakdown and financial size of individual institutions, despite the importance in financial terms that each institution has on the local and national economy: through the employment of staff, the attraction to the local area of an influx of students, the related 'multiplier effect' on the local economy and the extent of its overall purchasing power.

This ignorance of the financial environment within which an HE institution operates contrasts markedly with the situation within private industry and commerce. The turnover of Company A or Company B and their related profitability are often quoted to emphasize the importance and status of the organization. When one is seeking to make a judgement as to the nature of financial management within an HE institution, it is important to relate the function with similar sized organizations in the private sector, as well as within the public sector, of the economy. This is not to adopt an attitude of slavish adoption of practices in other sectors but to realize that an HE institution is a sizable and complex organization and that the requirement for a strong professional financial support service is paramount in the underpinning of a successful institution. Indeed, the knowledge that, during the period 1990–4, twenty institutions faced a situation of actual or potential financial difficulty (National Audit Office, 1994) is a salutary reminder of the need for sound financial management.

The relationship between the funding council(s) and individual institutions

When one is seeking to assess the scope of the range of the requirements for the finance function, it is important to understand the relationship between each HE institution and its respective national funding council. For the purposes of this chapter, I will use examples from the Higher Education Funding Council for England (HEFCE), but similar arrangements exist between the Welsh and Scottish Funding Councils and their institutions. This relationship is governed by a financial memorandum (HEFCE, 1993a), which sets out the terms and conditions under which a grant is made to English HE institutions and covers such matters as the necessity for sound financial management and control, the need to ensure overall financial solvency, the rules for property acquisition and disposal of land and buildings, the rules for borrowing and leasing, the requirement to maintain proper accounting records and to prepare financial statements for each accounting period, to assess the full cost of research contracts and other services, to appoint an audit committee, to arrange for both internal and external audit and to provide information to the funding council.

It is the responsibility of the governing body of each HE institution (usually the 'board of governors' in a statutory university and the 'council' in a chartered university) to ensure that the conditions contained within the financial memorandum are met. In turn, the governing body designates the principal officer of the institution, with the responsibility of satisfying the governing body that all the conditions contained within the memorandum have been complied with. The principal officer is accountable to the funding council and may be required to appear with the chief officer of the funding council before the House of Commons' Public Accounts Committee on matters relating to the grant paid by the funding council to the institution. The interest of the House of Commons relates to the proper use of public money in as efficient, effective and economic a manner as possible. Therefore, the offices of the Comptroller and Auditor General, on behalf of the Public Accounts Committee, and the National Audit Office, on behalf of the funding council, have the right to inspect the financial records of any HEI in receipt of grant from the funding council and to carry out value for money investigations.

In addition to the overriding constraints of the financial memorandum between the funding council and individual HE institutions, the funding council consolidates its role of monitoring the financial health of institutions through the receipt of the annual accounts from individual institutions by 31 December following the accounting period; by the requirement to provide annually a copy of the institution's strategic plan and financial forecast for the current financial year and the following four financial years; and by the mid-year financial forecast for the current and the succeeding financial years.

Internal and external audit

A further obligation is placed upon institutions through the HEFCE *Audit Code of Practice* (HEFCE, 1993b), the major requirement of which is to appoint an audit committee. The responsibility of the audit committee is to ensure that there are appropriate performance measures for internal and external audit, and that there are satisfactory arrangements in operation to promote the three objectives of economy, efficiency and effectiveness. The prime responsibility of internal audit is to provide the governing body of the institution and senior management with assurance as to the adequacy of the internal control system. This includes, among other things, ensuring that all the financial and operational procedures are effective; that assets are adequately safeguarded and recorded; and that management policies, authorization and approval procedures and regulations are adhered to. In addition, the internal audit function through a series of value for money audits is able to advise on the success in meeting the three objectives referred to above. Indeed, on the subject of value for money, the funding council itself was active in promoting the subject across the sector (HEFCE, 1994a).

The internal auditors have the right of access to the chair of the institution's audit committee and can request that a meeting of the audit committee be arranged as necessary. In carrying out the internal audit function, there are a number of possible alternatives:

- in-house;
- external provision (for example, local authority internal audit or a firm of accountants);
- joint provision of an internal audit facility for a number of institutions.

An internal audit plan should be approved by the audit committee annually, the major criterion being to ensure that over a period of time all the major financial elements are consistently monitored and reviewed.

The primary task of the external auditors is to report on the financial statements of the institution, and to carry out such tests and examinations in order that they can reach an opinion on these statements. The HEFCE *Audit Code of Practice* (HEFCE, 1993b) sets out a model engagement letter to be used on the appointment of the external auditors, in setting out the respective duties of both the institution and the external auditors. The external auditors should have unrestricted right of access to the chair of the audit committee. The external auditors have a responsibility to report within two months, by way of a management letter, on their opinion of the annual accounts. This letter and the response of the institution are forwarded to the funding council. The external auditors have to be reappointed each year, while the funding council recommends that tendering procedures for provision of the external audit function are carried out at least once every seven years (HEFCE, 1993b).

R. M. S. Wilson (quoted in Lockwood and Davies, 1985: 26), considering the subject of financial management within chartered universities at the time, was critical of what he concluded was 'A matter of some concern that the orientation of the finance office in so many educational institutions is towards *stewardship* rather than towards *service*.' Within the context of the external requirements demanded through the financial memorandum by the funding council, the need to maintain this stewardship role has not diminished. Indeed, there is a clear onus placed upon individual institutions and in particular on the principal officer to meet the overriding objective of ensuring the accountability of public money. This places increased pressure on senior financial managers and their staff, in ensuring that the twin objectives of stewardship and service are both met equally, since it is not sufficient in the context of a modern professional finance operation to concentrate on one objective at the expense of the other.

The role of the finance department

Financial management is concerned with two distinct functions. The first is financial accounting, which is primarily concerned with the recording of all the transactions that make up the income and expenditure account and the related matter of payment of creditors and collection of income and debts. The second is management accounting, which is primarily concerned with the key areas of budgeting and forecasting, the reporting of financial information to budget holders and related financial support to budget managers.

Financial accounting

The major functions that comprise financial accounting are:

1. The preparation of annual accounts.
2. The maintenance of a nominal ledger, which comprises details of all transactions that have taken place. This incorporates details relating to income and expenditure as well as balance sheet accounts.
3. The maintenance of an accounts receivable ledger, which records details of all debts owed to the institution. This includes the raising of invoices for services provided by the institution, the production of monthly statements, the generation of aged debtor reports together with reminders to be sent to outstanding debtors.
4. The maintenance of an accounts payable ledger, which records details of all payments made to suppliers of goods and services. This includes the payment of invoices either by cheque or through direct credit facility.
5. The maintenance of a fixed assets register.
6. The provision of a payroll facility, which may be undertaken either in-house or through a computer payroll bureau. It may also be the responsibility of the personnel department rather than the finance department.
7. VAT and taxation issues.
8. The investment of surplus cash funds through adequate treasury management.
9. The provision of a cashier function.
10. The provision of audit arrangements.
11. When required, the undertaking of purchasing and maintenance of purchasing procedures.
12. The maintenance of the institution's financial regulations.

Treasury management

The majority of the functions described above have an application within financial accounting in all commercial organizations. In relation to HE, there have recently been specific developments within a number of key areas of finance. One area has been treasury management. The fundamental features of treasury management are looking after cash to ensure that the institution maximizes its cash resources, while at the same time minimizing its interest payments. This involves ensuring that funds are acquired at the cheapest rate, while the return on any surplus cash is maximized. The aim of cash management is to improve liquidity by bringing money into the institution quickly, while paying suppliers at the last possible moment. Surplus cash must be invested overnight. Two reports – including *The Pearce Report on Capital Funding and Estate Management in Higher Education* (1992) and *The Bain Report on Private Sector Funding in Higher Education* (1994) – have been prepared in connection with the raising of capital by

HE institutions. Recently, a statement of best practice, *Treasury Management in Higher Education* (CIPFA, 1994) has been published with the objectives of:

- promoting and supporting the quality and status of treasury management in higher education;
- providing guidance on the proper practices to be employed for treasury management, including avoiding the dangers of depositing monies with weak banks offering interest rates over the odds.

Purchasing

Purchasing has also arisen as a further area of concern to HE institutions. This is as a result of a report of the House of Commons' Public Accounts Committee, *University Purchasing in England* (Committee of Public Accounts, 1994). This was, in part, a response to ensure accountability in the use of public funds, but also, to ensure value for money from the purchasing function, since this offers a very real opportunity for reducing the operating costs of individual institutions through the achievement of lower prices for the goods and services they purchase. In seeking to address this concern, institutions need to have regard to the fact that after salaries the purchase of goods and services is the highest element of expenditure within an HE institution.

A report originally commissioned by the Universities Funding Council (UFC), entitled *Good Management of Purchasing* (HEFCE, 1993c), recommended the following factors as essential:

1. That purchasing should be coordinated across the institution to maximize purchasing power and minimize duplication of effort.
2. That purchasing should be organized so that staff with the required purchasing skills are available throughout the institution, but without undue duplication of effort.
3. That purchasing should be focused on key activities, where maximum benefit to the institution is obtained.
4. That purchasing should be organized such that buyers operating remotely in individual departments have access to a common supporting infrastructure.
5. That purchasing policies and procedures should be well documented.
6. That there should be adequate controls to enforce the proper procurement procedures to protect the institution from fraud, provide assistance in supplier management and help to ensure that the institution receives best value for its expenditure.
7. That a purchasing information system should be established that provides the processing and management information to support procurement.
8. That professional support is provided through adequate training, career development and effective performance measurement.

Within the majority of industrial and commercial organizations, centralized purchasing is the norm. In this context, with requisitions being received centrally and the subsequent order placed by the central purchasing department, it is comparatively straightforward to enforce agreements with approved suppliers, to ensure that tenders are placed and to attempt to ensure that purchasing power is maximized, while obtaining best value for money.

However, in many HE institutions, especially where devolution is strong, the purchasing function is a combination of both centralized and departmental purchasing, where faculties and other budget managers are able to take advantage of centrally negotiated contract agreements, including consortia arrangements. In this environment, it is absolutely vital that clear communication of all purchasing arrangements is made to all those having responsibility for purchasing within the institution. A 'buyers' guide' detailing these arrangements is of necessity. This should be regularly updated.

Outsourcing

In addition to effective and efficient purchasing as a means of maximizing the use of public funds, outsourcing of support services represents an option for senior institutional management to consider in the pursuit of value for money. Outsourcing as an option has not become strongly developed within the HE sector. This is perhaps surprising, even if one ignores the experience of the private sector. Within those areas of the public sector where outsourcing has been adopted, savings of at least 20 per cent have been achieved in the areas of catering and cleaning. Among the advantages claimed for outsourcing are that it leads to improved quality at a lower price and that it permits senior management to concentrate on the core activities of the organization without the distraction of managing support services that are peripheral to its core function.

When one is seeking to determine whether outsourcing is appropriate, a number of factors need to be taken into account. For instance, how close is the service to the core objectives of the organization? As an example, it is a fact that in the case of services such as cleaning, no government department now undertakes its own, since it is unable to undertake cleaning as cheaply or as well as a specialist cleaning company. In addition, through total facilities management companies, better deals can be obtained through the contracting out of a number of support services rather than one-by-one contracting out.

In order to determine whether outsourcing is desirable, benchmarking of both internal and external services is required. Essentially, this involves an examination of the in-house support services against external competitors, through comparison of the cost and quality of outputs.

Costing and pricing in research and consultancy

Another key subject within financial management in the HE sector relates to the costing and pricing of research and consultancy. The primary mission of all HE institutions is the provision of teaching and research. In the prevailing situation of encouragement by both the government and the funding councils to widen the funding base from non-governmental sources, in order to offset the effect of a real term reduction in funding per student of over 20 per cent in recent years, HE institutions have sought to increase their funding from both research and consultancy. The financial memorandum between the funding council and an individual institution states (HEFCE, 1993a: 10):

> In determining the price to be charged for research contracts and other external services, the institution shall have regard to the need to assess the full cost and to recover full costs unless the institution considers it appropriate to do otherwise having regard to the circumstances of the particular case. The institution should ensure in such circumstances that it is aware of the extent to which it will be providing its own resources towards the cost of the project.

Professor Graeme Davies, Chief Executive of HEFCE, in a speech at the Fifth Annual HEFCE Conference on key issues in higher education at the University of Warwick on 26 April 1995, noted that:

> Contrary to government policy, only twelve HEFCE institutions can demonstrate recovery of costs from externally sponsored contract research at greater than 30 per cent. It must be acknowledged that most of the institutions with the worst performance in this area have low activity in contract research but the implication remains that institutions are subsidising commercial work from the public purse.

He added that:

> The recovery rates, as the difference between income and expenditure as a proportion of total expenditure for 1993/94 for the former UFC sector institutions by the various sources of research, were:

Research Councils	23.3%
UK Based Charities	2.0%
UK Central Government	26.2%
UK Local Authorities	25.7%
UK Public Corporations	41.9%
UK Industry and Commerce	25.0%
UK Health and Hospital Authorities	7.5%
EU Government Bodies	16.8%
Other Overseas	19.3%
Other Sources	6.8%

However, there is a dilemma for financial management in that academic staff and HE institutions tend to be driven by academic rather than financial criteria, and are still keen to undertake research even at less than the real overhead cost. Indeed, the problem is increased by the approach adopted by, for instance, the research councils, where a maximum contribution of 40 per cent of direct staff costs are aimed at meeting the indirect costs of the research. Currently, under the rules of the EU, the maximum contribution towards the institution's indirect costs is 20 per cent, while charities make no contribution towards the indirect costs.

In 1988, the Committee of Vice Chancellors and Principals (CVCP) issued guidance to chartered universities in *The Costing of Research Projects in Universities* (CVCP, 1988: 2). Under the chairmanship of Professor H. J. Hanham, this sought 'To consider and prepare draft guidelines for universities on the principles for determining the full costs of research and other services financed by grants and contracts from external sources and to make recommendations.'

Support for the approach of ensuring that the 'real' cost was paid by industry and commerce was contained within a White Paper (HMSO, 1987: 3): 'Institutions should not subsidise the clients – public or private – for whom they carry out research and consultancy. Clients should normally pay not only the direct costs involved, but also an appropriate share of general overheads.' Yet evidence provided in *The Financial Health of Higher Education Institutions in England* (National Audit Office, 1994), from a National Audit Office survey, concluded that a quarter of HE institutions had not determined the full overhead recovery rate to be charged, while only ten institutions confirmed that they were recovering the full costs of the activity. Can institutions continue to subsidize research from their teaching funds? In the short term, it may be that information as to the full cost of research will open internal debate as to the financial costs of undertaking research, but at least then, institutional management will be in the game with its eyes open. However, the long-term solution must be to recover all the costs involved by convincing sponsors of the full cost of the research.

Taxation

HE institutions are exempt charities by virtue of either the Charities Act 1993 or the Education Reform Act 1988. This status provides exemption to HE institutions from corporation tax, income tax and capital gains tax, while providing tax advantages on donations by individuals and commercial organizations, investment income and capital transfer and capital gains tax. However, the Inland Revenue became particularly concerned as to whether HE institutions were carrying on activities that were liable to tax, particularly in the areas of research and consultancy, and vacation lettings for conferences. These concerns were addressed in a fact-finding exercise carried out by the Inland Revenue in 1992, and guidance notes have been issued to universities as a result of this exercise, to enable them to assess their liability for tax.

The Inland Revenue has concluded for both vacation lettings and research and consultancy that it will not regard a university as trading in these areas unless the income covers at least 75 per cent of direct and attributable costs. It does not automatically follow once this threshold has been crossed a trading activity has commenced, but universities will need to examine their activities in each area, in conjunction with their professional advisors, in order to assess any liability for tax to the satisfaction of the Inland Revenue.

Higher education institutions are partially exempt bodies for the purposes of Value Added Tax (VAT). The provision of education and research is exempt from VAT. The supply of goods and services incidental to the provision of education is also exempt. However, certain commercial services, such as consultancy or catering facilities specifically for staff and visitors, are subject to VAT. VAT paid to suppliers cannot be recovered unless it relates directly to services where the HE institution itself has charged VAT on the supply. (See Chapter 9 for discussion of the problems in defining research as opposed to consultancy, and hence in determining VAT liability.)

Management accounting: devolved budgeting

For the majority of managers within an HE institution, the major focus of their involvement with finance relates to the management of their own budgets, and they are therefore far more concerned with management than with financial accounting. In this context, the major development within HE institutions within recent years has been the evolution of devolved budgeting. This development has arisen as a result of the realization that detailed hierarchical control is not an effective method for running an organization, since decisions and effective responses are better achieved through decentralized management. However, devolution must be contained within a framework of a broad strategy outlined within the strategic mission statement of the institution. Faculties cannot be construed as totally autonomous bodies – they are not subsidiary companies. Each budget holder needs to work in the context of a clearly defined plan, as otherwise a situation of sub-optimization can arise, whereby a function will maximize its own goals or objectives, although the impact on the institution may not be beneficial. Devolution is a means to permit flexibility in response, but within the context of an overall institutional strategy.

The main thrust of devolved budgeting is contained within the context of the constraints of a specific set of objectives, through which senior managers can hold subordinate managers accountable for the results of their actions. In the context of higher education, this means that managers have the discretion to determine the use of their budget to achieve predetermined objectives agreed with senior institutional managers, and at the year-end are then held to account for the achievement of these objectives, within the overall budgetary constraint. Rather than day-to-day accountability, the budget centre manager is provided with time to discharge the agreed obligations and responsibilites. This derives from the assumption that there are limits to the ability of senior management to make decisions concerning individual budgets throughout the organization, and therefore devolution aims to move decision-making to the lowest possible level.

A variety of models of delegated budgeting exist within the HE sector, from control of a fixed non-pay budget of consumables and equipment, to control of a rolling payroll and non-pay budget, which is regularly adjusted to reflect the degree of additional income that is generated through the financial year. In addition, under well developed models of delegation, the costs of the central management are charged to faculty budget holders through an apportionment methodology designed to reflect the pattern of services and resources that they consume, in order to encourage the efficent use of resources within the institution.

However, a recent study (National Audit Office, 1994: 59) concluded that delegated budgeting is not an overall panacea:

> Delegated budgets can be a means of securing the most efficient and effective use of resources by empowering those who are most directly involved in the delivery of core and support activities. But poor control and monitoring of delegated budgets can lead to over-expenditure and hence financial difficulties.

Delegated budgeting is concerned with ensuring that managers are able on the basis of accurate and timely financial information to make informed decisions. The dilemma for senior institutional managers is where to place the professional finance support to support budget managers. Two options exist:

1. The provision of professional financial support by the centre to individual budget managers.
2. The provision of professional financial support within the budget managers' area of responsibility.

Under the latter option the centre's role is reduced to setting standards and consolidating information received from individual budget holders. In this context the dangers of fragmentation, the lack of consistency of approach, additional operating costs and minimal cost-benefit may mitigate against adoption of this option. Budget managers require up-to-date on-line information to make good decisions. Good decision-making requires professional support and advice, from a responsive, proactive finance core team that is supported by modern information technology.

Information technology

The principal reason for having an accounting system is to produce the annual accounts, to control the organization's finances and to provide the necessary information for the major stakeholders, which in the case of HE institutions include Parliament, the general public, grant-awarding bodies, donors, the institution's bankers and current and prospective lenders. The information that is used for management accounting purposes is generated from the financial accounting system. However, the information presented within the constraints of financial accounting is not appropriate in the planning and control of an institution. The key role for management accounting is to adapt the information contained within the financial accounts through access to the information, combined with an ability to use the information in a meaningful manner. This can only realistically be achieved through the use of modern accounting software packages. In addition, in setting up the system, great attention must be given to the coding structure to be adopted, since the frustration for users of information will be increased if the means to access data are complex and difficult.

Institutional managers require an efficient and effective information supply in the context of their managerial activities. The requirements are to ensure that the right information is available at the right time, in the right place. Additionally, those responsible for provision of information must avoid the temptation to deliver as much information as possible, but must select and filter information, so that it is manageable and comprehensible to the user. Managers only have a limited time to digest the flow of information available. It is therefore essential that information is presented in a form through which a manager can monitor specific activities. Exception reports should be produced, highlighting specific areas of concern, while the manager should have the ability to drill down to examine individual transactions where greater detail is required. Through the use of tools such as spreadsheets and databases, and integration with other financial applications, the scope for production of meaningful information is increased.

In the context of HE, in 1988, the UGC launched the Management and Administrative Computing Initiative (MAC Initiative). This was in recognition of the need to replace existing systems and provide an integrated management information system. One million pounds annually has been provided by the HEFCE and its predecessor funding councils to the cost of the initiative, with the balance being provided by individual HE institutions. The aim of this initiative was not confined to finance but incorporated four other areas: staff, students, research and physical resources. However, the initiative has to date experienced delays in the implementation of its programmes of up to one year.

Conclusion

HE institutions live in challenging times with continuing downward pressure on resources. The challenge for finance professionals and for HE managers will be to manage an environment where financial regulations are maintained, and where probity and stewardship of public money and the avoidance of the 'sleaze factor' are sustained, while, simultaneously, high quality financial management is ensured through timely and accurate financial reporting and professional support. Budget managers and finance departments have often established a situation of 'them' and 'us' – an unhelpful attitude and an impediment to ensuring the collective well-being of the institution. Organizations survive and flourish in an environment where there is the recognition of the interrelationship and interdependence of the various units. Financial managers must establish relationships with budget managers that focus on the professional qualities and advice that they bring to the relationship and the added value that they contribute to the decision-making process. Issues such as effective purchasing, the opportunities for outsourcing, and the movement towards full recovery of all direct and indirect costs on research and consultancy represent opportunities for HE institutions to bring about significant reductions in their cost structure, while maximizing their income. Devolution and devolved budgeting provide HE managers, supported by proactive finance professionals with modern information technology, with the opportunity to deploy effectively the resources under their control. The budget manager is no longer a mere bidder for funds, but a manager of financial resources with a real interest in the effective and efficient meeting of financial management objectives.

6

Decision-making and Committees

Paddy Stephenson

Editors' introduction

The author of this chapter has provided a comprehensive and authoritative analysis of decision-making in HEIs. He has highlighted the differences between chartered and statutory universities, but also pointed out the many similarities. Readers from HEIs that have not yet gained a university title can regard the remarks about statutory universities as referring to their institutions as well. Indeed, even though every HEI is *sui generis* with regard to its formal and especially its informal decision-making process, the author has succeeded in providing a general account that will be readily recognizable and intelligible to everyone.

Introduction

In everyday usage, the act of making a decision about something is to determine, settle or resolve it. It follows that, in the day-to-day routine of any HEI, numerous decisions are constantly being taken. These will range from routine ones to those involving major policy issues. The variety of decisions taken by an HEI is illustrated by the following list of examples:

- decision to introduce a new method for allocating resources to academic departments;
- decision to dismiss a non-academic member of staff for gross misconduct;
- decision to raise catering prices;
- decision to introduce semesters and modular-based course structures;
- decision to increase car-parking charges significantly in order to recover the full cost of providing and maintaining car parks;
- decision to change the overseas mail carrier;
- decision to set up a quality assessment and audit unit.

The aim of this chapter is to explore the process whereby decisions are made and the role of committees in that process. First, the formal framework within which decision-making takes place will be considered; then decision-making in practice will be explored, with particular reference to the informal processes and the checks and balances within the system; finally, conclusions will be drawn about the changing nature of decision-making and the role of committees in that process.

Framework

The authority of an individual, or group of individuals (for example, a committee), to take a particular decision derives ultimately from an HEI's instrument of government. This instrument will define the powers of the HEI and its basic structure of governance, including major committees and officers.

In the case of those universities founded before the 1992 Further and Higher Education Act (the chartered universities), the instrument of government is, in all but a few special cases, a charter with supporting statutes. The conferment of a charter and subsequent amendments to either the charter or statutes require the approval of the Privy Council. This ensures a degree of consistency in the powers and structures of the chartered universities, which is reinforced by the Privy Council's practice of seeking the views of the Department for Education and Employment before approving any proposed changes to either the charter or statutes of a university.

The relationship between the charter and its statutes is not unlike that between a company's memorandum and its articles of association. The charter sets out the broad powers of the university and its basic structures, while the statutes fill in the detail. Thus a typical charter will state that 'there shall be a vice-chancellor who shall be the chief academic and administrative officer of the university'. The statutes, however, will indicate who has the authority to appoint him or her and what his or her main responsibilities are. For example, the statutes of most chartered universities include the following among the vice-chancellor's responsibilities:

- shall have a general responsibility to the council for maintaining and promoting the efficiency and good order of the university;
- may suspend any student from any class or classes and may exclude any student from any part of the university or its precincts provided he [*sic*] shall report every such suspension or exclusion to the council at its next meeting.

Details of the formal powers and composition of the main committees, such as council and senate, are also defined in the statutes. The charter simply describes the broad powers. Thus a typical charter states that 'the council shall manage the whole of the affairs of the university, and shall appoint, and if necessary remove, the vice-chancellor, the pro-vice-chancellors, professors, lecturers and other officers and servants of the university, and shall determine the fees to be paid by students of the university, and shall discharge such other functions and exercise such other powers as the statutes shall from time to time prescribe.' These broad general powers are in contrast to the detailed powers set out in the statutes. A random sample of several chartered universities show that, normally, there are between twenty and thirty specific powers of council set out in the statutes.

The powers and responsibilities set out in the charter and statutes provide the framework within which the whole decision-making process takes place. Failure to be aware of, or to observe, this formal framework can lead a university to act outside its powers – that is, it would be *ultra vires* – which in turn could lead to a challenge in the courts about the validity of a particular action.

The statutory universities, founded subsequent to the Further and Higher Education Act 1992, operate under articles of government that have been approved by the relevant secretary of state and follow a common pattern. For example, the board of governors in all the statutory universities has the following responsibilities:

- the determination of the educational character and mission of the institution and its activities;
- the effective and efficient use of resources, the solvency of the institution and the safeguarding of its assets;
- approving annual estimates of income and expenditure;
- the appointment, grading, suspension dismissal and determination of the pay and conditions of service of holders of senior posts;
- setting a framework for the pay and conditions of service for all other members of staff;
- the appointment of external auditors.

The responsibilities of the vice-chancellor under the articles of government of a statutory university are much more explicit than is the case in the charters and statutes of the chartered universities. Thus the articles of government state:

Subject to the responsibilities of the Board of Governors, the head of the institution is the Chief Executive of the institution and is responsible for:

- Making proposals to the Board of Governors about the educational character and mission of the institution, and for implementing the decisions of the Board of Governors.
- The organisation, direction and management of the institution and leadership of its staff.
- The appointment, assignment, grading, appraisal, suspension, dismissal and determination – within the framework set by the Board of Governors – of the pay and conditions of service of staff other than the holders of senior posts.
- The determination, after consultation with the Academic Board, of

the institution's academic activities, and for the determination of its other activities.

- Preparing annual estimates of income and expenditure, for consideration by the Board of Governors, and for the management of budget and resources, within the estimates approved by the Board of Governors.
- The maintenance of student discipline and, within the rules and procedures provided for within the articles, for the suspension or expulsion of students on disciplinary grounds and for implementing decisions to expel students for academic reasons.

It is interesting to note that the vice-chancellor of a statutory university has the power to expel a student for disciplinary reasons, whereas in the chartered universities that power usually rests with council itself, with the vice-chancellor's power limited to suspension and exclusion. Thus, in one case the formal power to expel a student rests with an individual officer and in the other with a committee.

Another interesting contrast concerns responsibility for academic matters. In most chartered universities this is, subject to the overall control of council, the responsibility of the senate. But in the case of the statutory universities, the vice-chancellor is responsible for 'the determination, after consultation with the Academic Board, of the institution's academic activities, and for the determination of its other activities' (see above).

Thus, in both chartered and statutory universities, the governing body has final responsibility for academic matters. But below that level, detailed responsibility lies with a committee (the senate) in the case of chartered universities, and with the vice-chancellor in the case of the statutory universities. In the latter case the role of the academic board (which in many institutions has now been retitled 'the senate' just to increase complexity) is essentially consultative, since its defined powers are subject to both the overall responsibilities of the governing body and those of the head of the institution.

These examples illustrate the importance of understanding the role of managers and their relationship with committees when one is considering the part played by committees in decision-making. The charter and statutes of the chartered universities state the officers that shall be appointed (for example the vice-chancellor), and in addition make provision for the appointment, by the council, of such other officers as may be required from time to time (director of finance, deans, etc.). In most cases, the duties of managers are determined by the committee that has the power to appoint them, although the statutes of some chartered universities will specify certain responsibilities of other managers (for example, one university's statutes state that the registrar shall be secretary to the court, council, senate and any committees of these bodies). On the whole, where powers are specified for managers, they are expressed in fairly general terms.

Similar provision is made in the articles of government of the statutory universities for the designation and appointment to senior posts. These must include the head of the institution and the clerk to the board of governors.

An important point that arises from the relationship between managers and committees is that ultimately all managers are accountable to a committee, even if this accountability is through another manager. Thus, vice-chancellors are accountable to their councils or boards of governors for the good order, efficiency and general management of their institutions. Subordinate managers may be managerially responsible to the vice-chancellor, but account will still need to be given to the authoritative body with responsibility for the relevant area – for example, senate/academic board for academic matters, council for financial or estates business.

The framework within which decisions are made is, therefore, set by the charter and statutes or articles of government of a university. These set out the objectives of the institution and the basic structure of governance for carrying through those objectives in terms of committees and managers and their respective powers. The relationship between committees and managers will vary from university to university and will be subject to the formal powers contained in the university's charter and statutes or articles of government. In all cases there will be a route of accountability that ultimately ends with a committee.

Decision-making in practice

Although the constitutional framework of universities, particularly in the chartered universities, vests much of the significant power regarding formal decision-making in committees, in practice committees cannot and do not provide an efficient and effective way of making decisions in a modern HEI. Committees operate to a timetable that is governed by the need for committees to report to a 'superior' committee within a cycle culminating in meetings of senate or academic board and council or board of governors. Committees also involve considerable numbers of people who have many demands on their time, and there is thus a constant pressure to reduce the number of meetings. These factors make committees an inefficient means for rapid decision-making where this is necessary.

In the introduction to this chapter, there is a list of examples of the kind of decisions that an HEI might be expected to take from time to time. The way in which those decisions are dealt with will obviously vary from one HEI to another, depending on its charter and statutes or articles of government, culture, the personalities involved and so on. However, given the range of decisions represented in that list, it is highly probable that a number of different approaches will have been used in any one HEI. For example, the decision to dismiss a non-academic member of staff for gross misconduct will require, in terms of good personnel practice, a rapid decision. In the chartered universities, the power to dismiss a member of staff is usually vested in the council. Given the need for speed in such cases, it would be clearly impractical to await the next scheduled meeting of council before a decision on the case was made. Thus, it is the normal practice for a council to delegate to an officer, such as the registrar, its power to dismiss. That officer is then accountable to the council for the exercise of that power. In the statutory universities, the power to dismiss is given specifically to the vice-chancellor. Although that power may be delegated, the vice-chancellor will remain accountable to the governing body for its exercise.

Another approach is shown by the decision to raise catering prices. This decision will be taken by the catering manager in response to market forces, seasonal prices, etc. Again, it would be wholly impractical for such decisions to have to await the next scheduled meeting of any relevant committee, although catering managers will probably have a responsibility either directly or through their line managers to account to a committee for their management of the catering function. In terms of good management practice and customer relations, it is likely that the catering manager will have a mechanism for obtaining feedback and comments from his or her customers about any significant changes being proposed. This may take the form of a users' committee – another variation on the role of committees in the decision-making process.

On the face of it, the decision to change the university's overseas mail carrier is a straightforward managerial decision. The two principal considerations are the cost of the service and its efficiency. However, it is a decision that could affect the effectiveness of both academic departments and such central functions as international student recruitment. Thus, the person taking the decision would need to be able to account, probably through his or her line manager, to both the finance committee, or its equivalent, regarding the cost implications of the decision, and the relevant committee(s), regarding the effectiveness of the service.

Different considerations apply to decisions that affect the basic academic activity of an HEI. Decisions regarding the introduction of a new resource allocation methodology, the introduction of semesters and a modular course structure, and the establishment of a quality assessment and audit unit affect the whole of the academic community. Each of these topics is likely to be controversial, and it is probable that the final decision to take the proposed action will have been the culmination of a lengthy process of iteration within the academic community, through working parties, consultation with departments, faculties, schools, etc. Thus the process of considering these topics will, in the vast majority of institutions, have involved the use of the formal committee structure, thereby ensuring the involvement – and it is hoped the commitment – of the various academic units concerned.

The decision to introduce car-parking charges falls somewhere between the two categories of decisions set out above. In one sense, it ought to be a straightforward managerial decision. Car parking is a staff and student facility that is not directly concerned with academic activity and where a simple calculation can be made regarding the cost of providing and maintaining car parks. However, in reality it tends to be a highly sensitive and controversial area. Demand invariably exceeds supply, the local council may wish to discourage the use of cars by refusing planning permission for more car parks, staff and students who use public transport resent the hidden subsidy that car users receive where there is no charge or one that is well below the true cost and unions may claim that free car parking is part of a member of staff's conditions of service and should, therefore, be the subject of negotiation. This kind of decision is likely, as a consequence, to involve both widespread consultation through users' committees, staff committees and their like, and formal processing through such bodies as finance committee and estates committee. Because of its controversial nature, it is the sort of decision that most institutions would not take outside the formal committee structure.

In all of these examples committees have a role to play. But it is one that varies from actually taking the decision (for example, to introduce semesters and modular-based course structures), legitimizing decisions taken by managers (for example, the decision to dismiss a member of staff), serving as a means of consultation (for example, through a users' committee) to acting as the formal body to which individuals must account for their actions if called upon to do so.

HEIs are complex organizations, whose operations are increasingly influenced by external constraints and requirements. There is no doubt that these developments in HE over the past several years, coupled with the major expansion that has taken place, have changed the way in which HEIs are managed and the role played by committees in that management. The examples given in this section show the varied roles performed by committees. Arising from these examples there are two other aspects of decision-making that need to be addressed. The first concerns the informal processes that underpin the formal process, and the second is the way in which committee and officer structures provide appropriate checks and balances.

Informal processes

Informal processes have become more prominent in recent years for a variety of reasons. These include the increasing complexity of HEI business, the pressure of deadlines and timetables – invariably externally imposed – that do not match committee timetables and the demands on the time of individuals. Informal processes are widely used to carry out consultation and to obtain information and feedback prior to a decision being taken. Committees can have an important information-giving and exchanging role but, depending on the nature of the decision, it will often be the case that the membership of a committee will not have the appropriate balance of members to ensure the degree of iteration needed for important or controversial decisions. Thus, informal processes can be an important way of helping to obtain widespread 'ownership' of difficult decisions.

In addition, decisions are increasingly being taking *de facto* through informal processes. There are a number of manifestations of this. The increasing use of chairman's action between meetings is one example. The growing use of project teams or task forces to sort out particular problems and come forward with solutions is another.

Perhaps the single most important manifestation has been the development of the vice-chancellor's management team. This goes under different names in different universities (for example, senior management team, vice-chancellor's advisory group, Monday morning meeting), and will typically comprise the vice-chancellor and the university's level 2 managers (normally the pro-vice-chancellors, the registrar and the director of finance or their equivalents), usually making a meeting of between six and ten people. It will normally meet on a weekly basis throughout most of the year, and will be concerned with the coordination of the HEI's business. This coordination will cover both short-term issues and longer-term strategic matters. The members of the management team may well include the chairs of most of the key committees (other than those chaired by lay members of the council or board of governors), and they will be well placed to ensure that policies emerging from the management team are subsequently endorsed by the formal system.

The vice-chancellor's management team is by definition not a formal committee. It is not referred to in the charter and statutes or articles of government of any university and, as a result, in most instances there is neither a formal reporting mechanism nor a specified route of accountability. In these circumstances, the constitutional position of a vice-chancellor's management team can best be described as follows. Vice-chancellors have statutory responsibilities, which are set out in the charter and statutes or articles of government. They are responsible to their council or board of governors for the exercise of those responsibilities. In carrying out those responsibilities, they find it useful to call upon the support and advice of a group of senior managers, who, together with the vice-chancellor, comprise the management team. Thus, in the majority of cases, management teams are not a committee and have no formal powers. They exist to support vice-chancellors in the exercise of their responsibilities. It follows that accountability lies in the vice-chancellor's relationship with, and responsibility to, the university's governing bodies.

This somewhat ambiguous definition raises the second of the additional matters arising from the growth in importance of the informal processes; for example, the need for, and place of, adequate checks and balances in the decision-making process. This is of particular importance in view of the government's concerns about accountability for the use of public funds and the need, therefore, to be able to demonstrate that an HEI is acting within its powers and is not misusing public funds. The basic checks and balances are enshrined in the charter, statutes and articles of government of universities. For example, there must be a lay majority on governing bodies of all universities (except Oxford and Cambridge, which have no lay member

involvement): this means that in theory the power to make the really important decisions (for example, the appointment of senior staff, the setting of
budgets, the determination of strategy) lies in the hands not of staff of the
institution, but of a group of disinterested persons who have nothing to
gain in a personal sense from the decisions being taken.

Checks and balances

The unavoidable development of and reliance on informal processes has
heightened the need for an awareness of the checks and balances that exist
within the system. One aspect of this is in the role played by the representation of various groups, such as students and non-professorial staff, on
various committees. Not only does this provide a check against ill thought
through decisions affecting these groups; it also should enable a more
widespread 'ownership' of the decisions being taken.

Another significant check lies in the existence of the committee system
itself. More and more decisions are *de facto* being taken outside the formal
structure. However, each university is obliged by law to act within the powers and structures laid out in its charter and statutes or articles of government.
This means that all major decisions will at some point have to be reported
to and endorsed by the body that, under the university's instruments of
government, has the formal power to take those decisions. Thus, an increasingly important role of committees is in the legitimization of decisions
taken outside the formal structure; for example, by the vice-chancellor's
management team. In understanding an HEI's decision-making process, it
is of the first importance, therefore, to know where formal authority lies for
a particular decision.

Finally, the role of lay officers, and in particular the chair of council or
the board of governors, needs to be examined in the context of checks
and balances. Lay officers are roughly equivalent to (unpaid) non-executive
directors. They will chair the governing body and in most institutions the
key council committees, such as finance committee and estates committee.
Part of the role of lay officers, as it is for non-executive directors, is to
ensure that the objectives of the 'business' are being pursued in an effective
and efficient manner. The relationship between the chair of the governing body (non-executive) and the vice-chancellor (executive) is therefore
of considerable importance and is likely to have a strong influence on the
extent to which the governing body acts, or needs to act, as a counter-
balance to the institution's managers.

Checks and balances therefore exist through the instruments of government, the representation of various groups on committees, the role of the
committee system as a legitimizer of decisions and the role of lay officers
and lay members of the governing body. These checks and balances, coupled with external ones imposed by legislation (for example, the requirement to appoint an 'accounting officer' accountable to the relevant funding

council for the university's use of public funds), should safeguard the objectives of a university and ensure that its powers are not misused. However, experience suggests that these checks and balances do not always work as effectively as they should, and that there is generally a need for a better understanding of the interaction between the different elements in the decision-making process and of the checks and balances that exist within that process.

Final thoughts

Decision-making is a fluid, multi-faceted activity carried out by a wide variety of people. It takes place within a quasi-legal framework that includes, in the case of HEIs, a formal committee structure. It follows that, while the formal structures of two institutions may look very similar, the actual operation of their decision-making processes may be very different. These differences will arise from, among other things, different personalities, different traditions and different cultural values. In particular, the leadership from the vice-chancellor and his or her senior colleagues can affect crucially the way in which the process works. Where there is trust and confidence in the senior management, the informal, more efficient processes are likely to hold greater sway. Where there is mistrust and suspicion, it is more likely that those disaffected will seek to use the checks and balances within the formal process to try to influence events.

In reality, all HEIs are likely to make decisions in a variety of ways, ranging from the very formal to the entirely informal. Some of those decisions, particularly in the academic area, will be taken in a collegial manner. Others, mainly in non-academic fields of activity, are increasingly being taken in a managerial mode. This issue is dealt with in much greater depth in Chapter 2. Changes are taking place: of that there is no doubt. These changes reflect the rapidly changing external world within which HEIs have to compete to survive. But HEIs will use the mode of decision-making that best suits a particular decision and their own cultures.

The instruments of government of the chartered and statutory universities do contain significant differences regarding the distribution of powers. Generally, in chartered universities, committees are given a greater range of formal powers than is the case in the statutory universities. On the other hand, the vice-chancellors in the statutory universities are given much greater specified powers than their counterparts in the chartered universities, powers that subordinate the role of committees such as the academic board. In terms of their formal constitution, therefore, the chartered universities tend to more collegial mode of decision-making, while the statutory universities have a framework that is more conducive to a managerial mode of decision-making.

It is clear that the role of the committee system has changed and is continuing to change. In many institutions its role has increasingly become that of legitimizing decisions taken elsewhere and of providing a framework of checks and balances. To use Walter Bagehot's terms, there is a growing tendency for the committee system to become the 'dignified' part of a university's constitution, in contrast to the 'efficient' part. He described the dignified parts of government 'as those which give it force – which attract its motive power. The efficient parts only employ that power.' The 'dignified' part is there to be used – if needed. (Editors' note: see Farrington (1994) concerning the law of meetings, governance and trusteeships, all discussed briefly in the 'Notes on the Legal Framework within which HEIs operate' at the end of this book.)

7

Personnel Management

Alison Hall

Editors' introduction

The very title of this chapter plunges us into an important debate: should the function under consideration be called 'human resource management' or 'personnel management'? The author plumps firmly for the latter, while one of the editors has already argued to the contrary in his recent book for the Open University Press entitled *Human Resource Management in Higher and Further Education* (Warner and Crosthwaite, 1995: 3–4). Such is the cut and thrust of academic debate. Whatever your position, the author provides a chapter that comprehensively, concisely and with clarity sets out the key tasks of the function. Readers who wish to protect their institutions should particularly note the sections on part-time employment, waiver clauses, and stress, the last item probably being the health and safety issue of the next decade.

Introduction

From conversations with personnel specialists outside HE, it quickly becomes clear that we seem to have a greater understanding of each other's role in (and contribution to) our respective organizations than do our colleagues within those organizations. Cynics would argue that this is evidence of the self-importance of personnel specialists, who have an inflated opinion of their value. However, I would suggest that the lack of understanding arises because the personnel specialist working in a large, complex organization (such as a modern higher education institution) has a multi-faceted role and that few colleagues from other specialisms (including academic ones) ever see more than one or two facets of that role.

In this chapter, I shall begin with a brief overview of the range of activities that personnel departments engage in and of the variety of ways in which the personnel function in HEIs is organized. I shall then use the idea of the multi-faceted role to illustrate the breadth of the personnel department's contribution to achieving the corporate objectives of universities and other HEIs. I shall conclude with a consideration of some of the challenges that are likely to face personnel specialists in HE.

It will already have become apparent that I prefer the term 'personnel' to 'human resource'. This is in part because the latter term is still viewed with some suspicion in the HE sector, but more importantly because I have yet to come across anyone who appreciates being described as a 'human resource'.

The tasks

Salary costs account for approximately 60 per cent of the annual expenditure of a university or HEI in the UK (CVCP, 1994). HEIs are no different from other public sector organizations whose income from government is strictly controlled but that cannot pass on increased costs to their customers. It is vitally important, therefore, that staff are effectively managed for optimum performance and it is the primary function of an institution's personnel department to advise and assist management, at every level, in achieving this.

The range of tasks performed by personnel specialists is much the same in HEIs as it is in other organizations. These tasks can be organized into three main areas.

- *Resourcing*: ensuring that the optimum number of appropriately qualified workers is available for the organization to achieve its objectives. This can be more simply put as having the right number of people with the right skills at the right time. This clearly includes recruitment and selection, redundancy and dismissal, but also covers workforce planning, organizational development and job design.
- *Relations*: ensuring that the organization's employees are appropriately rewarded, optimally productive and adequately protected. This can also be more succinctly stated as keeping people working happily, effectively and safely. This includes, among other things, remuneration and other reward mechanisms, health, safety and welfare, industrial relations and discipline and grievance procedures.
- *Development*: ensuring that the workforce has the necessary skills to adapt to the changing needs of the organization. This includes not only training and development in vocational and management skills, but also appraisal and mentoring.

The higher education context

While the range of tasks may be similar, the nature of HE in the UK influences how they are carried out. For example, although all HEIs are autonomous employers, a variable but large proportion of their funding is obtained from the government (via the national funding councils) or other public bodies (including the research councils and training and enterprise councils). This has implications not only in terms of accountability and how much an institution can afford to pay its staff but also in terms of the amount of externally imposed change institutions are compelled to accommodate. In 1991 the then Vice-Chancellor of the University of Essex, Professor Martin Harris wrote: 'The central problem springs from an attempt to achieve simultaneously three policy objectives; to increase access to higher education, to constrain public expenditure and to maintain quality' (Harris, 1991a: 4). These external pressures on HEIs (including worsening student : staff ratios, reductions in the unit of resource year on year and the selective funding of research) have required significant changes in institutional management. Elsewhere in 1991, Professor Harris commented:

> most of those involved in the management of UK universities would not have made frequent use of the terms 'cost effectiveness' or 'efficiency' before the start of the 1980s. Indeed, even the word 'management' itself was generally avoided in the university context until fairly recently.
>
> (Harris, 1991b: 2)

One of the major reasons why 'management' has been (and, in many institutions, still is) viewed with deep suspicion in higher education is the high proportion of the workforce made up of highly qualified knowledge workers – the academics. Academics tend to conform in almost every respect to Raelin's (1985) definition of a 'cosmopolitan professional'. Such professionals generally have only a marginal loyalty to the organization in which they work, preferring to align themselves with their peers within their discipline for the purposes of recognition and evaluation. As employees, they demand high levels of autonomy and participation in their work and resent close supervision, particularly by a manager. The management of academic staff had been likened to 'herding cats' (Partington, 1994). This means that one of the most interesting challenges facing the personnel specialist when advising management is how to motivate the academic staff to achieve their creative potential, while at the same time achieving the institution's corporate objectives.

Organization

There is considerable diversity between HEIs in the way in which the personnel function is organized. This is because the history and culture of an institution has a significant effect on both the division of tasks (health and safety, staff training and development, payroll, etc.) between functions and the contribution made by its personnel specialists to strategic level decision-making.

Beck (1985) traces the growth of personnel specialists in chartered universities in the early 1970s to two factors, one internal and one external. The internal factor was the establishment of the Central Council for Non-Teaching Staffs in Universities. This joint employer and union body was set up with the aims of promoting good industrial relations, of providing guidelines on dispute procedures and of overseeing the joint committees for the major groups of non-teaching staff. The external factor was the Industrial Relations Act 1971, which, while short-lived, served to draw attention to the need not only to formalize union recognition arrangements locally as well as nationally but also to review employment contracts and individual employment rights. Mackie (1990: 56) has pointed out that 'academic staff were judged at that time to be largely above the personnel fray', and many universities restricted the activities of their personnel specialists to non-teaching staff (this is still the case in a small number of chartered universities, including and especially at Oxford and Cambridge, where the academies are *de facto* the institution: they are not employed by a lay member dominated council or board of governors; they employ and govern themselves).

The development of the personnel function in the statutory universities has more recent origins. Until 1988, these institutions were under the control of the local education authorities, and much of the growth in the function dates from that time. Warner and Crosthwaite (1992/3) found that on average the number of professional personnel staff in the statutory universities more than doubled in the period between incorporation and the survey. They also found that an overwhelming majority (86 per cent) of heads of personnel had been appointed in the five years prior to the survey and half had previous experience of personnel outside education. This is in contrast to the situation in the chartered universities, where fewer than 38 per cent of heads of personnel had been appointed in the five years prior to the survey and only one-third had previous experience outside education.

The survey revealed other contrasts. While 80 per cent of heads of personnel in the statutory universities report directly to the executive head of their institution (or his or her deputy), the vast majority of heads of personnel in the chartered universities report to the head of administration. These different reporting routes are not simply niceties of organizational structure, but reflect and colour the perceptions of the role of the personnel function in the strategic management of the institution. In the chartered universities there is still a tendency to see personnel as just another aspect of the central administration. As Keep and Sisson (1992: 73) have pointed out, 'active management of personnel issues at a strategic level is relatively unknown, and the integration of personnel considerations into wider planning, within institutions . . . remains rare.'

Roles

The personnel specialist in an HEI is nowadays required to wear many different hats: lawyer, negotiator, conciliator, police officer and counsellor to name but a few. Below, I hope to give a flavour of the variety of work undertaken by someone in personnel in higher education by examining five of these roles in detail.

Lawyer

The rapid expansion in legislation impinging on the relationship between an HEI and its workforce has almost certainly been the single most important factor in the 'professionalization' of the personnel specialism in HE. Less than a dozen major statutes relevant to personnel were enacted in the 100 years prior to 1970, but in the 25 years since then, 18 major pieces of relevant domestic legislation have been passed. While it is not yet necessary for a personnel specialist to be legally qualified, he or she must have a working knowledge of statute and case law across a broad range. (Moreover, it is not sufficient to be aware of UK legislation alone – HEIs are currently seen as 'emanations of the state', and European Union directives therefore have direct effect.) Legislation applies throughout the employment relationship from recruitment and the treatment of the employee while in employment to the ending of the relationship.

In recruitment, the personnel specialist must be able to draft (or advise on the drafting of) advertisements that comply with the Sex Discrimination Act 1975 and the Race Relations Act 1976. Similarly, the personnel department must ensure that the selection processes used throughout the institution are free of both direct and indirect discrimination on the grounds covered by legislation. This will almost certainly include providing training for line managers to cover those occasions when a representative of the personnel department is not involved in the selection process. (It is likely that anti-discrimination legislation will soon be extended to cover the employment of disabled persons, as the Disabled Persons (Employment) Act 1944 is widely regarded as being woefully inadequate.)

Once the successful candidate is chosen, one area of the law comes into play for HEIs to a much greater extent than for other employers – that governing the employment of overseas nationals. For many academic and research posts the labour pool is international, but there are strict rules governing the employment of nationals of countries outside the European Economic Area (the EEA, being the European Union plus Norway). Owing to the low pay levels of academic and research posts in the UK relative to industry or commerce, overseas applicants often outnumber EEA ones in certain disciplines. This means that some personnel specialists, particularly in those HEIs with significant research activity, spend a great deal of time obtaining the necessary permission to employ the best candidates for vacant posts.

Most if not all HEIs will have well established forms of contract that comply with the requirements of the Employment Protection (Consolidation) Act 1978 (EP(C)A) and the Trade Union Reform and Employment Rights Act 1993 (TURERA). However, in small institutions where staff turnover is low, or in larger ones where new contracts are being considered, it is worthwhile to check that all the elements specified in the legislation have been addressed.

While a detailed knowledge of the law of contract is not required, it is helpful to be aware of the legal tests used to determine whether a contract is one 'of service' or 'for services'. The nature of the contract, whether written or verbal, is important, as it will determine whether a worker is an employee or not, and this has consequences for the extent of the institution's liabilities and the worker's rights. This has recently become an important consideration with regard to the employment of part-time teachers in higher education. It has been common for such workers to be described by institutions as 'casual', and full contractual benefits (including pension rights) have not been extended to them, even though they may have worked for the same institution for several years. As a result of the European Court of Justice ruling in *Vroege* v. *NCIV Instituut voor Volkshuisvesting BV and Stichting Pensioenfonds NCIV* (1994, IRLR 651) this practice has been called into question.

Another aspect of the employment contract that is of particular relevance to HE is the use of waiver clauses in fixed-term contracts. Such contracts (usually, but not exclusively, covering short-term externally funded research posts) are becoming increasingly prevalent throughout the sector. The EP(C)A specifies the circumstances under which an employee may be asked to waive his or her rights to make a complaint of unfair dismissal or to claim a redundancy payment in the event of the expiration and non-renewal of his or her contract. Some HEIs also have their own policies regarding the use of waiver clauses (for example, not requiring employees to waive their rights to claim a redundancy payment once they have accrued three or five years' continuous service).

While there has been a shift in the emphasis of employment legislation from employee rights to union containment in recent years (Torrington and Hall, 1987), there still remains a substantial body of statute, regulations and case law that applies to the treatment of employees during the course of their employment. These rights, which are mainly contained in EP(C)A and TURERA, range from the right not to suffer a detriment on the grounds of sex, race or trade union membership and the right to be notified in writing of variations in the employment contract to eligibility for maternity leave and/or pay. In most cases, the role of the personnel specialist will be to ensure that line managers are aware of the legal rights of the employees under their supervision, but where problems arise it is often necessary to advise individual employees too.

Universities (and other HEIs) are, like all workplaces, potentially hazardous, and many regulations have been introduced under the Health and

Safety at Work Act 1974 to minimize these hazards. Frequently, the day-to-day responsibility for implementing the legal requirements in an HEI rests not with the personnel department but with a separate health and safety office. However, even where health and safety is not the direct responsibility of the personnel department, personnel specialists need to be aware of legal requirements that impinge on the employment relationship. For example, the case of *Walker* v. *Northumbria County Council* (High Court, Queen's Bench Division, 1995, IRLR 35) has highlighted the employer's duty of care in relation to the employee's mental health. Where an employee is thought to be at risk from stress induced by his or her job or working conditions, the personnel department should liaise with the employee's department and the health and safety specialists to assess the risk and take any necessary remedial action. Similarly, with risk assessment during pregnancy (required by the Management of Health and Safety at Work (Amendment) Regulations 1994), the personnel department should ensure that if risk is identified and the work cannot be changed to eliminate it, then the employee must be transferred to other work or suspended on full pay.

If senior managers consult their personnel specialists at no other time, they will do so during a dispute. As mentioned above, the main thrust of domestic employment legislation introduced during the 1980s was the curtailment of trade union rights and activities, so it is important that personnel specialists are conversant with the legislation covering the proper scope of industrial disputes, the holding of ballots on industrial action and picketing. One area where trade unions have regained some ground recently, courtesy of the EU, has been consultation. The unions' right to be consulted with a view to reaching agreement has been confirmed with regard to both redundancies and the transfer of undertakings. This is of particular relevance to institutions that are taking over other organizations or services (for example, nurse training) or that have a high proportion of staff employed on fixed-term contracts (because the expiration and non-renewal of a fixed-term contract is a dismissal in law, usually by reason of redundancy).

In an ideal world, employees would always part from their employers by mutual consent. However, HEIs and their personnel specialists have to operate in the real world and it is sometimes necessary to dismiss staff because they are incompetent or too ill to work, or because of indiscipline or redundancy. After two years' continuous service, employees (both full and part-time) gain the right not to be unfairly dismissed and to receive a redundancy payment if appropriate (except in the special case of fixed-term contracts containing waivers discussed above). It is the personnel department's responsibility to ensure that the institution has fair policies and procedures in place for discipline, medical review and selection for redundancy, and also to ensure that line managers implement those procedures correctly.

Until the introduction of the Education Reform Act 1988, the majority of academics in the UK's chartered universities enjoyed tenure. This meant that they could only be dismissed for 'good cause', which typically included gross misconduct, incompetence and incapacity, but definitely not redundancy. The 1988 Act provided that any member of the academic staff appointed or promoted on or after 20 November 1987 would not have tenure, although staff appointed before that date retained tenure. As the statutes governing the terms of academic appointments varied from one university to another, the Act provided that university commissioners would be appointed to make or amend charters, statutes, articles and so on in order to ensure that all universities would be able to dismiss academic staff by reason of redundancy or financial exigency. The 'model statutes' drafted by the commissioners for each institution were finally given Privy Council approval in late 1992 and early 1993. In some instances, where universities already had provision in their statutes for the abolition of academic posts, the model statute has imposed mechanisms that are more time-consuming than those they replaced.

Negotiator

Torrington and Hall (1987) trace the development of the bargaining role for personnel professionals back to the period immediately following the Second World War, when there was relatively full employment and labour was scarce. However, while national salary scales for academic staff were introduced between 1946 and 1949, negotiating machinery involving the Association of University Teachers was not established until 1960. For technical staff, some local scales were set up immediately after the war and nationally negotiated scales were introduced in 1953. However, pay bargaining of any description did not come into being for the majority of support staff until 1970, with the setting up of the Universities Council for Non-Teaching Staff.

Today, the scope of consultation and negotiation with trade union representatives varies between chartered and statutory universities and also within institutions, depending on the staff group concerned. However, as a general rule, pay for academic staff is negotiated nationally and conditions of service (holidays, hours of work and so on) locally. For support staff, both pay and conditions are negotiated nationally, but with local variations in conditions of service. At present, there are nine separate negotiating bodies covering the majority of staff in both chartered and statutory universities. However, there are some chartered universities that implement local government pay awards for some groups of support staff even though they are not party to the negotiations. This is a historical anomaly incorporated into the conditions of service of individual members of staff, dating back to the time when these institutions were under local authority control.

There is a growing tendency in both chartered and statutory universities to move towards local determination of both pay and conditions, at least for some groups of staff. Warner and Crosthwaite's (1992/3) survey data suggest that the statutory universities, with a relatively high proportion of recent personnel appointments from outside education, might be better prepared for such a move than the chartered universities, which have until recently tended to appoint 'administrators' rather than negotiators.

Negotiating with the representatives of the workforce is not the only type of negotiation that personnel specialists engage in, or even the most time-consuming. Much more time is spent negotiating with other managers. For example, it may be necessary to negotiate with senior management about the introduction of a policy that may cost more in the short term, but will protect the institution from legal challenge. With the devolution of respons-ibility to line managers within departments, it is often necessary to persuade them to comply with institutional policy (for example, that all vacancies should be advertised in the interests of equal opportunities) without the back-up of realistic sanctions.

Police officer

While the stable conditions to which Weberian bureaucracies are best suited no longer pertain in HE, HEIs are large, complex organizations that still require some rules in order to avoid a descent into anarchy. From the point of view of the personnel department, the institution requires rules (in the form of internal policies and procedures) to address three major aims:

1. To ensure that the institution does not break the law (for example, having procedures in place to ensure that nationals of countries outside the EEA are not employed without permission, or that job applicants do not suffer unfair discrimination).
2. To ensure that staff are treated equitably and consistently according to their conditions of service and the institution's own rules (this can be important in defence of a claim of unfair dismissal or discrimination).
3. To ensure that there is proper accountability in decision-making pro-cesses relating to employment (for example, by having procedures in place to guarantee that offers of appointment are only issued after proper authorization has been obtained).

Personnel specialists have to be particularly sensitive in this role because the personnel department's primary purpose is to facilitate departments to achieve their own and the institution's goals, and it is not helpful if person-nel specialists are perceived as interfering bureaucrats. Although sensitive enforcement is very necessary, so too is the ability to step outside the role of enforcer, to review the appropriateness and effectiveness of the policies and procedures that are in place.

Honest broker

I alluded earlier to the exclusion of the head of the personnel function from the senior management team, particularly in the chartered universities. This is not simply because of a lack of understanding on the part of vice-chancellors of the contribution that personnel can make to strategic issues, but also, in part, because of the historical association of personnel management with the workforce. Torrington and Hall (1987: 14) express this sometimes uncomfortable position very succinctly: 'Although indisputably a management function, it [personnel management] is never wholly identified with management interests, as it becomes ineffective when not able to understand and articulate the aspirations and views of the workforce.' Personnel specialists acting in this role are not just a buffer between management and the workforce, but a conduit for communication, explaining management's expectations to the workforce but also conveying to management the fears, uncertainties and insecurities of the staff. This can be at the level of acting as a conciliator between a member of staff and his or her head of department, or at the level of informing policy formulation.

I would argue that this role, which seems to be increasingly disregarded, is crucially important in higher education. Most senior managers in universities (both chartered and statutory) are academics, and some of them need to be gently reminded, from time to time, of the aspirations and needs of the majority of their staff, who are not.

Conscience of the organization

This role is related to that of 'honest broker' but should still be found even in those institutions where the personnel specialist is fully identified with management. Torrington and Hall (1987) locate the roots of this role in the nineteenth century, before personnel even appeared as a distinct management activity, with the social reformers (such as Lord Shaftesbury) who tried to protect vulnerable workers from the more exploitative actions of ruthless industrialists.

It could be argued that with the legal protections now enjoyed by employees, the need for this role no longer exists. However, by and large, employee rights can only be exercised through the industrial tribunals and the courts. At a time when trade unions are weak and unemployment is relatively high, many employees will opt to stay silent rather than risk their jobs. Higher education institutions have, historically, been regarded as good employers, owing, in part, to their liberal traditions. However, as the unit of resource continues to decline and funding becomes increasingly dependent on external measures of performance, there is an understandable tendency not to embrace best practice voluntarily, unless it saves money. Personnel specialists will sometimes need to remind senior management that the stick may be effective in the short term, but that a diet supplemented by carrots will yield long-term benefits.

The importance of personnel specialists setting an example to their organizations in terms of ethical standards has been recognized by the Institute of Personnel and Development. At the time of writing a new code of ethics for members is under production and a book on ethical leadership (written by Steve Connock and Ted Johns) was published by the IPD in the autumn of 1995.

Future challenges

The HE system in the UK has undergone enormous change in the past 15 years and, although the rate of externally induced change may now have slowed, the evolution of internal processes has yet to catch up with the change that has already occurred. The changes that face personnel specialists in the next few years are therefore both specific (in the sense that they relate to the personnel function) and general (relating to the broader issues of institutional management and culture).

Of the specific challenges, those arising from the increasingly selective funding of research are among the most pressing, particularly for those institutions that are not yet recognized as 'research universities' or those whose research status is declining. The research rating of a department has profound effects on its ability to recruit or even retain the most able academic staff. When several institutions are recruiting lecturers in a particular discipline at the same time (which is not infrequent), higher rated departments will tend to have the pick of the best qualified and potentially more productive candidates, who are attracted to a well resourced, intellectually vibrant environment. The challenge for the personnel specialist working with lower rated departments is to counteract this inherent bias, by, for example, motivating existing staff to be more productive in research and finding ways in which 'home-grown' talent can be nurtured and retained.

External measurements of teaching quality are bringing their own challenges. For several years chartered universities in particular have been seeking to create a strong research ethos in response to research assessment. It has been true in many of these institutions, and openly admitted in some, that promotion to senior lecturer was only available to the best researchers, irrespective of the quality of their teaching. However, the realization has dawned that the majority of prospective applicants for undergraduate programmes are likely to be swayed more by external indicators of teaching quality than by research ratings. The challenge for personnel specialists in these circumstances is to work with senior managers, staff development specialists and the academic staff to create a climate where teaching is valued and excellence in teaching is rewarded. Some universities have gone down the road of introducing staff development programmes in teaching skills for new lecturers and of assessing the teaching performance of probationary staff. Others have begun to develop promotion criteria based on excellence in teaching, and are assessing the teaching performance of all candidates for promotion to senior lecturer. Some institutions are working towards a fully integrated approach to teaching quality at every level.

Personnel specialists in HE undoubtedly have the skills and expertise to make an effective contribution to facing the challenges described above. Whether they are permitted to depends on the institution's management culture. Keep and Sisson (1992: 68) argue that well developed personnel management systems have not evolved in the UK's universities because the institutions have failed to 'accept responsibility for managing the employment relationship'. Institutions have tended to blame the government for staffing problems arising from under-funding (recruitment difficulties, demoralization owing to deteriorating research infrastructure and so on), while the government maintains that the funding councils allocate the funds and that it is for the institutions, as the employers, to manage the funds they are allocated. While there is an ideological component in the institutions' position (that higher education benefits the country and therefore the state should fund it adequately), there is also in it an expression of an inherent reluctance to 'manage'.

When the first universities were established in the medieval period the masters' guild was the 'effective hub of university government' (Cobban, 1988: 99), being responsible for the selection of new masters, regulating the masters' duties and determining the academic regime. The senior officers of the university (the vice-chancellor and the proctors) were elected by the masters' guild and served for limited periods. The idea of academic self-governance was not as strongly developed in the 'redbrick' universities established in the late nineteenth and early twentieth centuries (indeed, it could be said that the sponsors of these institutions would have preferred to have kept the role of the academic staff in internal governance to a minimum). In spite of this, highly autonomous forms of government based on the idea of consensus among the academic staff developed and have persisted throughout the chartered universities. It is not surprising that the leaders of institutions which have retained the collegial ethos (or a 'folk memory' of it) find it difficult to accept that they are the managers of their academic colleagues.

The general challenge facing HEIs at the end of the twentieth century is to accept that 'management' is not a dirty word and that the effective management of people is the key to unlocking the creativity of all who work in HE.

Final thoughts

I hope that in this chapter I have conveyed some impression of the stimulating, but at times uncomfortable, position that personnel specialists occupy in their institutions. Those readers with experience of personnel in other settings will recognize that many of the sources of friction are not unique to HE, but 'go with the territory'. The contribution that specialist personnel management can make to achieving the institution's goals is beginning to be recognized, particularly in the statutory universities, but also (albeit more slowly) in the chartered ones. Personnel specialists will continue to live in interesting times for a little while yet.

8

Student Management

John Gledhill

Editors' introduction

As the author indicates in his first and second paragraphs, this subject is 'the least well covered by published guidelines' and there is no 'serious study of student management practices in HE'. This chapter goes some way towards rectifying this situation with an excellent summary of the key aspects of student management.

Introduction

Of all the areas of HE management, probably the least well covered by published guidelines and standard procedures is that of student records; even Lockwood and Davies (1985) have little to offer on this. The reasons for this are neither complex nor subtle, but neither are they easily remedied. Management of finance, staff, buildings and even social support services either has a legal or statutory basis or conforms to the norms of professional bodies. The way student records are managed, however, has, above a basic minimum norm, adapted to meet the needs of the individual institutions rather than external norms. HEIs have grown up along a wide variety of routes, developing their own traditions, structures and practices. As a broad generalization, HE management has tended to follow either civil service structures or those of local government, and these can lead to very different assumptions; for example, about centralization or devolution, collegiality or managerialism. Attempts to use identical or similar records systems in different institutions have usually failed for this and similar reasons, even though the underlying aims and results may be very close to each other.

There is also a widespread assumption (periodically voiced by academic staff at meetings and in the press) that student management is a simple, easy, clerical activity, that anyone can do; this has suppressed any serious study of student management practices in HE. However, a large part of student management is no longer geared simply to recording students' enrolment and examination results: institutional and national needs for management information are driving records to ever-increasing detail, with a resultant growing complexity of collecting and maintaining the data. The means by which the data are collected change over time, and are often dependent on available technology and other resources rather than on different managerial principles, so they will not be discussed further here. As institutional missions cover wider types of courses and students, the resultant structures and regulations are possibly too intricate for any one member of the institution to understand. Because of the widely diverging practices, the sections below represent more of a discussion of the main issues rather than detailed solutions. Similarly, there is no discussion of the specialized needs of issues raised by what may be transient phenomena, such as modularization, semesterization, enterprise skills or awards classification systems, or transient technology such as bar codes, optical character readers or compact disc storage.

Enrolment

It is within the working memory of HE managers that enrolment consisted of little more than signing on at the start of the year. Where a mass of data has to be collected at initial enrolment, and confirmed at annual re-enrolment, this is more difficult to streamline, especially when several thousand students have to be processed in a very short period (typically one week). Some use of technology can speed up parts of the enrolment, but cannot eliminate the need to handle a very large number of students and a very large amount of data. There is an instant conflict between the need to enrol rising numbers of students quickly, and with minimum disruption of their teaching, and the need to confirm ever more detailed data with them at the same time.

Some policies can affect the speed and efficiency of enrolment. For example, if a system of identity cards is in use, are they reissued each year or issued once only on initial enrolment? To reissue them each year has better security, but adds considerably to the enrolment burden; to issue them only on first enrolment is easier but may leave ostensibly valid cards in the hands of students who have left prematurely. Procedures can be set up to prevent fraudulent use internally, but not outside the institution. There is no right or wrong on this: it is a balance between security and time.

Enrolment is a very demanding time for staff, but can also be a very frustrating experience for students. This should be minimized by the employment of 'one stop shop' techniques, to avoid the students having to attend too many different venues, having to stand in too many queues and needing to go too often round the circle as different parts of the management agree on their status. As far as possible, all activities related to enrolment should be in the same place, if possible with a single queuing system (though that is rarely fully possible); this involves the attendance at enrolment not just of student records staff but also finance staff able to issue invoices and collect money, and even non-records functions such as international students' advisors, module fairs and students' union enrolment. Decentralizing enrolment to departments can be a valid approach to sharing the load and reducing student queuing, but does risk losing the overall coordination, particularly of the financial side of enrolment. It also runs the risk that departments may concentrate on collecting only those data needed for local records, and either attach less importance to institution-wide or nationally required data, or impose local interpretations on the data values. There is almost certainly room for an acceptable balance here, created by keeping any devolved enrolment sufficiently large-scale for those involved to be fully aware of all the nuances of the mass of data collected.

The main scope for efficient decentralized enrolment is for part-time students; many of these have great difficulty in attending a day-time enrolment period if their normal classes are in the evening or at other centres, or if their personal commitments leave them little flexibility for lengthy queuing. These problems have to be considered sensitively if the institution is committed to part-time delivery, but it also has to communicate to such students that not all procedures can necessarily be adjusted to fit their domestic schedules.

Induction

Often confused with enrolment, but very distinct both in aims and in implementation, is induction. Enrolment is aimed at the needs of the institution, induction at those of the students; the correct balance is difficult to achieve. Many items of great importance have to be conveyed to students at the start of the year, particularly their first year, but trying to get all the information over at once – even over a full week – can lead to chronic information overload and so-called 'induction fatigue', where students are expected to assimilate so much that the later parts of the induction are not properly absorbed, especially where, as new students, they may be impatient to start their course. There is similarly an awkward combination of time-critical academic induction (for example, choice of optional subjects, library tours) with social induction (societies, guidance services, etc.). To cut out induction sessions and rely entirely on handbooks and information sheets is probably an equally bad mistake, and a potential impoverishment of student experience. The most important aim is to make students aware of the existence of the various services, so that they can follow them up in more detail as time allows or need dictates; achieving this when each section involved wants to make its presence felt during induction is very difficult, and may need great tact.

Records

Traditional methods of recording student courses are no longer flexible enough in many institutions. Until the mid-1980s almost all students graduated on the course on which they first enrolled: most courses were straightforward full-time three-year courses, and transfers were difficult to obtain and unusual. The use of modular schemes radically changed this, though even here the concept of 'course' usually still has a place. Within modular schemes it is important to appreciate the distinction between what can be called a modular 'scheme' and a modular 'framework'. In a modular 'scheme', the institution will typically offer a wide range of subjects in a compatible format, from which students will have a very wide choice of routes, with possibly a few special modules to link the subjects; their final award may contain a combination of the subjects they happen to have studied (for example, 'Bachelor of Arts in French, Law and Sociology'); the concept of 'transfers' is often alien to this structure. In a modular 'framework', on the other hand, the institution may well offer something more akin to the traditional 'course', where each award has a predefined name, structure and compulsory elements, but all constructed according to a unified model. This encourages options from other areas (since they are guaranteed to be of equal value to other modules), and can also facilitate course transfers without actually encouraging them. Also distinct from either of these is the use of 'unitization', where an institution simply ensures that all the course components or modules are defined in a standard unit; for example, credit units, percentages or module weights. This is a prerequisite of modular structures, but does not have to lead to them. A unitized structure can accommodate courses and 'modules' of different overall course loading, with, for example, one course counting for 120 units per annum and another course for only 100 units per annum.

Whether the institution is modular or not, records are hard to keep up to date in large institutions: central and local management can seem remote from students and unsympathetic to their needs. The more complex the course structure and the more flexible the possibilities for changing route or course, the harder it is to ensure that the records are fully up to date; even more so if the students are on franchised courses at partner institutions. Not all statutory statistical returns are able to cope with fully modularized structures, and they can regard a student's choice of new programme or emphasis within a modular scheme as equivalent to a 'course transfer' under non-modular structures, with all its overtones of instability and fluctuating commitment. Where student financial arrangements are predicated on stable course enrolment (for example, by allowing only one course transfer), students run a real risk of having their financial support withdrawn because the funding authority's record system is based on these different assumptions (for example, those of local education authorities). This has the undesirable effect that educationally valid course structures cannot be operated properly because of funding bodies' records system.

The same can happen with multi-exit courses, such as foundation course, diploma, degree, honours degree, leading to time-consuming and unproductive correspondence with the student's funding body.

Of almost equal difficulty, under the more flexible systems, is keeping track of which elements or modules a student is taking. Allowing students to try several additional modules at the start of each year before settling on their final choice may be academically desirable but can wreak havoc with the timetable, forward planning and resource allocation; restricting this opportunity can be deemed unresponsive to student needs. Many institutions allow a month for module choices to be settled: two weeks is probably better. Operating provisional module choice in the previous year is rarely worth the effort if it is subject to too much subsequent change. Institutional resource distribution methodology cannot run successfully on the current year's subjects if the choice is delayed for too long, and in some cases it may be better to fund departments on the basis of the previous year's module choices, despite the time lag that this builds into the resourcing of new courses.

Tracking students' progress and attendance during the academic year is in some ways more sensitive than ensuring accurate enrolment at the start. Students, as mature adults, frequently resent the use of registers in classes and signing-on procedures at the start of each term, and in many HEIs there is no formal requirement to attend most individual classes. However, these methods may have to be used if the institution is to be able to guarantee to auditors and funding bodies that the number of students is accurate. The institution also has a duty of pastoral care for students, as part of which a regular monitoring of attendance may have a vital role to play in spotting absences and identifying the reasons before they become serious.

During enrolment at the institution a student will have to meet the needs both of the centralized records and of his or her home department. The former has to be able to record and analyse the basic student management information (age, sex, course, attendance mode, etc.), and the latter also has to be able to monitor the more routine matters, such as sickness, essay deadlines and tutorial groups, with which the central records are not concerned. This distinction still exists where the records are largely decentralized to departments. The different functions of basic records and transient domestic arrangements have to exist, and the different needs of each must not distort the efficiency of the other.

Archiving

Once students have left, the records system has to cope with the increasing problems of archiving. The ability of computerized record systems to carry out diachronic surveys of trends makes it very important that the complete records of students are preserved for as long as possible after they have left. It is also far from unusual to receive requests for transcripts for students who left over twenty years previously, especially from those now living in countries with a longer tradition of computerized records. Many parts of the student's record will become less useful as time passes. As course structures change over the years it becomes of less use to the institution to undertake cohort analyses of previous intakes. Experience suggests that the full computer record of the student should be kept for ten years if possible, after which (if space or processing time becomes a problem) the record should be reduced to simple data required by alumni organizations (for example, full names, last address, sex, birth date, date of entry, date of award, award on leaving), dropping much of all of the intermediate data (such as resit decisions, year's progress flags, financial information). Paper records can probably be archived one or two years after the student leaves, using any suitably compact document storage and retrieval system: the method is less important than the space and the ability to find records when necessary.

In the question of archiving, as with records on current students, it is of the utmost importance that the computing staff involved in maintaining the software fully understand the needs of the bureaucracy. Computer programmers share the same frailties as other people, and tend to write systems that are easy to maintain but might not produce exactly what the users want: in an intensive records system this can lead to very inefficient systems being used. The student records managers must set the brief and monitor the programmers' interpretation of it.

Examinations

Academic staff debate at great length the relative merits and burdens of the different forms of assessment: essays, invigilated written examinations, multiple choice questions, computerized tests and so on. Few of these debates touch on the logistical problems of managing the examinations: the collection of interim marks, printing mark sheets for examination boards, processing results, issuing letters to students, coping with amendments and appeals, and the perennial search for errant examination desks. As pressure on academic time increases, and student numbers grow, the examinations systems find themselves under pressure from both ends. Teaching time encroaches more closely on to the start of the examination period (or vice versa), shortage of accommodation extends the timetable later into the term, the examination marking period then extends into the early vacation, results are later and so on. Where there are large numbers of part-time students there is similarly a conflict of pressures in the instability of much modular data if the structure is too flexible, and the need to get the examination timetable out early enough for part-time students to make the appropriate domestic arrangements. Computerization can help with a clash-free short examination period, but expectations of students and academic staff that all their preferences can be accommodated are often unrealistic: not every examination can be early, not every student can avoid two examinations in one day, nor can the use of Saturday morning and some weekday evening slots always be eliminated.

Cheating

Pressure on students brings an increase in attempted (and successful) cheating, not only in invigilated examinations but also in coursework. The onus for ensuring that students are fully aware of the perils of cheating and plagiarism falls on academic staff and management alike; cheating cases can frequently fail if the student can demonstrate that he or she was not informed how to avoid it. It is vital to ensure that the procedures for handling these are watertight and cover all likely eventualities. Institutions must also make sure that their own cheating and plagiarism rules are consistent with those of any professional bodies whose examinations they organize. Some professional bodies make no mention of plagiarism, so that a successful internal charge of plagiarism accompanied by 'not guilty of cheating' may inappropriately but legally be treated as simply not guilty of cheating under the terms of the other body.

As students also get more litigious, institutions may become swamped with large numbers of appeals against decisions, and requests for reviews of marks. The traditional approach of HEIs appears to be still correct: marks and results themselves cannot be challenged, only whether the procedures leading to them were correctly carried out and all relevant information taken into account. Provided that no marks have been lost, no arithmetical errors made and no mitigating circumstances ignored, students should not be able to appeal to the courts (or for chartered universities, to the visitor) against the academic judgement of the institution (see Farrington, 1994 on 'expert judgement', pp. 358–65).

A further frequent cause of misunderstanding between students and management during examinations is the regulations about what students may take with them into the examination. Students have great emotional attachment to various pieces of equipment, mascots, dictionaries, calculators, pencil cases and other items of stationery. All can be used for cheating, and the ingenuity of determined students frequently outstrips the letter of the cheating regulations: notes are discovered in dictionaries and pencil cases, sophisticated calculators have notes stored in their memories, some calculators have means of communicating with similar models elsewhere in the room, personal audio systems may have course notes rather than music on them, mobile phones are used to receive answers during a visit to the toilet facilities, electronic dictionaries often include spelling checkers and a thesaurus, giving a distinct advantage to their users.

The 'simple' solution for management to prevent cheating is to ban all the items mentioned above, but that is very unpopular with students, and does not always enjoy the full support of academic staff; controlling calculators, for example, is notoriously difficult. Similarly, tutors of international students may place a greater emphasis on the needs of their students to be able to understand the question paper via a dictionary than on the risk of cheating this introduces. The alternative, and equally 'simple', solution is to allow students to take any materials they wish into examinations. This makes the setting of papers very awkward and is not usually acceptable to academic staff as a global solution. Avoiding impersonation during examinations can be achieved by checking identity cards, though this slows things down. The answers to these questions are, as so often, not purely administrative or managerial, and may be a compromise between a clear but rigid rule and sensitive but vulnerable flexibility.

Anonymous marking

As distinct from the managerial problems of cheating and plagiarism, much debate of a more philosophical and idealistic nature has been held on the question of anonymous marking. Sometimes presented simplistically as an easy means of ensuring lack of prejudice, it can often have punitive side-effects on the workload of management and academic staff alike. At its simplest, it can be achieved by telling students to write their number rather than name on the answer scripts, but there is much more than this to a proper system, to say nothing of setting up procedures for making sure that the student has put the correct number on the work. An institution using anonymous examining must decide how far it wishes the anonymity to be preserved. Anonymous marking of scripts and coursework is the lowest level, but need not always be accompanied by anonymous decision-making; it depends on whether there is as much fear of bias and prejudice at the examination board as during the marking. If there is equal concern at this level it involves not knowing the names of the candidates at any stage during the examination board's deliberations. This sits uneasily with the legitimate role of the examination board to take into account any special circumstances of a student. The nearest solution to these competing ideals is to preserve anonymity during marking and any discussions on the course element or module itself, when, for example, it may be decided to carry out some overall scaling to the module marks. At the examination board that makes the final decision, anonymity can still be preserved until all cases have been considered on their marks alone. At that stage, when mitigating circumstances are brought up at the end, anonymity may at best be a fiction and it helps no one to pretend otherwise. Even when all these procedures work smoothly, they may cause delays in the publication of results while students' names are being matched to their identity numbers. The system can work, and often works well, but it is not as efficient or speedy as non-anonymous procedures; mark entry on to computers, for example, can take longer, as more validation of identity may be required.

Internationalization

As HEIs expand their horizons beyond their home shores and build more intimate relationships with overseas institutions, the complexity of coordinating the examination requirements can often get overlooked, or assumed to be simply addressed. The more obvious point about transporting examination papers to the various international partners can significantly affect deadlines for submission of question papers for printing. More subtle are the questions of simultaneous timing of examination sessions, and this is not restricted to examination centres at opposite sides of the globe. Even within Europe, the different time zones can present logistical problems. If a different question paper is set for the various centres, the timing problem disappears but is replaced by the question of comparability of assessment. If the same paper is sat by students at the various centres, the difference in local time must be taken into account, as otherwise some students may find themselves sitting the examination at dawn or in the late evening. If the times are not coordinated exactly, the HEI must obviously try to ensure that no student who has left one centre before the end of the examination has had the opportunity to convey information about the contents of the paper, and the communications technology available at present makes international cheating a very real possibility. The only failsafe procedures are: different papers for each centre, run each centre simultaneously or prevent students from leaving early or starting late at any centre. None of these solutions is without problems. The above comments relate mainly to examinations held as part of a formal arrangement between two institutions; much the same comments apply to examinations held away from the HEI as part of a special arrangement for individual students; for example, because of illness. Increasing the number of international students at an HEI increases the pressure for them to be allowed to take some of their examinations (particularly resits) in their home country. Although considerable moral pressure can be exerted by the students in this position, such arrangements are best avoided except in most exceptional circumstances. Attending an HEI in a particular country should imply an understanding that one has to attend for all required teaching and assessment, including resits.

External examiners

The problems associated with the selection and appointment of external examiners, and with the submission and analysis of their reports, are not confined solely to student records management, but overlap into quality assurance generally. The role of the external examiner is too broad a subject to be covered in detail here.

Financial and legal requirements

Financial systems

Few good student records systems can be run in total isolation from the financial records system. Some institutions try to run the student or sponsor invoicing system as if it were part of the normal sales or services system. In pure accounting terms this may make sense, but such systems are rarely as good as one that links the student or sponsor invoicing system more directly to the student record. Ideally, the systems should be fully integrated, but as the financial system also has to cope with non-student invoices it is not always possible to guarantee a fully integrated institution-wide system. The close relationship between the student or sponsor invoicing system and the student records system must be paramount, as otherwise there are long-running internal wrangles when differences arise between the 'registry view' of how many students have enrolled and the 'finance view' of how many are to be invoiced. At the very least, this can lead to discrepancies between forecasts of student numbers and of fee income, which can make planning less effective. At worst, it can mean the two parts of the system (student records and finance) having to exchange notes on student status or the students having to tell both offices separately: the latter is very poor in terms of customer service.

Assuming that there is agreement between the financial system and the enrolment records system on the number of students or sponsors to be invoiced, the other main linkage between the two parts arises when non-payment of fees occurs. From a purely financial view a student (or his or her sponsor) who does not pay fees is a debtor or defaulter, and may be treated in the same way as any other customer. HE tradition tends to try to divorce such matters from the purely academic concerns. For this reason, management may find itself in conflict with academic staff, who may feel that debt chasing is unnecessarily bureaucratic, heavy-handed and insensitive, putting pressure on students who are trying to pass examinations. Conversely, management may find academic staff unwilling to enforce any financial sanctions required by the institution for non-payment of fees. Both viewpoints are understandable, but must be reconciled. In particular, it is incumbent upon management not to invoke on small debts the same Draconian pressures that it uses against those owing large amounts. To expel a student for total non-payment of fees may be understood by most academic staff, but to threaten expulsion for non-payment of a disciplinary fine will not gain the same level of support. Care must also be taken not to penalize the students for non-payment by their sponsor, though the influence that a student under threat of expulsion can have on a tardy sponsor should not be underestimated.

The sanctions available for management against small debtors have been affected by new technology and data protection legislation. Whereas under a manual system it is straightforward to withhold a student's examination results without jeopardizing the marking and decision-making process, this can be very cumbersome if computerized mark records are maintained. If the student has a right to see computer records under data protection legislation, to try to withhold results as a financial sanction may require the institution not to enter the marks on the system at all, resulting in a large increase of manual procedures and special action by the chair of the examination board when a debt is cleared. This is not conducive to the smooth management of examination results. However, the withholding of results can be a very powerful sanction and should not be avoided altogether; to process all results regardless of financial matters can lead to students waiting to get their results before deciding whether to pay their debts or not. The best compromise is to use such blocking procedures only for serious large-scale debt, such as the non-payment of the fees, and not to use them for smaller debts (library, discipline, car-parking fines, etc.); the appropriate sanction for the latter is denial of enrolment the following year or the withholding of the actual award and certificate. This avoids examination boards having to keep updating their decisions as minor debts are cleared.

Legal aspects

Very few legal requirements affect student records as such, though there are statutory requirements to submit periodic enrolment returns to the statistical agencies. Other legislation directly affecting student records management is typically the need to issue certificates of enrolment as required by some benefits and tax legislation, and the requirement to abide by the terms of the institutional registration under the 1984 Data Protection Act (basically the need for records to be accurate, up to date and relevant to needs). Students' right of access to their records may affect the possibility of withholding results as a financial sanction, as mentioned in the preceding section, but otherwise has little direct effect on the content or processing of the student records system. This assumes that the institution is only going to use the student data for genuine educational purposes: the Data Protection Act (1984) does not prevent any registered user from carrying out any acts provided they are registered by the user under the Act (and are not otherwise illegal). Any normal activity of an HEI, registered openly under the Act, can therefore continue. Non-educational activities could be challenged by students on the grounds of use or holding of records not relevant to the institution's educational function; for example, if an institution maintained computerized records of students' criminal activities or sexual orientation, or used legitimately held data to approach students whose birthday was due to canvass them to use institutional catering facilities for their party. Similarly, students could claim that passing their address to insurance companies or mailing list agencies was not consistent with the institution's functions: registering this under the Data Protection Act may make it legal, but does not guarantee that it is seen as acceptable.

Graduation

The range in style and function of awards ceremonies at different institutions is quite wide, and reflects the underlying choices that have to be made about the ceremonies.

The fundamental choice that has to be made is whether the ceremony is to be the formal act of conferral or merely a celebration of a conferral already made within the committee structure of the institution. There is no legal constraint on this choice, but the effect of the choice must be clearly understood. If the ceremony is deemed to be the formal conferral a student is not technically a 'graduate' until the ceremony has been held. This means that no certificates can be issued in advance and the students should not add qualifications ('BA', 'LLB', etc.) after their names. It also means that students who complete their course (or pay overdue debts) in the middle of the normal academic year have to wait until the next ceremony before collecting their award and certificate. (A way round this is to frame the regulations such that the vice-chancellor, acting alone, can constitute a minimal conferral ceremony.) On the other hand, making the act of conferral at a committee reduces the ceremony itself to little more than a celebration without formal status.

A less fundamental point, but one still of great importance, is whether it is a 'degree ceremony' or an 'awards ceremony'. This is not mere semantics but governs whether only degrees are conferred at the ceremony or whether diplomas, certificates and other awards are also conferred. At the very least, the decision crucially affects the size and frequency of the ceremonies, particularly in institutions with large diploma and certificate populations, such as the statutory universities. There is a very strong argument for including in the ceremony all those who have successfully completed a course leading to an award, whether at degree level or not, although this can add large numbers to the ceremonies.

The selection of venue for the ceremonies is not always simple, and the choice between having many small events or a few larger events is often constrained by the availability of venues. Institutions with a large central hall of their own may choose to hold the ceremonies there, while others with nearby cathedrals or similar large buildings may prefer the public pomp that they can impart to the ceremony. However, both of these types of arrangements can be under considerable strain when there is growth in student numbers. Institutional halls are frequently not big enough to cope with large numbers, and universities find themselves having to have 15 or more ceremonies for about 800 people at a time. The larger public facilities may be able to cope with 2000 people at once (typically 600 students with two guests each), but may be unwilling to make themselves available for a whole week to enable eight or ten ceremonies to be held. The hire fees charged, even by cathedrals, is also of relevance. Whichever venue is used, HEIs must always remind themselves that the ceremonies are principally there for the students and their parents, rather than for the institution itself. This is not to belittle the events: the celebration by the HEI of the success of its students is very important psychologically, both for the students and for the institution, and a splendid show can increase confidence in the standards of the institution. Some institutions choose to have separate ceremonies for their international students: these can either be at the HEI itself (typically held soon after the end of the course, while students are still in the vicinity), or, if numbers make it sensible, in the students' home country. The latter present considerable logistical difficulties and are not always to be recommended.

When drawing up their regulations for ceremonies, HEIs must give careful attention to two other legal points covering rules for attendance by officers and students. Most HEIs require the presence of a senior officer to legitimate the ceremony. This is crucial if the ceremony is the formal act of conferral; as described above, the persons empowered to confer an award must be clearly identified in the basic regulations of the institution. Typically it is restricted to the chancellor and vice-chancellor, but may also include pro-chancellors and pro-vice-chancellors. In most cases it is also possible to write into the regulations that the vice-chancellor has the power to nominate others to act on his or her behalf. However, this needs checking in case the formulation of the regulations already defines the vice-chancellor to be acting on delegated powers from the chancellor or other body, since a person holding delegated power cannot normally further delegate the powers at his or her own discretion. If the ceremony is not a formal act of conferral, the attendance of one of the senior officers is no longer a legal requirement but a matter of public relations. A good idea, if the regulations permit, is to make the quorum for a formal act of conferral to be one person. This enables the vice-chancellor (for example) to confer a single award or supplementary list without convening an actual ceremony, and it can also be used, for example, for the vice-chancellor to confer an award on a terminally ill student who cannot complete the course or attend a ceremony.

Attendance by students is clearly also affected by whether the ceremony is the formal act of conferral. If it is not, then the absence of a student (whether notified or not) is of no legal importance; nor is the presence or omission of a name from the order of proceedings. If the ceremony is the formal act of conferral there should be a point in the ceremony where the presenter or vice-chancellor (or perhaps a walk-on role for the registrar) utters words to the effect that 'Those students named in the proceedings but not in attendance are also admitted to their degrees and awards.' The precise wording is less important than the formal act of recognition of the conferral. A note in the order of proceedings is probably not enough to confer the awards, and a statement such as the above ought to be read out orally. It must be noted that this imparts greater status to the order of proceedings, in that it thereby becomes the formal record of awards made at the ceremony, and the omission of a name could be deemed to call into question the legitimacy of the award (additional names can be read out if necessary, or supplementary lists appended).

A rather vexed legal question, on which legal advice is not always unanimous, is whether awards can be made posthumously. The 'common sense' view that often prevails in this lack of united legal opinion is that since aegrotat awards can be made to students who fail to complete their course because of illness, a posthumous award can also be made to students who fail to complete their course because of death. In both cases the HEI is making an award in the absence of the full normal evidence of achievement, and is in effect treating death and illness on a par. The legal point is not about the HEI's rights to decide this, but about whether an award can be made to a person who no longer exists. A distinction is made by lawyers between awards which are earned by meeting formal criteria (such as degrees) and awards which are discretionary (such as military medals), and between achievements which can be passed on as part of the estate (such as titles) and those which die with the person (such as degrees).

Final thoughts

In many organizations there is a potential tension between those sections which have an exciting 'can do' entrepreneurial brief and those which press on with the more prosaic routines in a steady, economical and efficient way. The former may get the attention, but the latter are still of major significance. Student management is very much of the latter ilk. Banks have a similar inbuilt potential tension (in the allocation of resources and senior management attention) between the need for failsafe, efficient and economical routines (for example, for handling cash) and the flexible, responsive delivery of fast-moving, cutting-edge merchant banking style financial advice to corporate customers.

Moreover, if the various aspects of student management are undertaken sloppily, there is a growing likelihood of litigation between the student and the HEI. To this end, readers should be aware of D. J. Farrington's *The Law of Higher Education* (1994), and especially the chapter on 'Students: Scholars, Clients and Customers'. *Inter alia*, this chapter analyses the contract for admission and the contract of matriculation, the legal issues surrounding academic progress and the complexities of student discipline. Finally, a new legal twist is the degree to which recent legislation on unfair contract terms (for example, small print, over-complex language, weak customer versus mighty supplier) may apply to the student–HEI 'contract'.

9

Postgraduate and Research Organization and Management

John Hogan and Mark Clark

Editors' introduction

This chapter is in two separate sections: the first (by John Hogan) deals with general issues of postgraduate education, including the development of graduate schools; the second (by Mark Clark) examines in depth aspects of research management.

There is no doubt that there is an inexorable growth of postgraduate education in the UK. Even if the research assessment exercises had not produced financial carrots for such development, it would still take place. The virtual tripling of undergraduate numbers since 1980 entails exactly the same increase in the number of students wanting and expecting to be able to proceed to postgraduate work. In fact, this very undergraduate expansion will cause an even larger percentage of the annual cohort to seek postgraduate qualifications as the scarcity value of the first degree becomes less and less. It seems certain, therefore, that there will be insufficient funded full-time postgraduate places to meet this demand, and consequently that there will be a huge increase in students wishing to study part-time. Traditionally, the statutory universities have been far stronger than the chartered universities in this type of study. It remains to be seen, however, if adequate provision can be made for research work on a part-time basis in the laboratory-based subjects. The editors expect that there will be some innovative solutions to this problem.

1 POSTGRADUATE EDUCATION

Introduction

Postgraduate education covers a wide range of activity, from short conversion courses through to PhDs in the most obscure of topics. The administrative and organizational problems presented are equally wide-ranging.

Table 9.1   Postgraduate students at chartered universities in the UK

	Number	% of full-time student population
Full-time		
1953–4	12,284	14.8
1963–4	22,943	17.6
1973–4	47,625	19.0
1983–4	48,355	16.1
1993–4	85,105	18.1
Part-time		
1953–4	4,799	29.8
1963–4	7,163	41.7
1973–4	20,884	85.6
1983–4	30,160	83.0
1993–4	67,393	80.9

All statistical information is taken from DFE Statistical Bulletins, CVCP, HESA and USR.

This section will examine some of the major issues and trends in postgraduate education and some of the managerial responses.

The scale and nature of postgraduate education

Postgraduate education developed comparatively slowly in the UK. In 1938 there were only 6000 postgraduate students, representing some 6 per cent of the higher education student population (Rudd, 1975). There was a substantial increase in the number of postgraduates during the 1960s, when more state studentships were provided to help to increase the number of trained academics required to fill posts in the rapidly expanding higher education sector (Table 9.1).

Nevertheless, UK higher education institutions (HEIs) did not develop separate organizational structures to cater for the requirements of teaching postgraduates and conducting research. In the main, the administrative structures of HEIs developed primarily to manage the demands of undergraduate teaching. In the vast majority of HEIs, undergraduate students represent over 75 per cent of the student population and, for 30 weeks in the year, institutional energies seem to be directed primarily to teaching undergraduate students.

There are now clear indications that postgraduate education is becoming increasingly important and demanding new managerial responses. The very rapid expansion in undergraduate numbers during the late 1980s and early 1990s is well known. What is not so well appreciated is the similar rate of expansion for postgraduate students (Figure 9.1).

Traditionally, most postgraduate education, particularly research training,

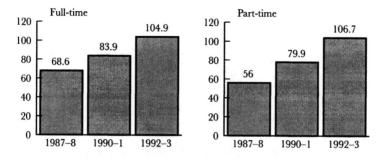

Figure 9.1 Growth in UK postgraduate numbers excluding Open University (thousands)

has taken place in the chartered universities. In 1987–8, for example, only 9 per cent of postgraduate research training occurred outside the chartered universities (Henkel and Kogan, in Clark, 1993). In 1992–3, 76 per cent of full-time postgraduates and 57 per cent of part-time postgraduates were studying in chartered universities. However, the recent rate of growth in the former 'public' sector has been particularly impressive.

Postgraduate students represent almost 20 per cent of the higher education student population. Just under half study on a full-time basis and just over half are registered as part-time students. Most postgraduate students are men (58 per cent of full-time population, 55 per cent of part-time population in 1992–3), but the rate of growth for women students has been much more rapid since the mid-1980s. In the chartered universities, 40 per cent of the full-time postgraduate population follow research degrees and one-third of the part-time population are registered for research degrees. The portion following research degrees in the statutory university sector and colleges of higher education (CHEs) is lower.

While many full-time students commence their postgraduate training shortly after completing their first degrees, most postgraduates have some work experience and are significantly older or more 'mature' than their undergraduate compatriots: 53 per cent of full-time postgraduates and 92 per cent of part-time postgraduates were 25 or over before commencing their postgraduate work in 1992. This, coupled with the fact that many are self-financing, makes them potentially a much more demanding and discerning group of students.

While education is the single largest subject area for postgraduate study, the rate of expansion has been much more rapid in certain other large subjects, notably mathematics and computing, social sciences and business and finance (Figure 9.2). A large proportion of part-time students in the new universities and CHEs follow programmes in business and administration.

Postgraduate programmes are particularly important for the UK's international reputation. In 1992 over one-third of international students in UK higher education followed postgraduate programmes and one-third of the

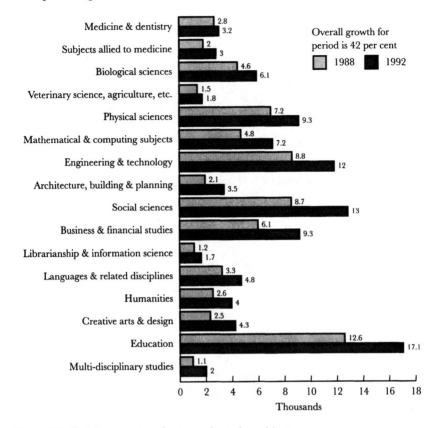

Figure 9.2   Full-time postgraduate students by subject

full-time postgraduate population was from overseas. This was a much higher proportion than for undergraduate full-time degrees (where 6 per cent were from overseas) and is an important factor in shaping the character of recruitment, teaching and supervision.

Future growth

It is probable that the recent rapid growth in postgraduate numbers will continue. The abolition of the 'binary line' proposed in the 1991 White Paper, *Higher Education: a New Framework*, has increased the number of HEIs that regard the provision of postgraduate education as part of their core activities. Some 165 HEIs are now offering research degrees and over 200 provide taught postgraduate programmes (Higher Education Business Enterprises (HEBE), 1994a, 1994b).

The government's decision in November 1993 to hold the age participation rate for full-time undergraduates steady at a level of around 30 per cent until October 1998 has meant that HEIs have looked to alternative areas of growth. Most seem to have decided to increase their postgraduate populations. The HEFCE has noted that nearly all institutions have a strategy for strengthening research, and among the common elements identified is a growth in the number of postgraduate research students (HEFCE *News*, 1994). There has been an increase in the number of institutional scholarships for postgraduate study and an expansion in the number of taught master's programmes. *The Times Higher Education Supplement* in February 1995 advertised almost 7000 postgraduate courses, of which almost 10 per cent were new programmes. With a larger number of qualified undergraduates, and record levels of unemployment for new graduates (11.7 per cent in 1993), it is not surprising that there is a demand for postgraduate places. A postgraduate qualification may give a competitive advantage in the employment market and is preferable to a period of unemployment (Higher Education Information Services Trust (HEIST), 1994/5).

HEIs are fully aware of the importance of postgraduates, particularly research students, in the research assessment exercise. The number of research students is not only one of the factors considered in the assessment of research quality, but is also used as one of the volume measures to help to determine the level of research funding allocated by the funding councils.

While postgraduate education is likely to continue with its rapid growth, there are factors that may cause problems. It is possible that the pressure in the early 1990s to increase the number of research students will cease once the results of the 1996 research assessment exercise are known. The HEFCE has warned that the constraints on research funding and the requirements for the selective allocation of such funds mean that the aspirations of many institutional missions will not be matched in reality (HEFCE, 1995c).

Recruitment and admissions

Compared with recruitment to undergraduate programmes, the recruitment and admission of postgraduate students is a confusing muddle. For most postgraduate programmes there is no national application system comparable with the Universities and Colleges Admissions Service (UCAS) for undergraduates. There are important exceptions, including the Graduate Teacher Training Registry, which acts as a clearing house for postgraduate certificate in education (PGCE) applications. In the main, the recruitment of postgraduates is determined by individual institutional policy, with little inter-institutional cooperation. Applicants are free to apply to as many institutions as they wish and accept whatever offer they see fit. However, a large proportion (42 per cent in 1993) apply to only one institution (HEIST 1994/5), and in many respects postgraduate admission is a less competitive process than recruitment to undergraduate degrees, although, again, there are some notable exceptions, particularly master of business administration (MBAs) programmes. While there are no national figures available, information from some HEIs indicates that over half those offered a place on a postgraduate programme fail to register, either because they have accepted an offer elsewhere or, more probably, because they have failed to raise the necessary funds.

The evidence available suggests that there are two main motives for undertaking postgraduate study: a desire to learn more about a subject in which a student has a particular interest, and a desire to enhance skills for vocational reasons (Policy Studies Institute (PSI), 1994). There are other motives, some students just drift into a further period of study, but most make a positive decision to apply to a particular course at a particular institution (HEIST 1994/5).

Funding

The main obstacle to postgraduate expansion is financial: both personal finances for the individual hoping to study at a postgraduate level and institutional funding.

Many postgraduate students fund their studies from their own resources. About half of full-time research students in the chartered universities are funded by the research councils (ABRC, 1994), but this group is the exception. Most postgraduates are not eligible for a mandatory grant or a student loan (PGCE students are an important exception to this). Career development loans and other forms of personal finances are required. A survey undertaken in 1992 at the University of Edinburgh showed that 20 per cent of postgraduates had considered withdrawing at some stage because of their financial problems, and some 80 per cent used their own savings to help finance their studies (*The Independent,* 19 November 1992). Institutional responses to the funding problem have included the targeting of access funds or hardship funds to postgraduates, but such funds are limited. There is little doubt that if more funding was available, or if the student loan scheme were extended to all postgraduates, there would be a further boost to the recruitment of postgraduates.

The means of providing institutions with funds to teach and train postgraduates are confused. For most full-time programmes, whether taught or research, HEIs charge a fee to home students recommended by the Department for Education, £2350 for 1994–5. Fees for part-time students are much lower: many HEIs now charge half the full-time fee, but most charge a lower rate. This common flat-rate fee disregards the obvious differences in the costs of providing training between different subject areas. There is no attempt to distinguish between even broad bands of subjects (clinical, laboratory science, other), which are used to help to determine the level of undergraduate fees and are often applied to the full fees paid by many international students.

In addition, institutions receive funding from the Funding Councils for teaching home postgraduate students. However, this funding is included in the general grant for teaching and, for research students, as an element in research funds. Under the current funding methodologies, it is not possible to determine how much public funding is made available to support postgraduate training, since decisions over funding allocations are taken by individual HEIs. Nevertheless, there are indications that the level of public support for postgraduate programmes is inadequate. Given the growing recognition of the need to provide postgraduates with the level of facilities comparable with their advanced level of study (see, for example, National Postgraduate Committee, 1995), this is a major problem for institutional managers. Such facilities include, for example, laboratories, IT facilities, offices and common rooms.

There is little firm evidence available on the actual institutional costs of postgraduate research training: on the best data available, a working group of the Advisory Board for the Research Councils (ABRC) concluded in 1994 that 'it looks very unlikely that the sums provided specifically to underpin the work of PhD research students are sufficient to cover the expenditure made by departments' (ABRC, 1994: A2.24). The working group recommended that a system of differential fees should be introduced to reflect the different costs of research training in subject areas by creating a series of fee bands. However, the effect on the market of introducing differential fees is far from clear.

It is at least arguable that institutions are underfunded for postgraduate teaching and training, and this is likely to cause increasing strains given the efficiency gains imposed upon higher education generally, and the increasing number of postgraduate students.

Taught programmes

Taught programmes are typically managed as an extension of undergraduate degrees – taught in the same departments and drawing heavily on the same staff. The elements involved are familiar to the newly registered student, typically an advanced course followed by a substantial dissertation. A taught programme usually lasts for between nine and twelve months if studied full-time, probably twice as long if studied on a part-time basis and longer still if taught by distance-learning.

The number of taught programmes available in the UK is impressive. For example, some 48 HEIs offer 135 taught programmes in economics, 38 HEIs offer 70 taught programmes in physics (HEBE, 1994a). The range of postgraduate activity covered by these taught qualifications varies considerably; postgraduate certificates, diplomas or master's degrees are familiar titles, which cover a wide variety of different programmes, employing different methods and producing different outcomes. At least five general types of taught postgraduate programmes can be identified:

1. A specialist course building on an undergraduate degree taken in the same subject area.
2. A conversion course offering specialist training, which is only open to those without a first degree in the same subject.
3. A general course covering a wide range of material.
4. A postgraduate course that leads to a professional qualification or exemption from part of such a qualification.
5. A research preparation course designed to lead to a doctorate.

These definitions are not mutually exclusive, and many qualifications cross one or more boundaries. Nevertheless, managers of postgraduate training should be clear about the different range of programmes to be offered and the different demands that are made upon facilities and staff time.

Research degrees

There has been an important change in the nature of postgraduate training, particularly research training, during the 1980s and early 1990s. Traditionally, postgraduate research training has followed an apprenticeship model of a research student being allocated a single supervisor and working in a related field. The period of study for a research degree is usually longer than for a taught qualification, typically two years full-time registration for an MPhil and three years for a PhD (DPhil at Oxbridge). Normally, the students require an additional period to write up the research (an extension or continuation period). However, there has been a great deal of concern over the completion rate for research students. The ABRC report (1982) on postgraduate education was extremely critical of the length of time it took students to complete, and recommended that full-time PhD students should complete within four years, with the investigation being completed within three years and the writing-up within the fourth year. The report identified three main causes for the poor completion rates: poor supervision, especially in the early stages; a lack of adequate knowledge about research techniques; and inadequate motivation by the student. The four-year submission rate policy for full-time PhDs was adopted by the research councils, which refused to award studentships to institutions that failed to secure the submission of a certain proportion of their PhDs within a four-year period. This sanctions policy was a success, with a dramatic improvement in the completion rates for social sciences and improvements in the completion rates for humanities and sciences (which achieve the best submission rate figures).

The submission rate issue helped to focus the debate about the nature of the PhD. It is now widely accepted that, while the PhD must be a significant original piece of work, it is also a research training process and must not be regarded as the apex of a career in research. This has changed institutional perceptions about the mechanisms and techniques required to facilitwate and monitor progress. All institutions have introduced a greater degree of control or 'centralization'. It is now commonplace to find a system for monitoring progress via annual reports and work in progress seminars, with initial registration for an MPhil and upgrading to a PhD only permitted on evidence of satisfactory progress, and an institutional word limit for research degrees. It is now more common for a research student to undertake a taught element, probably a master's degree, before proceeding to research. The Economic and Social Research Council in its training guidelines issued in 1991 requires institutions to provide formal training programmes for up to 60 per cent of a student's time during their first year of registration.

The PhD has been criticized as being too specialist, providing an opportunity for detailed research on one narrow subject, but often neglecting the broader discipline. Partly as a response, taught doctorates, traditionally associated with North American postgraduate education, are beginning to emerge as a significant development. In engineering, clinical psychology and education, taught doctorate degrees are now well established.

Graduate schools

A growing number of HEIs have responded to the changes in postgraduate education and research by establishing graduate schools. The graduate school concept was originally a North American one, where most of the leading research universities have had a long-standing commitment to the promotion of postgraduate work and research. Postgraduate education and research in North America is widely recognized as being a great success, with a large number of students following well resourced and well taught programmes of advanced study under the protective umbrella of a graduate school. One recent authority has suggested that 'for university organization, the most distinctive American contribution has been the evolution of the graduate school as a formal higher tier of operation on top of the undergraduate college' (Clarke, in Whiston and Geiger, 1992: 143). A graduate school is a body for the management of graduate education within an institution working with departments and faculties. It plays a crucial role in championing the cause of graduate education within an institution. It is typically responsible for a full range of administrative services, from admissions through to graduation.

A number of European countries have looked to the North American model of a graduate school as a starting point for the reform of their own administrative support structures. France, the Netherlands and Germany have all established graduate schools within their HEIs to promote interdisciplinary research, collaboration with industry and postgraduate training.

Over the past five years, an increasing number of HEIs in the UK have adopted a graduate school model. To date, 33 universities have established graduate schools and a further 23 universities have definite plans to establish a graduate school or are considering such a move. By the end of the decade, over half of all UK universities could have established specialist organizations concerned with the management of postgraduate education.

Some 85 per cent of the graduate schools that have been established to date are located in chartered universities (UKCGE, 1995).

The graduate schools that have been established are rather different from their North American and European counterparts. UK graduate schools are more concerned with policy-making for postgraduates. Their primary purpose is to improve the quality of postgraduate education and most intend to increase the number of postgraduate students. They tend to be responsible for policies across the entire institution or within a particular faculty. Few, however, have been given primary responsibility for the management of institutional research. No HEI in the UK seems to have adopted the full North American concept of membership of the graduate school being reserved for staff with the best research records.

Normally, graduate schools have a head, a governing body, which includes postgraduate representatives, and administrative support. A number of core activities can be identified for most UK graduate schools. Typically, responsibility for policy-making for research students, monitoring student progress, approval of academic programmes, degree regulations, course reviews and coordination of training programmes are regarded as core functions. Perhaps surprisingly, other administrative functions typically associated with postgraduates (for example, admissions, maintaining student records, registration, and grievances and appeals) have not necessarily fallen into the graduate school's area of responsibility. This suggests that in many cases graduate schools are being used to concentrate on policy-making, while implementation may be handled through a variety of existing institutional structures.

Conclusion

There has been a significant change in the nature of postgraduate education over the past fifteen years. This requires a response by HE managers. Clear policies need to be in place for the promotion of certain forms of postgraduate activity, coordination of research training, monitoring of student progress and improvement in the quality of postgraduate education. These factors explain why there has been a very rapid development in the graduate school structures. It is likely that the general trends of increasing student numbers, concerns about quality and declining units of resources will force more institutions to adopt new management structures for postgraduate education.

2 RESEARCH

Introduction

The functions of a research support manager can be divided into two activities: first, the support and stimulation of research within the institution;

second, the management of contracts for research funded by sponsors external to the institution. This section of the chapter gives an outline of the general research support role and then concentrates on some key issues in research contract management and negotiation.

The research support role

There is no doubt that across HE the management of research has assumed greater strategic importance. This, combined with financial cuts and the reduction of the student unit of resource, has made the funding of research from the institution's own resources more difficult. The problems differ with the type of institution; nevertheless, the strategic importance of the quality and volume of research has increased for all institutions except those few HEIs that have made it a feature of their strategy to concentrate on a teaching mission. For the majority of HEIs that have seen it as an integral part of their role to develop research, an important goal has been to increase the level of externally funded research from non-funding council sources.

That we now have a far more competitive environment for research funding is, of course, no accident. The changes in policy and management for the sector as a whole have resulted in institutions operating in an increasingly competitive market-place for the supply of higher education. One may have one's own views as to how even the playing field is in practice, but the abolition of the binary line, the transfer of significant research funding ('dual support' or DR) from the funding councils to the research councils, the increased selectivity of funding of HEIs and the monitoring of research through the research assessment exercises have been policy drivers that have intensified the market for externally funded research. As a result, the customers of HEI research, such as the research councils and the academic foundations, have experienced significant increases in the number of applications for funding.

The change in emphasis of research council policy, to include explicitly in the criteria for funding the contribution to the national economy and the quality of life, has focused attention on the needs of users of research and the support (not necessarily financial) of industry. The Realising Our Potential Awards, named after the White Paper, are only made to academics who have a track record of working with industry and securing industrial funding.

Against this back-drop, institutions have created or strengthened the management units responsible for the support of research. The research manager in an institution that has a research culture has an advantage in further developing external funding. Gaining research grants and contracts is the norm, and policies will already be in place that reward the obtaining of research funding. The direct costs of the contract will fund the project costs and will be managed by the academic responsible. A further incentive common in HEIs is for a proportion of the overhead recovered to be allocated to the academic department (or even to the individual academic's salary!). It is also common for departments highly rated in external research assessment exercises to have this recognized in the institution's academic resource allocation procedures. External funding and research students can also be recognized. It is normal for institutions to have a financial incentive to encourage commercial exploitation of research as a *quid pro quo* for the institution having ownership (and responsibility for the full exploitation) of intellectual property.

An important stimulus for new research initiatives is an institutional pump-priming fund for innovation. Research initiatives may have to compete directly with teaching and learning developments, but it is important that this source of finance is separately allocated to general departmental resources and that there is an input to the decision-making by the research support manager.

Other schemes that can benefit the institution's development and renewal of research by the involvement of the research support manager are academic staff promotions and study leave. These are central to any research strategy and are important factors in the recruitment and retention of quality academic staff (see Chapter 7, this volume).

Research planning is a difficult area, but coordination of central research planning and strategy is a role of the research support manager. The arguments for and against centralized research planning are well known, but none the easier to evaluate for that. The purpose of a plan is to set priorities for development and influence the deployment of resources. Institutions in today's highly competitive environment cannot hope to be strong in all areas of research, and not to concentrate and build on strength could seriously disadvantage the research profile of the institution as a whole. The opposing argument is based on the fundamentally correct view that research initiatives are generated by individual academics who champion their project. If the best opportunities are not to be taken as they come along, initiative will be stifled, and the research plan is in danger of becoming counterproductive. The usual way through this dilemma is to attempt to do both – set a small number of priority areas and retain development funding for the best new initiatives that arise outside the priority areas – as far as financial constraints will allow.

A corollary of the competitive market-place for research is the need for the staff of the research support unit to be proactive. The role of the unit includes identifying research funding opportunities, following through with academics and working with them to prepare submissions to the prospective sponsor. This calls for specialist knowledge of different sectors of the research market, notably the research councils, industry and the European Commission. The knowledge and approach required for each are different. A selling and business development approach is required for dealing with industry. A penchant for walking the corridors of the directorates general and actively lobbying the researcher's case is required in Brussels. Research sponsored by users and industry is crucial as direct funding or to unlock funding from the EU and the UK research councils. To be successful, these staff have to be credible with the research staff of the institution and industry and have commercial management skills that cover not only contract negotiation, but also business development.

Research contract management and negotiation

The research contract

The agreement between the institution and the sponsor funding the research can take many forms, from a simple exchange of letters to a weighty document consisting of numerous clauses. The simple exchange of letters can often suffice, as long as it covers the key points to the satisfaction of the institution and the sponsor. The normal sequence is that the academic prepares a proposal for the work to be carried out, the sponsor makes an offer to the institution and the institution accepts the offer. At each stage, the sponsor and the institution should be satisfied with the preceding stage or seek clarification or changes. The basic points to include are:

- a clear definition of the project (cross-referenced in the letters to the agreed proposal);
- project start date and end date;
- project milestones to be achieved by set dates;
- form of and dates for the final (and interim) reports;
- the price to be paid.

This form of exchange of letters can often suffice for smaller value projects, particularly where no additional staff are to be appointed to carry out the research and where the output is limited to a report rather than an invention or development in the physical sciences. Further points – regarding, for example, the ownership of copyright or publication – can be added, but the discipline of using a simple standard contract signed by both parties can be helpful once the agreement goes beyond the basic points. In many cases, and in particular for science and technology and most work for government departments, the sponsor will want to impose its standard contract or at least use it as the starting point for negotiation.

The termination clause is of key importance, particularly where additional staff are to be appointed for the project on fixed-term contracts. In these cases, the institution incurs a significant financial commitment and it is advisable to negotiate a termination clause that ensures that the sponsor is liable to pay the institution the outstanding financial commitment should the sponsor decide to end the agreement early.

It is worth emphasizing that, apart from small personal awards to individual members of staff from academic societies, the research agreement should be between the institution and the sponsor. This enables the institution to exercise control over the agreements that it is entering into and protects the individual, as the liability is the responsibility of the institution, which should limit the liability to that covered by its insurance.

It is easy to lose sight of the basic points when negotiating the finer points of a contract. The use of a checklist such as included in the CVCP's guidance on research contract issues (CVCP, 1992), rather than this short piece, is recommended. An outline of the main issues for a few critical areas in the management and negotiation of research contracts is given below.

Value Added Tax (VAT)

Before August 1994, research work carried out by HEIs was not liable to VAT, whereas consultancy services, applied research and development work carried out by HEIs were liable for VAT. The test for any research-related work was that it was liable for VAT if it solved a particular local problem (consultancy) rather than adding to the general stock of knowledge. This has never been an entirely straightforward matter, but research grants from the research councils or academic foundations – for example, the Nuffield Foundation, the Leverhulme Trust or medical charities – did not attract VAT, as these grants were not considered to be solving a particular local problem.

With the introduction of the VAT (Education) Order 1994, the decision as to whether the sponsor should be charged VAT for a particular piece of work had to take account of not only the nature of *what* was being done (research or not), but also the *type of sponsor* and whether it counted as an eligible body. Eligible bodies do not have to pay VAT on the price charged for the work, provided the work being carried out by the HEI is defined as research. There are two kinds of eligible bodies: first, public bodies, including government departments, the research councils, health authorities, local authorities, HEIs and colleges; second, charities. There are two further conditions that must be met for the sponsor to qualify as an eligible body. The sponsor's circumstances must prevent it from distributing, and it must not distribute, any profit it makes to individuals as personal bonuses or the like, *and* – if the sponsor is itself a provider of education, research or vocational training – it will only count as an eligible body if it applies any profits it makes from its own supplies of education, research or vocational training to the continuance or improvement of those supplies.

If there is any doubt as to whether a particular organization – a public body or a charity – qualifies as an eligible body, the best course of action is to write to the organization, setting out the relevant definition from the legislation, and ask that an appropriate officer of the organization certifies that it is an eligible body. Self-certification by the sponsor at least shows that the institution has taken reasonable care if later challenged by a VAT officer.

The simple matrix in Figure 9.3 shows when VAT is chargeable to the

	Research	Consultancy
Non-eligible body	VAT at standard rate	VAT at standard rate
Eligible body	VAT exempt	VAT at standard rate

Figure 9.3 VAT matrix

sponsor. However, whatever the matrix gains in clarity, it still leaves the question as to whether a piece of work is research or consultancy. It must be borne in mind that, even though the terms 'research' and 'consultancy' may have very clear meanings in your institution, these will not necessarily be shared by the VAT inspector from your local office. Although the definition of research for VAT purposes has broadly stayed in line with that operating before August 1994, it is probably the case that the boundary between 'research' and 'consultancy' is moving to include more work in the 'consultancy' category and tending to increase the scope of work that is subject to VAT.

Some of what has been said about which work is liable to VAT smacks of verbal wrangling, but remember that the VAT inspector has considerable powers, including fines and back-assessment. The VAT officer auditing your institution's VAT return will spend most of his or her time in the commercial world, will rely to a very large extent on the written contract between the institution and the customer, and will not wish to debate about the work's place in a larger academic game plan. The basic test is that the work is consultancy if it solves a particular local problem rather than adding to the general stock of knowledge. It may help to guide difficult decisions to use two commercial tests. If either of these indicate that the work is consultancy, this should weigh heavily on the side of assessing the work as liable to VAT. These tests are as follows.

1. *What does the customer intend to buy?* If the contract passes ownership of the results of the work (the intellectual property rights) to the customer *and* bars the institution from publishing the project results, this suggests that the service being purchased is consultancy.
2. *Could the work be carried out by a firm of consultants?* Commercial consultants and market and social survey companies have to charge VAT. If the work could be carried out by a firm of consultants or if work that includes a survey as part of the methodology could be carried out by a market or social survey company, then VAT should be charged.

All that has been said here about VAT applies only to research supplied by HEIs to UK sponsors. It should by now be clear that expert advice should be obtained from the institution's finance office or, if necessary, from a firm of accountants.

Intellectual property, confidentiality and publication

In research agreements, intellectual property (IP) is often divided into two types: background and foreground. The background is the IP that the research team brings to the current project from its prior work. The foreground is the IP that is generated on the current project. In this area the focus of a contract negotiation is generally on the ownership or access to the foreground. It is not uncommon in scientific or technological research sponsored by an industrial company for the company to want ownership of the foreground. The company will, if it intends to exploit commercially the project results or foreground, want unrestricted access to develop a new or improved product or process.

The company will be very clear about what it wants from the contract. The reason for considering IP, confidentiality and publication together is to ensure that the institution is in a position to be clear about what rights to the IP it is prepared to give up and what rights it wants to maintain.

The ownership of IP resulting from a project has received considerable attention, most particularly in the area of science and technology sponsored by companies. Institutions have increasingly become willing to form companies based on IP they have generated. However, it is true to say that these remain the exception and, though this option should be considered, the priority for the majority of generic research is to ensure that the right to publish is maintained and that the future funding of projects by different sponsors is not put in jeopardy.

The key point is that the foreground IP from a project sponsored by company A becomes the background IP for a future project sponsored by company B. If the institution passes the ownership of IP from the first project to company A, or grants company A an exclusive licence to the IP, this can block further work sponsored by other companies. Companies want an unimpeded route to commercial exploitation, and if the exploitation depends on background IP owned or controlled by a competitor, this will act as a block to the company sponsoring a project.

It is not uncommon for research contracts with HEIs to have the company owning the foreground IP and agreeing to pay the institution a royalty on successful exploitation. In this case, the institution should negotiate the right to use the IP for its own research and also aim to include in the contract the right to sub-license the IP to another company after an agreed period. Another option is to grant the company an exclusive licence for a period (rather than ownership of the IP), and then a non-exclusive licence. Both these options give the institution some freedom to carry out research for other companies who want access to the IP. Passing the ownership of the foreground IP to the first company does not give this freedom.

With an eye to publication of the project results, are the confidentiality restrictions reasonable? A company will normally want to vet the publication to ensure that no confidential information is disclosed. It is wise to stipulate the period of delay before publication. The institution will have higher degree regulations that cover the submission and examination of theses. To protect the right to publish of sponsored postgraduate students, these regulations should cover acceptable restrictions to access to the thesis and its publication. It is then possible to negotiate agreement with the sponsor as to access to and publication of theses, subject to the institution's regulations governing higher degrees.

It is not only the sponsoring organization that has confidential information that it will want to restrict. Any confidentiality clause in the contract should be even-handed to protect the institution's background information and information from other projects, both sponsored and internally funded.

One final point is that it is often said with some justification that it is difficult to specify the project in advance. The temptation is then to leave the project definition vague. However, time spent on the specification is time well spent. For objectives that may or may not be completely achievable, use terms such as 'reasonable endeavours to . . .' (rather than 'best endeavours'). The scope and clarity of the project definition not only underlies what does and does not have to be done as part of the project, it is also the basis for the IP rights (see Farrington, 1994).

Liabilities and insurance

The institution's insurance will generally be managed outside the research support unit, and a key role is for the contract negotiator to ensure that the new contracts are covered by the institution's insurance. The insurance that comes to mind for research and consultancy is professional indemnity for errors and omissions, as its purpose is to indemnify the institution for negligent advice or errors and omissions in the report to the sponsor. However, the division of different types of risk under different types of policy is secondary. What is essential is that the different policies dovetail together and in combination cover the range of risks that the institution faces (across all its activities), bearing in mind the need to keep levels of cover in place that match the size of settlements in personal injury cases and the ever-increasing costs of litigation. This is the job of the institution's insurance manager, with appropriate advice.

The basic idea of a liability is that the person or organization responsible for causing harm to another should make good the harm or compensate the victim. There are some liabilities that the institution cannot exclude or restrict (personal injury or death resulting from negligence); other liabilities (for example, consequential damage or loss of profits) can be excluded or limited as long as the restriction is reasonable. What is reasonable in any particular case is difficult to guess, but limiting the liability to the limit of the institution's insurance cover (say £5 million) is likely to survive.

It is in the interest of both the institution and the sponsor to minimize liabilities. There have been cases when, in the negotiation of a contract with a large sponsor, the sponsor has demanded high levels of liability from the HEI. This can be made worse when the starting point for the negotiation is the company's standard contract and the advice from the company's legal department is that there can be no movement on the liability clauses.

Insurance underwriters regard certain sorts of research as higher risk, and some risks may have special treatments in the policy. The most common forms of these are exclusions and risks that are required to be notified to the broker before a decision to insure the risk or not is made. An exclusion of a type of activity not covered by the policy – for example, aerospace or work for US organizations – and any exclusions that apply will be detailed in the policy document. Risks that have to be notified to the insurer (including any risk that *might* form part of an exclusion) will be similarly detailed in the policy, and there will be special arrangements for clinical trials. Always notify risks of this sort before signing the contract with the sponsor and before the work starts.

It is also worth pointing out that at the same time that insurers are scrutinizing the cover given to 'public sector' organizations, HEIs are carrying out work of a more commercial nature. Even within traditional areas such as environmental science, insurers are playing it carefully with risks associated with pollution. It is true that institutions are not in the business of operating large-scale commercial chemical plants, and they may regard the caution of the insurers as misplaced, but the professional management of research contracts and the risks associated with them is becoming increasingly important.

Overheads and pricing

It is a common experience when one is negotiating a contract to have the overhead element challenged by the sponsor. Part of this problem is owing to a belief that HEIs are paid for from public money and that charging an overhead is an attempt to recover some costs for a second time. This may not be true, but it is the job of the contract negotiator to explain why this is not the case and how the costs of the research are correctly reflected in the overhead rate being charged.

The direct or additional costs of a research project – research salary costs, consumables, travel and so on – are fairly straightforward to estimate. The more difficult question to answer is: what is the overhead cost (or indirect cost) of carrying out a research contract? This requires determining what proportion of the overhead cost – buildings, libraries, central services and departmental services – is attributable to research as opposed to teaching. This requires a cost model for the institution that is robust and defensible, and it is recommended that the institution's main businesses, teaching, research and anything else are identified separately. The derivation of a cost model and the calculation of overhead rates applicable to different activities is a technical matter, for which a professional cost accountant is needed. What is important here is that the overhead rate – usually expressed as a percentage of the labour cost of the project – is known and can be defended when challenged by a prospective sponsor.

The level of sophistication of the cost model to be developed will depend on the starting point and the likely additional return when using it to price research contracts. This will in turn depend on the overhead currently being achieved (rather than the current target) and the volume of the institution's research contracts. If at all possible, the cost model should not be limited to research. A cost model prepared for research alone runs the risk of some of the indirect costs of research being excluded and not being identified as loading teaching or other activities. A balanced view of the indirect costs attributable to the various activities is more likely if the cost model is a complete model for the institution.

Some thought should be given to the different costs of research in different disciplines. The indirect costs of laboratory-based disciplines will usually be greater than those of those not using laboratories. A model for research that differentiates between laboratory- and non-laboratory-based subject areas will make it easier to gain support from academic staff, for whom an overhead can be an irritant when they are primarily concerned with obtaining the direct costs for projects. It is worth investing a significant amount of managerial time in consulting academic staff at an early stage in the preparation of the cost model, and explaining and selling the benefits of the cost model and overhead rates once they have been adopted as institutional policy. No matter how large the research support office, research contracts will usually be initiated by academic staff, and their understanding and support aids the negotiation process and the successful recovery of the standard overhead from research contracts. It may be necessary to institute incentives to ensure early and full financial cooperation from academics; for example, a percentage of central overheads recovered above a certain minimum threshold might be fed through to the relevant departmental conference travel budget (or even to the salary of the individual academic).

Conclusion

The need has never been greater for institutions to increase levels of non-funding council research income, and the changes in the research market have made this far more competitive. Working with industry will assume a greater importance, both in its own right and to access other research funding. The policies and approach will in many ways have to be more commercial to succeed, yet simply offering and promoting relevant research is not enough, as the quality has to be maintained and improved.

10

Estate Management

David Adamson

Editors' introduction

It is salutary that, with the exception of the employment of staff, by far the largest element in an HEI's budget is estates management. It should also be pointed out that estates management comprises not just the up-front areas of new build and refurbishment, but also the more prosaic work of buildings maintenance, supply of services and the upkeep of grounds. However, these latter areas also involve considerable expenditure, but expenditure that it is vital to make on a timely and planned basis if even more horrendous sums are to be avoided in the future – 'a stitch-in-time'. Moreover, the estates director is responsible for the total physical environment of both staff and students at HEIs, and it would be most unwise for senior managers to underestimate the effect that this has on morale and thereby the ultimate success of their institution.

Introduction

Higher education institutions generally entrust the management of their estates to an 'estates director', although there are many organizational variations. The estates director should ideally report directly to the vice-chancellor, a pro-vice-chancellor or the head of the non-academic management. Professionally, the estates director may come from any one of many backgrounds, such as surveying, engineering, architectural, accountancy or the law.

The two main aspects of estates management are the strategic planning for the longer term and the day-to-day, term-to-term, running of the estate. In many ways, identifying decisions that need to be made about the future size and nature of the institution's estate is not only the most important but also the most difficult aspect of estate management. The time horizons are very long. Plans by local authorities about how land may be used and how buildings can be constructed take two years to finalize and are then valid for ten years, and so an HEI estates director has to think at least that far ahead. Given the cyclic popularity and the changing nature of academic disciplines, not to mention the very short notice that the government gives for substantial changes of policy or funding, it requires considerable foresight by estates directors and dialogue with academic staff to shape the longer-term HEI estate plan.

By contrast, the shorter-term management of the estate requires decisiveness, toughness and pragmatism in solving immediate or imminent problems and in optimizing short-term opportunities, such as the sudden availability of property, the chance of securing extra funding or the balancing of irreconcilable demands.

Strategic management of the estate

Like all aspects of management within an HEI, shaping the estate starts (just as it ends) with the core business of the institution – its teaching and research. The estates director therefore has to be fully aware of the institution's academic plan for the future; this should be in reasonable detail for the first five years and in some outline for the subsequent five. In fact, the estates director as a senior member of the HEI's management team should have played a major part in the drafting of the institution's academic plan.

From knowing what it is that the institution is planning to do, the estates director must make his or her judgement as to what estate will need to allow those activities to be successfully pursued. Comparing these requirements with the existing assets will lead the estates director to an assessment of the gap between what is and what should be in the estate; this exercise is generically known as *gap analysis* and leads to the formulation of the institution's estate plan as an adjunct to the institution's academic plan. The HEI will want to shape its estate plan in a form that it finds appropriate; for some HEIs a useful model would be the current Higher Education Funding Council format (HEFCE, 1993d). HEIs that have a particularly predominant aspect other than teaching, notably research, will need a modified format.

The assessment of what estate is required to meet a particular academic plan needs careful thought. Generally, a sound result is best achieved by pursuing and then comparing two approaches. First, it is relatively simple to consider the existing estate as a baseline, and to assess what changes to that existing estate would be needed to cope with academic changes. The more rigorous approach is to estimate from the academic plan the numbers of staff and students. Most HEIs have a good idea as to the amount of space needed for staff and for students to carry out their various activities, for each type of academic discipline. To these are added the needs of particular academic activities, such as those which require especially large equipment. Many institutions have found it helpful to develop what is sometimes known as 'space norms' (for example, those set out by the UGC, updated to allow for modern academic practices) to build up the total built space needed by the institution, department by department. This gives an absolute assessment of need for space in buildings; the first approach above merely gives a list of relative changes to an estate that may be too big or too small in the first place.

When the assessment has been made of how much and what type of built space is needed (and also how much land for recreation, sport, gardens, agricultural studies, etc.), the next step is to set up a database of what the estate already has in terms of amount, nature and quality of built space, and the location and type of land.

Built space is defined in terms of 'gross' area (the total space between the inside of external walls) or in 'assignable' (or 'net' or 'usable') space – the space that needs to be maintained and serviced – which is the gross area less circulation space such as corridors, toilets and stairwells. Assignable space is generally measured between internal walls (the space represented by walls makes a surprising difference). It may, at this stage, be worth categorizing the institution's estate into functional types and quality categories: high quality, well serviced laboratory space, low quality offices, etc. It is worth reducing the total space by a proportion to represent areas that cannot be fully used (for example, because of low ceilings, noise, temperatures) – such allowances are often known as 'bad fit'.

Having compared in detail what the HEI needs with what it already has (gap analysis), the estate plan will include a list of detailed space requirements. These are best grouped by urgency and by priority. (It is a common mistake to confuse these two; something immediate may have a lower importance than something to be done later.) The list of estate requirements will probably include needs for more or better built space, and this may be achieved by 'new build' or by refurbishing existing properties. There should also be a list of properties that can be sold or demolished.

Enhancing the estate

There are many factors that the estates director must assess before the institution commits itself to the traumatic experience of procuring a new building. Beyond the institution's control are the effects of the cyclic state of the British construction industry. The market was reasonably stable and sensibly priced in the mid-1980s, disastrously overheated and overpriced around the turn of the decade and then increasingly in depression into the mid-1990s. An HEI should reflect on whether its building projects should be brought forward or delayed (if either is possible), so as to procure a new building during a more favourable phase of the cycle.

From the institution's estate plan, there will be a summary definition of what the academic end-user of a new building will require. Then, the buildings department of the HEI will supplement these end-users' needs by a statement of its requirements for the fabric, electrical and mechanical services, data wiring, etc. These documents taken together constitute the 'employer's requirement' for the project; this crucial document should result from detailed discussions, which may have lasted several months and should be set down very clearly as the basis on which the HEI, as the project client, and the architects, consultants, contractors and so on who will join the team will translate these initial requirements into the final building. All the crucial aspects of the project – quality, time and price – flow from the employer's requirement, and at this early stage it is well worth doing the initial financial appraisal and a study of the best means of funding the project.

Option and investment appraisals of capital projects

In order to adopt a proposed capital development, an institution has to ensure that the project provides the best solution for the problems in hand and at the same time identifies the risks and the financial capital and recurrent commitment for the future. This appraisal process is not only an obstacle through which a proposal must pass in the final stages before implementation, it should also be done as part of the process of developing a proposal, contributing to the form and the choice of options to examine. The appraisal must be updated as design proceeds, and revised before and after tender.

The appraisal process begins with the clear identification of the problems. Since the HEI inevitably has constraints on its available resources, there is a need to prioritize and detail these problems.

Alternative means of meeting the objectives must be identified. The funding councils require the institution to demonstrate a suitable range of options. *Inter alia,* the institution has to examine the options of status quo (or 'do nothing'), of increasing the effectiveness and efficiency of the use of current space (and other non-capital solutions such as leasing space), and of collaboration with other HEIs, as well as new build. For each potentially worthwhile option, the costs, benefits, risks, timing and uncertainties should be assessed. As far as it is possible, the costs and benefits should be valued in terms of money and are discounted to present value. Options are assessed on a whole-life (for example, 50 years) costing basis that includes the cost of maintenance, running costs, staffing costs and major capital refurbishment during the life of the project. The source of funding for these costs (which over a whole life are much greater) is as important as it is for the capital costs of construction.

For costs and benefits that cannot sensibly be valued in monetary terms, such as the quality of education, a subjective scoring system is better; for example, a scoring scale of –5 (very much worse) to +5 (very much better) (see Table 10.1). The importance of each factor could be emphasized by putting a weighting on the scores. All the uncertainties of the options have

Table 10.1 Option and investment appraisals of capital projects: scoring system

Options	Do nothing	Project A	Project B
Teaching quality	0	+1	+1
Research quality	−1	+2	+5
Accommodation standards	−2	+2	+5
Recruitment of quality students	−2	+2	+3
Total	−5	+7	+14
Ranking	3rd	2nd	1st

to be weighed up by a sensitivity analysis. Factors that represent high risks to the HEI will have to be assessed by the decision-makers, balancing them with the costs and benefits of each option.

An example of the cost plan for the selected option is shown in Figure 10.1. If the project requires approval from the HEFCE then it should achieve a rate of return on capital equal to or exceeding the Treasury test discount rate.

Town and country planning for construction projects

Over the past fifty years, decisions as to how land and buildings may be used have become increasingly important. There is a great deal of town and country planning legislation and at times it may be necessary for HEIs to get professional advice on this, despite considerable cost. However, the Committee of Vice-Chancellors and Principals (1995) has had written and circulated to every university and local planning authority clear and helpful guidelines as to the significant aspects of planning law for universities.

The system that has become universal in Great Britain is 'plan-led'; that is to say, plans are drafted, deposited, subjected to public inquiries and the secretary of state's approval and then implemented at regional, county, local planning authority and village/local levels. Plans are generally valid for ten years and, once drafted, have statutory significance regarding planning applications and appeals against refusal. Generally, if a planning application by an HEI is in accordance with the local plan, then there will be a presumption in favour of approval, and vice versa. The plan-led system has made the planning aspect of estates management more predictable and stable, but of course there will always be other national and local political factors. It is therefore especially important that universities strike a careful balance between confidentiality and the considerable benefits that can be achieved by genuine consultation with community groups of local residents, pressure groups and the local Council itself. By these means, it will also be easier for the institution to hear of and cope with external pressures and events that could impair or restrict development.

Figure 10.1 — University of Poppleton estimated cash flow forecast

Header parameters:

- Cost of funds (note 3): 6.95% (LIBOR at 9.5%)
- Academic use: 3,440 m² (assignable space)
- Research Park use: 3,065 m² (lettable space)
- Rental rate: £183 per m² (excl. VAT)
- Vacancy factor: 20% (see note 2)
- RPI: 4%
- Project Costs: £M — Total project budget 10.19; VAT at 17.5% 1.76; Total 11.95

(All annual figures in £'k unless otherwise stated.)

Part A — Years 1–14 (1994–2007)

Item (£'k)	1 / 1994	2 / 1995	3 / 1996	4 / 1997	5 / 1998	6 / 1999	7 / 2000	8 / 2001	9 / 2002	10 / 2003	11 / 2004	12 / 2005	13 / 2006	14 / 2007
1. Funding costs														
Sinking fund payments	0	0	952	952	952	952	952	952	952	952	952	952	952	952
Notional Lease Premium	0	0	5	5	5	5	5	5	5	5	5	5	5	5
2. Costs of servicing/maintenance														
Academic space	0	0	299	311	323	336	349	363	378	393	409	425	442	460
Research Park	0	0	133	277	288	300	312	324	337	350	364	379	394	410
TOTAL COST TO UNIVERSITY	0	0	1,389	1,545	1,568	1,593	1,618	1,644	1,672	1,700	1,730	1,761	1,793	1,827
3. Forecast income														
Estimated Rental Income	0	0	(112)	(224)	(449)	(449)	(449)	(546)	(546)	(546)	(546)	(546)	(664)	(664)
Letting Fees	0	0	11	11	23	0	0	0	0	0	0	0	17	17
Service charge	0	0	(27)	(166)	(230)	(240)	(250)	(259)	(270)	(280)	(291)	(303)	(315)	(328)
TOTAL ESTIMATED INCOME	0	0	(128)	(379)	(656)	(689)	(699)	(805)	(816)	(826)	(837)	(849)	(962)	(975)
NET COST TO UNIVERSITY	0	0	1,261	1,166	912	904	919	839	856	874	893	912	831	852
Additional Research Grants/Services increased to fund net cost	0	0	5,044	4,664	3,648	3,616	3,676	3,356	3,424	3,496	3,572	3,648	3,324	3,408

Part B — Years 15–27 (2008–2020)

Item (£'k)	15 / 2008	16 / 2009	17 / 2010	18 / 2011	19 / 2012	20 / 2013	21 / 2014	22 / 2015	23 / 2016	24 / 2017	25 / 2018	26 / 2019	27 / 2020
1. Funding costs													
Sinking fund payments	952	952	952	952	952	952	952	952	952	952	3,089	0	0
Notional Lease Premium	5	5	5	5	5	5	5	5	5	5	5	0	0
2. Costs of servicing/maintenance													
Academic space	478	497	517	538	560	582	605	629	654	680	707	735	764
Research Park	426	443	461	479	498	518	539	561	583	606	630	655	681
TOTAL COST TO UNIVERSITY	1,861	1,897	1,935	1,974	2,015	2,057	2,101	2,147	2,194	2,243	4,431	1,390	1,445
3. Forecast income													
Estimated Rental Income	(664)	(664)	(664)	(808)	(808)	(808)	(808)	(808)	(983)	(983)	(983)	(983)	(983)
Letting Fees	33	0	0	0	0	0	0	0	25	25	49	0	0
Service charge	(341)	(354)	(369)	(383)	(398)	(414)	(431)	(449)	(466)	(485)	(504)	(524)	(545)
TOTAL ESTIMATED INCOME	(972)	(1,018)	(1,033)	(1,191)	(1,206)	(1,222)	(1,239)	(1,257)	(1,424)	(1,443)	(1,438)	(1,507)	(1,528)
NET COST TO UNIVERSITY	889	879	902	783	809	835	862	890	770	800	2,993	(117)	(83)
Additional Research Grants/Services increased to fund net cost	3,556	3,516	3,608	3,132	3,236	3,340	3,448	3,560	3,080	3,200	11,972	(468)	(332)

Notes:

1. Construction takes place in Year 1 and 2, with completion in October 1995 for academic space, January 1996 for Research Park.

2. Vacancy factor for 1996: 80%; 1997: 60%; 1998: 20%.

3. Sinking fund will commence on 31 December, 1996. (Assuming all costs are rescheduled.) The cash flow above is a rough estimate only, and requires fine tuning with actual financiers' proposal when the actual financing mechanism is known. The cost of funds is based on currently best available information from the possible financiers.

4. Rent review at 5 year interval at RPI compounded annually.

5. Costs of servicing & maintenance at £87.00 per m², increase annually at the RPI. Costs of servicing & maintenance on Research Park are rechargeable to tenant.

6. Letting fees is at 10% of the first year's rent. (Assuming 10 year leases.) Annual management fees, which is currently under review, have not been included. No initial premium for 'commercial' lets have been included.

Figure 10.1 University of Poppleton estimated cash flow forecast

Following an appropriate level of consultation, an HEI wanting a new building needs to make a detailed planning application, allowing enough time, generally two to four months (but possibly longer), for due consideration and decision on the application. In the event of refusal or unacceptable conditions, the institution may appeal by means of a written submission or a public hearing.

New construction procurement

Now the client must decide whether it is worth going any further with the project, and if so what should be the selected method of procurement for the building. It is possible to generalize procurement strategies under four main alternatives. These are set out in greater detail in Appendix 10.1.

Management contract. Less common than it used to be, this approach calls for the institution to employ a consultant advisor and facilitator for the entire project on a fee basis, which may well be unrelated to how well the contract progresses. This route is more suitable for HEIs that only rarely procure new buildings and therefore do not have much in-house expertise. Appointment of a poor management contractor, or poor appointment procedure, can leave such a client doubly exposed.

Construction management. The client effectively acts as its own main contractor, dividing the job up into a series of discrete packages, which are in turn contracted out, with the HEI retaining detailed coordination and management of the project.

'Traditional', architect-led procurement. An architect is selected (by interview or competition) from a shortlist and is appointed to carry out design and, in many cases, the coordination of the project; often, but not necessarily, including the supervision of the contractor on behalf of and under the guidance of the HEI as client.

Design/build. Under this system, once a detailed employer's requirement has been drawn up, a design/build contractor is appointed to take on the project through to completion for a fixed price (possibly with some allowance for inflation for a large and lengthy project). As the contractor is following his or her own designs, there is a much lower risk of conflict compared with the traditional form of procurement, but on the other hand it is more difficult for the client to secure the detailed architectural input that may be required; certainly, the cost in terms of time and money, of the client changing his or her mind is much greater in a design/build contract. Conversely, the total cost is lower, especially if there is a good employer's requirement.

Whichever procurement route is chosen, and this is one of the most important decisions that has to be made, the form of contract must then be selected; almost invariably, universities choose standard forms of contract, such as the JCT (joint contracts tribunal), the NEC (new engineering contract) or several others.

Having set out the employer's requirement for the new building, carried out the financial appraisal, ensured that funding is possible and decided on a procurement strategy, the HEI now has to spend substantial sums of money to proceed further. It will be necessary to appoint an architect (or perhaps one architect to do the design and another to supervise the contract), consultants such as electrical and mechanical services engineers, structural engineers and quantity surveyors. There may also be a need for town and country planning experts, VAT tax consultants and perhaps environmental or landscape advisors. A safety consultant is required from the time that the design begins. For each, a full and considered letter of appointment is vital.

If the procurement route is design/build, the project can proceed to tender, once a value engineering exercise has confirmed that the employer's requirement is both sound and cost-effective. It is good practice to invite not more than about three design/build contractors to tender, and they should be given from four to six weeks to tender for a normal, large project. (This period has increased because of added requirements for statutory safety checks on design and construction method.) If the contract is not proceeding by design/build, then the estates director, with appropriate institutional management support, will lead the process of design, the biggest danger being lack of coordination and integration as design and costing proceed.

Tenders from contractors must be assessed in accordance with the institution's financial regulations. This should involve the keeping of a formal record of the tenders and the associated discussions. Three to five weeks are then required for an assessment of the tenders and for post-tender negotiations about design matters, programme, price and quality; a good balance between low price and sound quality is important. It is then normal for a carefully worded letter of intent to be issued to authorize the start of work by the contractor.

During construction the client should maintain his or her leadership of the project (see Figure 10.2). The Latham Report (1994) is helpful in setting out the client's responsibilities. At the least, the client will need one or more clerks of works on site, weekly site meetings chaired by the estates director or the architect and regular progress meetings, to settle higher-level matters of policy and procedure; these are best chaired by the estates director for a large project. The appropriate committee of the institution will need regular updating on the three key aspects of any project – quality (fitness for purpose), progress towards completion on time and price as compared with the budget initially set by the institution – and on the trade-offs between these three. Finally, as the project nears completion, arrangements will have to be made for user manuals (particularly for building services and to comply with health and safety requirements), production of as-built drawings (for use during future maintenance and space management) and the opening ceremony, with all the political skill that that requires.

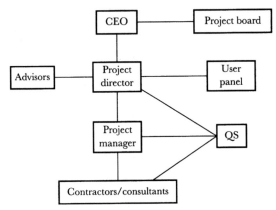

Capital investment manual

Project organization

Construction schemes

Figure 10.2   Maintaining control of the project

Refurbishment

New build has many pitfalls (and thrills): refurbishment projects seem less challenging, but this is not so. Changes in size and nature of HEIs and shortages of land or cash lead institutions to opt more frequently for refurbishment. The main challenge in refurbishment work is getting a good idea of the existing building: its structure, its condition, the state of its services, the likelihood of finding asbestos, dry rot, etc. This assessment is especially difficult if, as is usual, the building has to stay in full use until the works begin. Clearly, it is prudent to offset lack of knowledge by allowing a large contingency in the project budget (10 per cent may be necessary, rather than about half of that for new build); it is also sensible to allow for more float time in the project programme and to have better planning for the eventualities of money or time overrun. Further, it is especially important to have a suitable form of contract and to ensure that both formally and informally the contractor has as good an idea as possible of the building to be refurbished. There is a lot to be said for using design/build or even construction management forms of procurement, rather than a traditional and more formal route. Some HEIs have successfully used a staged contract, although in practice this can lead to longer project times. The involvement of the institution, particularly the clerk of works (building, electrical/mechanical), the end-user and the project officer, is vital for refurbishment work. Of the few consolations, an advantage of refurbishment work is the potential for securing a grant, particularly if the building is listed, as so many are nowadays. Care is needed, and probably specialist consultancy advice, in applying for listed building consent (LBC) where alterations are proposed, and in considering the potentially favourable VAT implications if the LBC alterations are to residential buildings, such as halls of residence (NB simple repairs and maintenance of listed buildings carry VAT). Even if the building is not listed, there may still be complications if it is within a conservation area (see Mynors, 1995 and Suddards and Hargreaves, 1996).

Reducing the estate: disposals

Every institution should keep its holdings of land and buildings under active review and rationalize and dispose of those which are no longer needed or can be better replaced by new. Regular physical assessment by users and officers within each institution will indicate how well or badly current activities are supported by the extent, location and quality of space. The inherent suitability of each building and site is thus assessed for fitness for purpose regularly, and disposals are planned. Although a new building may typically have a physical life of around sixty years, at several points during its life it must be refurbished and, at these stages especially, the relative merits of refurbishment versus disposal need to be considered. Location, nature and condition will largely determine the potential disposal price; another important factor will be the planning status of the land or building in question. The designated planning use class will have an effect upon the value of individual properties; generally for academic buildings the presumptive land use is D1 (academic) and residential properties can fall into classes C1, 2 or 3. B1 office permission is generally valuable. While the advice of professional valuers should be sought when disposals are being considered, individual institutions can enhance potential value by maximizing the potential for adapting properties to a more valuable use. For transactions involving capital sums of more than £250,000 for properties that were exchequer funded, the funding councils require consultation and will specify the conditions under which the requirement to repay the proceeds may be waived. While decisions over the disposal of property depend upon the institution's estates committee's recommendation being ratified by the governing body, it is often useful to have a group of certain senior people (for example, chairman of governing body, vice-chancellor, chairman of estates committee, treasurer) with corporate delegated powers to secure a good property deal at short notice.

Routine estate management

Most of the day-to-day challenges of managing the estate relate to allocation and management of the HEI's space, the maintenance of buildings, gardens and grounds, and the large range of management issues that any senior member of the institution has to deal with, such as staffing, budgeting and training.

Space management

For most institutions the management of space is a significant issue. Space is at a premium and is costly, so the amount of space provided for each student and staff member is accordingly kept to the minimum required and carefully monitored. Although traditionally space has tended to be 'owned' by departments or facilities, it is important that those responsible for managing space at any level do so in the context of the needs of other departments and the institution in general. Teaching space can be split into departmental space, which is used exclusively by a department, and bookable space available for use by other departments via an institution-wide booking system. This enables space to be used more efficiently and according to the priorities of the institution as a whole. Utilization rates (proportion of time used multiplied by proportion of capacity used) should be monitored and improved as an antidote to demand for new build. Central computer-based systems must have full information on the size, nature and capacity of the premises at the institution's disposal. A typical computer system will comprise an asset (capacity) record and a space allocation formula or system. The capacity record accurately reflects the total amount of academic space that each department has and how that space is used; the space holding of each department should be updated annually. The space allocation formula, driven by student and research staff numbers with localized variations (for example, for large equipment), leads to allocation of departmental space at present and as projected for some years ahead. The results of this allocation are compared annually, with each individual department's actual space holdings shown on the capacity record. The resultant surplus or deficit forms the basis for management decision-making regarding the reallocation of space. Transfer of space as needs change is vital, but expensive. This has been recognized by the funding councils, and annual 'minor works' grants are invaluable. It is useful to have an advisory group on space working within the HEI's planning committee to keep space allocation under review. In this way, the use of existing space can be optimized, thus reducing or avoiding the need to create more built space. A system of space charging can help to persuade the users of surplus space to offer transfer, but many institutions think charging is unnecessary and costly to administer. Allocation of spare space can be via a bidding process for heads of deficit departments through the appropriate academic manager. The funding councils are keen to encourage institutions to measure and judge the efficiency of their space performance and are seeking to introduce the use of simple measurement methods to manage performance and to draw comparisons, where appropriate, between subject disciplines, institutions and regions. The wide diversity of space uses, particularly in research-based institutions, means that appropriate performance indicators for comparing space utilization will prove extremely difficult to introduce, but each institution must regularly assess its own space management performance. An HEI needs to know how much space it needs and comparison with other comparable institutions is one management tool to set that scene.

Maintenance of buildings

When you have established the amount and type of space in the HEI estate, it is necessary to have a maintenance plan covering about five years, so that buildings can be maintained to the levels demanded by legislation, and by the need for efficient working of departments and support functions to provide for sufficient comfort and the morale of students, staff and visitors. If resources permit, a condition survey should be done about every five years on each building, with the results entered on the same database as the space records; some institutions have insufficient resources for this and others make a conscious decision to do condition surveys less frequently because there are insufficient resources to implement conclusions. The funding councils institute condition surveys from time to time. Using such surveys, plans can be drawn up for work that should be done in outline over the next five years, year-by-year, with particular detail for the immediate year ahead. Maintenance tasks will fall into categories: the fabric of a building, the electrical and mechanical services, data cabling, etc. There should be an overall categorization under the following headings.

- *Backlog maintenance.* Clearly, each HEI should set annual budgets so that the estate can be maintained in steady state without any degradation or build-up of backlog, but many institutions have been unable to sustain adequate maintenance programmes and have therefore built up a large amount of backlog maintenance.
- *Routine maintenance.* Once the budget is set for routine maintenance, the maintenance manager will need to decide how much needs to be spent during the year on meeting statutory requirements, on planned preventative maintenance and on reactive maintenance. Ideally, about 20 per cent of the budget should be spent on preventative maintenance, since a successful pre-emptive programme can prevent unexpected failure occurring, with all the associated extra expense and inconvenience to academic or residential users of the buildings. It is a matter of fine judgement as to the extent to which failure should be prevented, and the extent to which certain building elements should be allowed to remain until the very last moment. For example, a planned preventative maintenance programme for wooden windows is clearly cost-effective, and for heating systems the replacement of pumps before failure will generally be a good investment. On the other hand, roof coverings may well be allowed to run beyond their design life if there are no signs of significant failure, if one accepts the risks.

Most HEIs have the majority of their maintenance works carried out by in-house direct labour staff, but some contract out much of it to facility managers or other contractors, in spite of the likely VAT disadvantages of doing so. At the very least, a medium-sized HEI will need to have enough qualified staff to plan, assess and ensure the safe, efficient and cost-effective working of the various elements of buildings, including the fabric and the provision of utilities and communications. The estates director will be able to assess the performance of such staff by comparison with other institutions within and outside the HE sector, but this needs to be done carefully, given the fundamental differences between institutions and therefore between their estates. There is an annual review by estates directors of what all institutions are spending on the various aspects of maintenance (per square metre).

Provision of services in buildings

Services should be reliable, flexible and energy efficient, and should meet statutory requirements.

Mechanical services

A building's mechanical services comprise the heating, ventilating, air conditioning and ancillary piped gas and water services. The users' requirements and the function of each building must be clearly defined and predicted so that the provided services are fit for purpose. In particular, building loads and occupancy usage patterns must be carefully modelled, so that equipment is correctly sized to match the anticipated load. Internally, good environmental conditions should be achieved with the minimum usage of primary energy resources. Consideration should be given to the use of energy efficient and environmentally 'friendly' systems, high standards of thermal insulation, heat recovery techniques and the use of natural ventilation where possible. There has been a wonderful advance in the capability of control systems for heating, and an increasing number of other systems, such as security, ventilation and humidity control, analyse and display information of all sorts about the building and how it is being used: the generic name for such systems is building management systems (BMS). It is important to give a lot of thought to replacing old services so as to achieve compatibility with other current and possible future systems for the building in question and for the estate generally. In particular, the mechanical installations should have enough flexibility for future modifications to be made to the systems with the minimum of disruption to other building users (flexibility costs money but if there is a long life it is worth it). The installations should have an adequate life to suit the wear and tear expected for the type of building and working environment concerned. All items of plant and equipment must be installed with enough space for maintenance and servicing by people who may not be long-armed giants.

Electrical services

Most of the same basic design criteria apply as are listed for mechanical services. Connected loads, usage patterns and diversity factors will be used to assess supply requirement. The systems should allow for changing use patterns and should be designed so that disturbance caused by mains failure is localized and minimized, especially where there is scientific or medical research. Systems must comply with statutory requirements and meet British Standard Codes of Practice, noting such recent legislation as the Workplace (Health, Safety and Welfare) Regulations 1992 and the Health and Safety (Display Screen Equipment) Regulations 1992.

Energy management

An average-sized HEI will probably be spending in excess of two million pounds per annum on energy, and as institutions increase in size and in levels of research activity, so space becomes used more intensively and the demands for energy become greater. On the other hand, by the establishment of an aggressive energy policy, electricity and fuel bills can be substantially reduced. The main starting point is 'energy audit', which will include a review of metering arrangements, usage patterns for different parts of the institution and energy patterns. From this should come a programme of such energy reduction measures as temperature control installations, additional metering in problem areas, improvement of insulation in areas of high losses and campaigns for education and discipline in reducing waste. There should be one individual who has specific responsibility for energy management, possibly supported by a working group of user representatives enhanced by lay advice. Some HEIs charge directly for energy consumption; others give incentives for reduced demand, although care has to be taken in cases where departments have particularly energy inefficient buildings.

Purchase of fuel, water, electricity and gas

The Consortium for Higher Education Energy Purchasing (CHEEP) tenders contracts for gas and electricity, with final negotiations and decisions being made by each institution; however, even greater savings can currently be made on CHEEP prices, especially on electricity. Note that all sites of over 100 kW maximum electrical demand or consuming more than 2500 therms annually of gas can be put out to tender, and genuine competition in utilities is slowly spreading, so it is worth being imaginative and looking around. Hard negotiation with water companies, with the assistance of a good specialist consultant, can achieve substantial savings; recirculation systems are often worthwhile for high-use equipment. The Department of the Environment negotiates a bulk oil contract on behalf of institutions.

Telecommunications

A clear strategic approach to the provision of telecommunications services that will meet the institution's present and future requirements in a technically competent and cost-effective manner is vital. Factors that will have an impact on the way in which telecommunications services will develop and will be delivered include population growth, physical adjustment to the estate, technical developments in key areas and the need to optimize resources and expenditure. Many institutions will have ISDX–PABX systems, which can be developed to provide an integrated voice and data communications infrastructure that will assist in improving significantly the network performance and the quality of services, providing enhanced facilities at much reduced cost. As equipment replacement becomes necessary the opportunity should be taken for the development of wide-area, fully compatible, digital telephone networks that will open up many technical areas of communications. Generally, the management of institution-wide voice services should be centralized, as should the operator services, and there should be close cooperation between voice and data managers, both of whom need to be flexible and clear-sighted middle managers.

Maintenance of gardens and grounds

Most institutions have extensive gardens and grounds, and the maintenance standards should be set at levels appropriate to their importance to the HEI and the local community. In addition, there are usually extensive sports grounds providing a wide range of outdoor (and increasingly indoor) sporting facilities, many of which are used to generate income all year round. The management of the institution's gardens and grounds is usually the responsibility of a superintendent who is charged with their development and maintenance, with budgetary control. The superintendent has to keep work methods and mechanisms under continuous review to benefit from new developments. Maintenance standards must be set at a level that represents a compromise between the requirements of the users and the scope of the annual budget, so, as ever, prioritization is essential; it can be useful to introduce a system of grading garden areas (for example, elementary, standard and ornamental) to ensure an equitable distribution of available maintenance funds. Staff training and safety are important elements in management, particularly as the use of potentially dangerous machinery and chemicals is the subject of ever stricter controls and regulations. It is often the case that many gardens and grounds are used by the general public, and certain gardens may well be nationally listed where they form an attractive setting to historic buildings; gardens often represent an important local amenity. Conservation methods (and lobbies) are increasingly important, and a positive policy that represents good environmental concern on the part of the institution is helpful. One of the many ways of achieving this is through the development of natural grassland and woodland areas, with minimal use of pesticides and with weed control in planned areas by hoeing and mulching and the use of chippings of tree and shrub prunings to form compost.

External relations

A good estates director will establish links with a large range of external bodies, directly or indirectly. The Association of University Directors of Estates (AUDE) has a national, elected executive committee, which meets regularly and takes action on matters of national significance to the HE sector. Each region in the UK has its own regional AUDE organization, with termly meetings attended by all universities. The CVCP has a branch dealing with capital and estates matters, and organizes several committees and working groups on specific matters of importance, such as new build procurement, town and country planning, building design, space management, etc. There are HE representatives on various government and national committees, particularly those which shape policy in the construction industry and associated legislation. At a more local level, the estates director will need to have good working relationships with the chief planning officer and the housing director of the local authority, and with various professional and civic bodies from which the institution will seek advice and support in the development and the maintenance of its estate.

Appendix 10.1

Summary of the main contractual options available

This summary relates to a typical construction project. The specific requirements of each particular contract would need to be carefully reviewed to establish the most suitable contracting strategy.

1. *Traditional building contract (usually based on JCT form of contract).* Design function undertaken by consultants, with construction work, including management, the responsibility of a main contractor, selected by competitive tender. Overall supervision of the construction phase undertaken by the consultants, acting on the HEI's behalf. The consultant team would normally comprise architect, structural, mechanical and electrical engineers, and quantity surveyor.
2. *Design/build contract (usually based on JCT form of contract, with contractor's design).* Design and construction the responsibility of main contractor, selected by competitive tender. Tender exercise based on detailed brief of requirements (referred to as the 'employer requirements').
3. *Management contract.* Design function undertaken by consultants, with main contractor appointed to procure and manage direct contracts between HEI and specialist contractors (selected by competitive tender). Selection of main contractor based on competitive bids relating to fee for management role.
4. *Construction management.* Design and contract management the responsibility of the consultants, in conjunction with representatives of the HEI. One consultant (the project director) overall responsible for design, construction and quality control. Construction undertaken by specialist contractors selected by competitive tender, with direct contracts with the HEI.

Comparisons of available contractual options

	Construction management	Traditional contract	Design/build contract	Management contract
Relationship with employer				
Contractor	Adversarial position.	Adversarial position.	Joint interest in success.	No main contractor.
Consultant	Joint interest in success.	Adversarial position.	Joint interest in success.	Joint interest in success.
Design				
Quality	Consultants will aim to design and supervise to qualities imposed by cost limit.	Quality at risk by contractor's wish to maintain profit should problems arise.	Consultants and contractor have joint interest in achieving high quality.	Consultants and employer have joint interest in achieving high quality.
Employer's protection	Employer has direct control.	No protection for employer.	Employer has direct control.	Employer has direct control.
Overall cost	Longer time scale associated with traditional process will tend to increase total cost. No economies from contractor involvement in design.	Initial low tender, but safeguards needed to control cost of any changes.	Cost reduction likely if contractor is involved before completion of design. Contractor's fee fixed.	No economies from contractor involvement in design, but shared interest of consultants and employer in cost control.
Anticipated fee, inc. VAT (%)	18	12	14	12
Risk of cost increases	If design completed prior to tender, risk low subject to no client changes.	Risk higher as contents of 'employer requirements' will not be as conclusive as final detailed design.	Final price only fixed when last specialist contract package is signed. Risk is then low if design is already completed in detail and changes are avoided.	Final price only fixed when last specialist contract package is signed. Risk is then low if design is already completed in detail and changes are avoided.

Cost	Generally good.	Risk of contractor encouraging changes to maximize amounts payable to him or her.	Generally good, with benefit of contractor participation in design process.	Generally good.
Competition	Construction phase fully competitive.	Design and construction fully competitive in theory, but effective competition dependent on clarity of brief.	Construction phase fully competitive.	Construction phase fully competitive.
Quality control during construction	Consultants have full control, but are in adversarial position to the contractor. Possibility of consultants covering up quality failures arising from design errors.	Employer has limited control of quality and conflict is likely.	Contractor and consultants have joint interest in high quality control of subcontracted packages.	Consultants and employer have joint interest in quality control of subcontracted packages.
Overall programme length	As construction does not start until design and tender exercise are completed, overall programme is likely to be longer than design/build or management contract.	Shortest overall period, possibly three months shorter than any other	Base case.	Slightly longer than M.C.
Control of programme by employer	Reasonable degree of control, possibility of problems if design contains errors.	Dependent upon contractor's priorities.	High degree of control by employer.	High degree of control by employer.

	Construction management	Traditional contract	Design/build contract	Management contract
Client changes	Client changes offer contractor opportunity for claims.	Client changes offer contractor opportunity for heavy claims, which are difficult to resist.	Contractor has interest in controlling of client changes.	Client changes can usually be accommodated.
Design errors	Design errors offer contractor opportunity for claims. Consultants would normally take responsibility.	Contractor responsible for design and therefore for any remedial work due to errors.	Contractor has interest in minimizing design errors.	Consultants responsible for design errors.
Status within construction industry	Acceptable.	Acceptable.	Acceptable.	Limited experience.

Note: If considered necessary, it would be feasible to apply a points system to compare the probability of success of these options.

11

Campus Support Services

Derek Phillips

Editors' introduction

There are certain activities in HEIs that are regarded by all, except perhaps those who are involved in them, as 'Cinderella' functions. This is a mistake, because they are of considerable importance to the good running of the organization and, in particular, to its ability to recruit students and staff. However, unlike Cinderella, some of these functions may not even be allowed to go to (or at least stay at) the ball. All the areas covered by the author in this chapter (with the possible exception of telecommunications) have already been 'outsourced' at some HEI or other. Even the author, who provides a spirited defence against this phenomenon in catering, is prepared to accept it in printing.

Of particular interest is the section on security, which is an area of increasing concern in HE. A year or so ago, the editors ran a one-day conference on this topic, which was so popular that recruitment had to be closed at 140 participants and the event re-run! However, a word of warning. In the chapter, the author mentions the possibility of wheel-clamping. It is the opinion of the editors (and their legal advisors) that this should never be undertaken lightly as the legal consequences are (at least in England and Wales) as yet unclear.

Introduction

'Campus support services' is somewhat of a catch-all phrase and the precise areas of responsibility it involves will be interpreted differently at almost every HEI. I have therefore covered in this chapter the core activities of student residence management, catering, security, portering, cleaning, telecommunications, and printing.

Residences

Management of student residences is by tradition a mixture of welfare, discipline and property management. Prior to the mid-1960s, most student residences were constructed along Oxbridge college lines. In essence, this meant that they were separate buildings (halls of residence) providing a social and dining facility. In many cases the management was partly vested in a Warden, invariably a member of the academic staff who had a slightly reduced teaching role in order to carry out these duties, often helped by hall tutors. In most cases, the particular residence operated with a distinct amount of autonomy. The cost of building this style of residence was expensive and, until around 1970, fully government-funded. From that date a decreasing amount of government funds was made available, which had the immediate effect of reducing the style and thereby building costs. Residences built from the late 1960s onwards have usually been of a 'self-catering' nature. In effect, these have been flats for up to 12 or 14 students sharing communal lounge, kitchen, toilet and bathroom facilities.

The competition to attract students has increasingly focused on issues other than purely academic considerations. Institutions have needed to be able to provide residential accommodation, at affordable rents, to attract the best students. This has been particularly true in respect of international student recruitment. It is now common for institutions to guarantee a place in residential accommodation as part of the package to attract these full cost paying students.

Vacation lettings

The continued pressure on costs has led to changes in the operation and management of all student residences. More professional residential management has been engaged, and in most cases the role of the academic Warden, when retained, has been amended to concentrate on the pastoral care element. This has allowed a greater centralization of the services provided by halls, including the purchasing of various goods and supplies required for the services, and the movement of labour between establishments. These changes have had a marked effect on the viability of the operation. The continued pressure on student finances has meant that, for many years, HEIs have needed to maximize the income from the plant available; that is, the bedrooms and other facilities. This has led to an extensive conference and vacation lettings business. In 1970, a number of universities joined together to form the British Universities Accommodation Consortium (BUAC), which subsequently formed itself into a limited company and today represents over sixty institutions. The principal task of BUAC is to act as a marketing agent. A similar organization was formed by the non-university sector, known as the Higher Education Accommodation Consortium, the name of which has recently been changed to CONNECT. The growth in HEI conference business has been substantial and is estimated to have generated an income in excess of £100 million in 1994–5. This has led to a number of institutions building or converting premises to provide year-round, hotel-style conference facilities. These are extensively used by both HEI departments and the general business community, often for training activities and continuing professional development courses.

The substantial expansion in the vacation letting business has drawn the attention of the Inland Revenue. This in turn has led to long and complicated negotiations. Following initial pilot studies, in 1994 the CVCP compiled guidance notes with the objective of trying to minimize the tax potentially payable by universities. In order to do so, it is essential that all the various mechanisms are implemented, both to establish true profit (if any) and to ensure that the necessary steps are taken to avoid payment of corporation tax. As the guidance notes indicate, if a university is not recovering 75 per cent of direct costs, then in the view of the Inland Revenue it is not trading, and the matter is dropped. However, if the university is recovering over 75 per cent, then the operation must be examined to ensure that 'trading' is not taking place. Fortunately, a number of items of expenditure have been specified for special treatment. In particular, the decision to allow the cost of loan financing of residences against possible profits has for many universities virtually eliminated the profit potential for many years. The few institutions that have a very substantial vacation income business have, in the main, taken the route of forming limited companies to operate these services, covenanting any profits to the institution and thereby avoiding the liability for tax.

Funding of residences

The rapid expansion in student numbers has led to pressure on institutions to provide additional accommodation. In many cases, this has been triggered by local authority concerns about housing, particularly in areas where students make up a large proportion of the local population. The cost of funding such capital investment is high and has led to many institutions borrowing large sums. Although in most cases these would have been in the form of normal commercial loans from banks and building societies, a number of ingenious schemes have been developed, one of the most popular of which was the original Business Expansion Scheme (BES). This was heavily used by HEIs in the early 1990s until the Treasury ended the facility in respect of property development in the 1994 budget. The level of loan exposure is a concern to many institutions and the funding councils, and needs to be kept under constant scrutiny to ensure that over-exposure does not occur. The latest tactic is to raise a bond on the capital markets, in the name of a single university (as Lancaster has done) or a group of HEIs. This has been encouraged by the 1995 Budget and references to the Private Finance Initiative (PFI).

The future of student residence provision will need to be considered in the light of any changes in government policy. While the chartered universities have, on average, a university 'owned' provision of around 50 per cent of their student numbers, the statutory universities and other HEIs will have a much smaller figure. The often speculated move towards more home-based students would, of course, reduce the need for further provision. However, this would mark a fundamental change in the character of the British chartered university system, and may well place other pressures on institutions to create additional study space for day students.

In order to provide the necessary funding for student residence building programmes, continued change in government (Treasury) policy has been required. For example, in recent years (principally following the creation of the statutory universities in the early 1990s), the ability to use government funded land or buildings as collateral against commercial loans has been agreed. Previously such use was counted against the public borrowing figures and therefore required Treasury approval, through the relevant department (DES/DfE), with the attendant political implications.

During the past five years there has been a marked trend to build new accommodation with *en suite* facilities. This is partly to meet the growing aspirations of the very important conference and vacation lettings market referred to previously, but is also demanded by an increasingly selective student market. A substantial amount of the current HEI accommodation stock was built in the early to mid-1960s. This accommodation, predominantly of a traditional type (that is, halls of residence), is commonly in need of major refurbishment and modernization.

Legislation

Managers now also need to be aware of changes in legislation, particularly in areas that may be extended to cover student residences. At the time of writing there is considerable debate about the status of student residences with regard to fire certification and the legislation concerning houses in multiple occupation (HMOs). Much work and negotiation regarding these areas has already been undertaken, through the funding councils and the CVCP. The unique nature of the HEI operation will probably be accepted for halls of residence and college quadrangles (but not for real houses used as student accommodation), but it is always difficult to ignore national legislation, especially when there is often an EU background. However, the costs involved for HEIs would be enormous if the legislation were to apply rigidly, and undoubtedly the bulk of these costs would need to be passed directly on to the student body by way of increased residence charges.

Accommodation services

The provision of advice and help to students about accommodation in general is an essential part of the campus support services. In virtually all institutions the rapid rise in student numbers has meant that the percentage of students accommodated within the institutionally owned residences has fallen. It is therefore essential that an efficient accommodation service is established to assist students to find suitable accommodation within the private sector. To this end, many institutions have embarked on initiatives such as 'head lease' schemes. This allows the private landlord to lease the property to the HEI, and he or she is therefore assured of the management of both income and property. In turn, the institution is able to lease to the student under a privileged legislative position, thereby ensuring that the property is made available for return to the landlord at the end of the lease period. In this way, the HEI becomes the 'head tenant' but must consider important health and safety matters, for example the increasingly stringent gas safety inspection requirements.

Final thoughts

The requirement of successive governments, since 1970, for varying degrees of loan financing of student residences has placed increasing pressure on this sector. This policy, coupled with a decision to reduce or eliminate other state benefits to students in more recent years (for example, Housing Benefit and Social Security Benefit during vacations), has meant that more students have needed to take advantage of the loan scheme, and to become increasingly aware of their accommodation costs. This has placed pressure on both the private and HEI owned accommodation to be as cost-efficient as possible. Managers need to review all their operations on an ongoing basis to ensure that efficiency is maintained. Comparison of costs within the university sector has proved helpful to all in this exercise. For example, the annual 'performance indicators', produced by the Conference of University Business Officers, provides useful data in the fields of residences, catering and associated areas.

Catering

Catering services in HEIs have grown and developed substantially over the past forty years. Much of the change has been owing to the different style of student residences constructed in recent years. The move from traditional halls of residence to self-catering flats has generated the growth of 'meals for cash' facilities throughout HEIs. Student demand, no doubt partly fuelled by the change in state school meals provision, has encouraged the development of snack-style meal outlets. A common phrase within the catering trade is that there is now a tendency to 'graze' throughout the day rather than eat at traditional meal times. These changes have caused considerable difficulties within the operation of the relevant services. The uncertainty of income has meant that more dynamic management has been required to ensure that such services are financially viable. Fluctuation in demand varies considerably, often from day to day. Many factors can affect this phenomenon, including weather, examinations or even a student union meeting.

The need to meet fast-changing student tastes has meant that a great deal more investment has been required to develop the ambience of outlets, in addition to the normal expenditure on replacing catering equipment. The so-called 'fast food' phenomenon is as much a part of HEI facilities as of the general market-place. The requirement to engage key staff for 52 weeks has also meant a change in operations – as opposed to the days when, a century ago, Oxford college servants worked in seaside hotels during the long university vacations, having been laid off by their colleges! While many years ago it would have been possible virtually to close down services during vacations, this is no longer a viable option. Although a number of institutions still find it necessary to provide some subsidies to their catering operations, more and more are looking to have a fully self-funding service. This in itself has led to catering departments expanding their operation into a more commercial market. For example, many institutions utilize their restaurants and other facilities for an extensive 'function' market, including anything from professional association dinners and company dinner dances to wedding receptions. This market has grown substantially. Within some HEIs the income from this sector may even exceed that derived directly from staff and student catering.

New production methods

With labour costs being a very substantial element of the catering operation, a number of institutions have sought ways of reducing expenditure in this area. In most cases this has been accomplished by the introduction of 'cook–freeze' or 'cook–chill' operations. The rationale behind both schemes is to eliminate expensive weekend working and allow more scheduled production during the working day, avoiding the peak periods immediately preceding and during a meal service. Such schemes are expensive both in the initial capital investment and in operating costs, particularly in respect of the necessary refrigeration.

Legislation

Recent legislation on food hygiene has produced additional costs and the need for increased managerial control over catering operations. EU-based regulations concerning refrigerated temperatures have resulted in substantial investment in virtually every catering establishment throughout the country. The need, under the new legislation, for 'due diligence' to be shown has meant increased recording and training for the staff involved.

Purchasing

The purchasing operation has improved substantially in recent years. With the help of The University Catering Officers (TUCO) a number of national agreements have been achieved, with very useful financial savings. These contracts have, by and large, been negotiated and implemented outside the regional university central purchasing arrangements. In part, this has been because of the specialized nature of the particular commodity group (that is, fresh and perishable foods), the provision of which is difficult to control from any great distance.

Outsourcing

The reduction in subsidy has led to catering services becoming lean and efficient. Although a small number of the statutory universities have opted for the use of external contractors for their catering services, this has not yet been a particularly prevalent development. In most cases, such companies seek to achieve a management fee (plus VAT) above any charges recovered from the customer, and therefore, unless substantial savings are being achieved in staff costs and food purchasing, it is unlikely to be a viable option. It should also be remembered that such contracts require adequate managerial control, and the effort required to produce the initial and subsequent tendering information should not be underestimated.

In many cases the provision of these services is not necessarily in the hands of the central institutional management. In most cases the student union will provide a partial service, often in the respect of liquor bars and in many cases either limited or full food services. Through 'custom and practice', such arrangements are usually on a non-contract basis, with, particularly in the case of student unions, little or no overhead being charged.

Retail facilities

Another area related to the catering operation, and in many ways a direct result of the change in both the type of residences provided and the number of students accommodated, has been an increase in retail facilities at most HEIs. In many cases, the 'general store' provision is either directly operated by the institution or franchised. Where the operation is 'in-house' it adds an extra dimension to the catering operations as an additional outlet. There is also a potential 'knock-on' advantage in purchasing volume. Some HEIs manage their own bookshops on campus, and even newsagents.

Final thoughts

The future of catering within the HE sector must by definition be uncertain. Further expansion of student numbers, together with a possible trend towards more home-based students, will place pressure on existing facilities. It is unlikely that there will be much, if any, capital available to extend these facilities. On the other hand, the continued trend towards healthy eating and smaller snack-type feeding will enable existing facilities to feed potentially greater numbers. All these changes will require dynamic management, with an increasing entrepreneurial bias.

Security

The provision of security at all HE institutions has unfortunately become more problematic, in line with the general situation throughout the country. The obvious problem of 'controlling' a large and predominantly youthful population has been exacerbated by an increase in recorded crime. In part this has been owing to an increasing value of potential items of theft. For example, student car ownership has increased dramatically in the past twenty years, and theft of and from cars has sadly increased in similar terms. Bicycles, popular among students, have likewise exploded in value since the advent of mountain bikes. It is not uncommon for such vehicles to have an initial value of between £500 and £1000, and they are therefore objects of some desire to a would-be thief.

To counter this situation most institutions will have increased their staff numbers in respect of security. It is now very common for such services to be operating 24 hours a day, which may not have been the case in the past. This alone has not by any means solved the problem, and it is often necessary to install increasingly sophisticated devices. The most common of these devices is closed circuit television (CCTV), the installation of which has produced remarkable results in many HEIs, with very substantial reductions in theft and other incidents. It has also provided an increased sense of personal security, particularly to female staff and students.

In addition, increasingly sophisticated door entry systems have been installed in many academic and student residence buildings. These include various card entry systems and security locks. The provision of adequate security is an expensive commodity. The need for mobility has required the purchase or the leasing of suitable vehicles, together with the necessary radio link equipment. This has meant that managers have needed to consider the possibility of using specialized security companies, often to supplement internal arrangements (although great care is needed in the selection of such security firms, given that the industry as yet has little by way of regulation). Moreover, the specialist nature of the HEI community requires a more informed service than that required to safeguard, say, an industrial site. This is especially true in relation to dealing with student matters and such sensitive areas as drugs and sexual harassment.

Various political implications also need to be considered within the realms of security. For example, the additional pressures provided by section 43 of the Education (no. 2) Act 1986 place a responsibility on an HE institution to ensure freedom of speech. The activity of various pressure groups (for example, animal rights) usually requires additional security in certain vulnerable areas. HEIs also attract distinguished visitors, who often warrant specialized security (the Royal Family, ministers of state, etc.). Problems arise in maintaining the correct balance between providing a safe environment and allowing the traditional freedoms within the HEI system. It will undoubtedly be a fact for the future that unrestricted access to all HEI buildings is likely to become less and less available.

Control of car parking has tended to become an issue in virtually all institutions. The previously mentioned increase in student car ownership has invariably meant that regulations and restrictions are needed. This has led to the use of such devices as wheel-clamping to provide the necessary control. In many cases this creates a disproportionately emotive response from students and staff affected. A careful balance needs to be attained to ensure that the issues do not become disruptive to the general operation.

The public relations aspect of these tasks also needs to be considered in a changing environment. For example, the security staff or 'gate personnel' are often the first point of contact for visitors to an institution. The need to convey a polite and congenial welcome, and the ability to direct visitors to the right building, is becoming an essential element of the operation, and many HEIs take 'customer care' training very seriously.

Portering and cleaning

In most HEIs the portering operation in particular buildings is usually separate from the direct security role of the institution. However, porters carry out important individual tasks for particular buildings. With the demands on increased security it is often the building porter who is in the front line, and who is more likely to know more about matters relating to particular buildings than the central security service.

With pressures on expenditure, the roles of portering and cleaning have tended to merge. This creates some problems, but does allow a more organized service. Recent legislation (for example, control of substances hazardous to health, health and safety office procedures, materials handling) has led to the need to record and itemize a large number of the activities carried out in this sector. Similarly significant changes in the equipment available for cleaning tasks have produced useful savings, but require a more technical knowledge from the operational managers. In many cases institutions have appointed specialist teams to carry out cleaning and maintenance as opposed to the day-to-day routines. The greater use of institutional teaching facilities and other areas has also led to changes in the employment of cleaners, with many areas now subject to night cleaning, which carries added complications for management and control and with added cost. Specialized contract cleaning firms are used in a number of institutions, with differing results, not least dependent upon the availability of companies in the surrounding area. Urban institutions, for example, may well have a range of such companies operating, while those in rural areas would find difficulty in identifying a sufficiently large company to take on the task.

The increasing awareness of environmental issues has needed to be addressed in virtually all areas relating to the cleaning operation. Many HEIs have adopted a 'green' policy. This has meant that recycling issues have needed to be addressed and solved. In most cases the financial implications result in an increase in the actual operating costs. However, student and academic staff pressure is almost certain to mean that such issues will continue to require attention, with the likelihood of increased costs to the operating service. Current legislation also requires managers to be able to show they have taken the necessary steps to ensure that the disposal of the institution's waste complies with the various pieces of legislation – especially if it is from laboratories and mildly radioactive.

The provision of internal mail services usually falls within the purview of portering staff. It is essential that this service is as efficient as possible, to facilitate the smooth running of the operation. External mail services also need to be managed. The simple days of the Post Office being the only means of mail delivery have long since passed. There are now an increasing number of companies prepared to compete to provide improved customer services at reduced costs. It is necessary for managers within these areas to keep abreast of the changes on offer and the possibilities of regional or national terms becoming available.

The increase in the size of most institutions, often with several sites, has led to the need for improved transportation of both students and staff. This, in turn, has led to managers needing to be much more aware of the requirements for economical and effective transport management. The decision as to whether to buy or lease vehicles depends on individual requirements. Proper controls over this area are essential to avoid excessive costs.

Telecommunications

Telecommunications in HEIs are an expanding and important market for services to students, staff and the community in general. The fax machine is commonplace, and almost every office has one. Telex continues, but is now used only for communicating with Third World destinations that have not yet been able to afford the emerging technology. Competition is increasingly available for voice traffic, and British Telecom is responding to vigorous attempts from Mercury, Energis and the cable companies to attract new customers.

Electronic mail has been widespread in the HE sector for many years following the development of the Joint Academic Network (JANET). This is now exploding with interest as the internet develops, with exciting possibilities offered by the World Wide Web and connection to the business community. It is now possible to 'surf' the internet for news services, sound and graphics displays. There is no doubt that as the technology (for example, voice transmission over the Internet using multimedia PCs) and standards develop, and as this market grows with connection via telephone and cable links to every household, communication as we know it today will be transformed.

Mobile phones are having an increasing impact where the mobile facility offsets the increased cost of calls. Users have to choose the type of telephone, the service provider, an analogue or digital network, and the tariff to suit their needs. The provision of mobile telephones to members of staff is an area that in most cases has grown without significant central input, and will undoubtedly be a service for which managers will need to provide elements of control and advice in the near future.

The pressure for public telephones on campuses has also grown. It is not uncommon for several hundred such telephones to be available, with new student residences also providing, in some cases, direct telecommunications links to the individual student study/bedroom. This trend is likely to continue, although the advent of relatively cheap mobile phones is having an increasing impact.

Printing

Technology has had a dramatic impact on printing and reprographic services in recent years. Improvements have concentrated on improving quality and productivity; office workers may now create impressive documents from inexpensive word processing and desktop publishing software. Completed documents are commonly transmitted via a local electronic network directly to a printer for multiple copying, collating and stitching. Documents, reports, booklets and leaflets may then be despatched with a minimum of effort. Copiers and printers are available with spot and full colour, the standard of presentation is immensely improved and costs are comparable with black and white duplicating of only a few years ago. In parallel, relatively cheap office copiers now provide for automatic document feed, collating and duplex printing that had previously been available only at a substantial premium and was to be found only within a cumbersome central facility.

The very competitive 'free market' for print work has also changed the concept of 'in-house' printing. It has become increasingly difficult for such operations to remain financially viable when compared with the use of outside companies. The special needs of HEIs to safeguard such areas as the printing of examination papers needs further consideration, but many institutions have, in recent years, virtually closed down their central 'in-house' operations.

12

Student Support Services

Russell Rowley

Editors' introduction

Successful study can rarely be achieved if other areas of a student's life are unbalanced or causing problems. This 'study context' comprises numerous aspects, only one of which needs to go wrong at any one time for disruption to occur. But one dominant trend has emerged in the past couple of years as student grants have declined and other forms of financial support have been withdrawn, leaving it undeniable that money worries have increased significantly as a cause of disruption to academic study.

In this chapter, the author argues that just as students must be treated holistically, so should the support services involved be regarded as a necessary and totally integrated part of the HEI environment. Moreover, he urges that student support services should be proactive, rather than reactive, and completely responsive to developing customer needs.

Introduction

It is significant that a chapter on the management of student support services should be included within a book on the management of higher education in the 1990s. As I hope this chapter will show, the significance lies in the recognition that the skills and expertise of the staff within student support services contribute directly to the total student learning experience.

The UK higher education system has a number of characteristics that make it unique and have given it its worldwide reputation. One of these is a tradition of providing student support services, usually referred to as pastoral support. These characteristics have developed historically, extending back through the nineteenth-century public school tradition, through medieval church-based education, to the classical Greek period. This tradition views education as having aims beyond the imparting of information alone; knowledge is advanced through the questioning of assumptions. The early involvement of religious orders meant that the development of university life was similar to that of monastic life (Earwaker, 1992). This is the tradition embodied in the Oxbridge colleges and emulated in the establishment of universities – until recently. Thus university life existed in isolation from the rest of society. Student to student support became a feature of an elitist system in which students were required to live away from home in a predominately male environment.

Another significant part of this tradition has been the development of the role of the teacher as tutor. Students were assigned a personal tutor, who took responsibility for the student's moral well-being as well as his academic development. To some extent this may have been necessary because HEIs found themselves *in loco parentis* until the age of the majority was reduced from 21 to 18 in the 1960s. It could be argued that it was a form of social engineering to ensure the continuation of the tradition. More benevolently, it could also be taken as an early recognition of the importance of a holistic approach to education, because a student's academic progress is influenced by a range of factors, including social, cultural, political, emotional and spiritual. Therefore, it was important that the HEIs addressed students' accommodation needs; provided for their religious devotion, and their social and political life; and, of course, ensured that they had the opportunity for physical exercise through sporting activities, which not only meant a healthy body and healthy mind ('the body is the temple of the spirit', 1 Corinthians 6:19), but also allowed for development of a collegiate or team spirit.

It is important to recognize the impact of these historical characteristics upon the development of higher education, for I would argue that these characteristics have provided the model for the tutor–student relationship and for the concept of pastoral care in higher education. It is not until recently, probably since the late 1970s or early 1980s, that the attitudes and opinions engendered by these characteristics have had to change radically. Even the universities designed to cope with the expansion of HE in the 1960s (for example, Lancaster, Kent and York) retained a separatist, exclusive tradition by being built outside neighbouring towns, with campuses designed to accommodate, serve and entertain their students. Earwaker (1992) argues that even the polytechnics, which were designed primarily to be a service to their community, in many ways also continued the long established practices of HE and maintained the pastoral care model of student support services by providing on-site living accommodation, counselling and careers services, medical services, chaplaincy and student union facilities. Nowadays, it is generally the case that institutions provide at least this range of support services, which are being extended to include childcare, financial advice, learning/study skills and services to students with disabilities.

There is no one accepted model for the management or provision of this range of support services. In some institutions the students' union provides welfare and financial advice, in others they are managed as distinct entities. However, within the statutory universities and some of the colleges of higher education, there has been a tendency to group these support services together for management purposes, to form a student services department. This chapter will be concerned primarily with the management of this integrated model of student support services.

The integrated model

The integrated model of student support services is the outcome of the HE system in the UK maintaining a commitment to the concept of pastoral care, while responding to pressures for change within its operating environment. I shall shortly address these pressures more thoroughly, but suffice it to state here that a major pressure has been the increase in the number of students, especially an increase in the number of mature students, many of whom may be older and have more life experience than their tutors. The move to a mass higher education system has forced HE to become less elitist and separatist, while the close personal relationship between tutor and student has almost completely disappeared (and may always have been more of a fictional ideal than a mundane reality). Furthermore, there have been changes in the background of tutors, many of whom may have come from an industrial or commercial environment and are, therefore, not indoctrinated with the pastoral care model of HE. These changes have meant that the tutor's role has become more academic and teaching oriented, thus creating a vacuum, for the historical impact of the pastoral care model dictates that HEIs should provide a range of support services to students that were previously provided by tutors, who usually were untrained and carried out the pastoral care role through a sense of commitment and good will (helped by a common social and school background between students and academics in an elite HE system).

Apart from the increased demand for tutors to concentrate on academic matters, created by the changes to the system, the changes in the type of students have created new types of needs. Hence we have seen the development of professional support services, which, as already mentioned, include counsellors, careers advice and guidance, student financial services and childcare.

The bringing together of these professional support staff into an integrated student support service provision makes available to the institution the whole range of services previously provided by tutors. More especially, this integrated service means that a student needs to refer to only one point within the institution, and is not transferred from one department to another, or, as the student would see it, 'passed from pillar to post'.

The impact of external factors upon HEIs

I have suggested that these changes have occurred especially since the late 1970s and early 1980s, during which time HEIs have had to change because

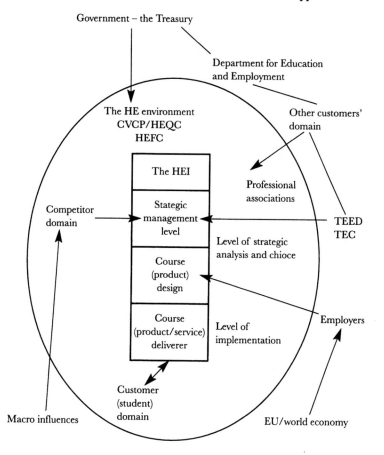

Figure 12.1 Environmental influences affecting HE management decision-making

of the influences within the environment in which they exist. These influences are illustrated in Figure 12.1, and include government policy, the national, European and world economy, local employers and the community, the professional associations and the funding councils. It is important to recognize how these operate.

The influence of central government

There is an increasingly direct intervention by the government, which takes a variety of forms, especially the restriction upon funding by the Treasury, whose demands are carried out by the funding councils. With the direct linking of funding to students, institutions have been forced to recruit more students. This has indirectly changed the status of students, so that in many ways they are like customers. There is nothing new about the power of the purse, so it is not surprising that the funding councils, on behalf of the government, want to be able to assure themselves of quality within the system, even if only as a simplistic perception of value for money (Holmes, 1993).

The change in attitude towards students is symbolized by the introduction of a Student Charter from the Department for Education in 1993. The effect of this is to put the student into the role of a consumer, with 'entitlements' as to what the service should provide. The Charter requires *inter alia* that:

- You should receive well-informed guidance from your tutors and careers staff and appropriate access to counsellors.
- In your first few days your university or college should make you familiar with the services available on site. These should include proper counselling for personal problems, medical help, arrangements for student security and safety, and careers advice.
- Universities and colleges should set out their policies on equal opportunities.
- Universities and colleges should set out in prospectuses or other booklets what accommodation they themselves provide.
- Universities and colleges should explain their policies for providing access to students with disabilities or learning difficulties.

The effect of these changes in attitude is to create a change in the underlying assumptions behind the provision of student support services. These are now aspects of the HE experience to which students are entitled. Therefore, the elitist tradition of HE, including the paternalistic assumptions of the pastoral care model, needs to be replaced. (Editor's note: see Farrington 1994 for an analysis of the changing relationship of student to HEI in terms of contract law.)

The demands of the economy

For some time now there has been a view that British industry requires graduates with good 'transferable skills', such as communication skills, self-development skills and team working. This was the underlying assumption of the Pegasus projects of the 1980s and of the Training, Enterprise and Education Directorate's funded *Enterprise in Higher Education*. The European Commission (1991) noted a similar skills shortage:

One feature of current skills shortages is the widespread lack of important generic skills and social skills such as quality assurance skills, problem solving skills, learning efficiency, flexibility and communication skills. These are in addition to shortages of critical scientific and technological skills.

(European Commission, 1991: 3)

These views reflect employers' expectations of graduates. In a separate survey of employers (Harvey and Green, 1994) the following skills were listed as essential: effective communication, team work, ability to solve problems, analytical skills, flexibility and adaptability, self skills (confidence, etc.), decision-making skills, independent judgement, numeracy, logical argument, enquiry and research skills, imagination and creativity, use of IT, relate to wider context, specialist subject knowledge.

The influence of student expectations

There is evidence that the views of students are influencing decision-making within institutions (Harvey and Green, 1994). For example, in recent years a number of institutions have introduced student surveys as an attempt to identify student expectations and adapt their institutions' plans accordingly. Such a survey has been carried out at the University of Central England in Birmingham since 1989. Here students regularly identify personal development and the wish to obtain a qualification as most important among their expectations.

In informal discussions, prospective students regularly identify intellectual development, personal autonomy, 'having fun' and meeting other people as their expectations of HE. Brian Caul similarly states: 'As a result of their time on campus, their lives should be enriched not just through intellectual stimulation but also socially, emotionally and culturally.' He goes on to say, 'the value added which universities should provide for individual people and for society as a whole, is freedom for critical reflection, questioning of assumptions, and opportunities for comprehensive personal development' (Caul, 1993: 9).

If we were to apply only the measure of consumer popularity to HE it would surely be the case that it is a highly valued commodity because the number of people wanting it has increased dramatically in the past decade. From an age participation rate of 15 per cent it has expanded to 30 per cent, and if we can judge its popularity by our European neighbours (for example, Netherlands 36 per cent, France 44 per cent, Germany 45 per cent, though even these figures are low compared with the USA at 65 per cent and Japan striving to achieve 90 per cent), it will continue to increase. In itself, the increased number of students becomes another influence.

HEIs' response to the external factors

The net effect of these influences and the transition from an 'expanded élite' (post-1960s Robbins expansion) to a 'mass' HE system by the mid-1990s has been to pressurize HEIs into being more economical with scarce resources and to look at ways of being more effective and efficient in using those resources to deliver high-quality outcomes. In response, institutions have adopted a model of management that emulates the large business corporation; however, they need to be recognized as diverse organizations, for unlike in business corporations, it is difficult to identify their product or output and to judge them by a simple 'bottom line'. Indeed, education is unique, in that students may be seen as an institution's product as well as its raw material. It is more appropriate to compare HEIs with service industries, though again it is possible to identify a range of services; for example, each undergraduate course that is offered, postgraduate research, specialist short courses, and conference accommodation. When HEIs are viewed in this way, it becomes clear that institutions have a variety of students, users and customers. Therefore, institutions will need to recognize that they have market diversity, product diversity, technological diversity and goal diversity (Handy, 1993), which may be reinforced by the devolved management structure adopted by many institutions, and which further reinforces the differences between one part of the institution and another. These differences are such as to create subcultures within the sub-units, be they departments, schools or whatever (Lawrence and Lorsch, 1967). The effect of these cultures is to create behaviour that conflicts with a coordinated approach to the achievement of the overall goal.

The skills of a student support services manager

In this setting of a multi-structural organization, the manager of a centralized student support service needs to be able to manage services in a manner that enables him or her to respond to the diversity of the organization. The management skills required include advocacy and negotiation skills; 'politicking', motivational and team-building skills; boundary management and change agent skills; financial and other resource management skills; human resource management skills; time management and organizational skills; decision-making and risk-taking skills. Additionally, the manager of student support services needs to be able to demonstrate his or her own authority and to take responsibility for the exercise of it.

These skills are very similar to those of managers in many other parts of the organization, and very similar to those which employers of graduates expect. The specialism of student support services is about people working with people.

A primary task for the management of student support services is to identify the range of services required by a particular institution. It is arguable that there is a range of student support services that might be described as core services, such as accommodation, careers guidance, counselling, health care, financial advice and disability services. However, some institutions will have differing needs. Therefore, the provision of services will be influenced by the institution's mission or purpose, as well as the needs of the students, so what is an appropriate provision for one institution is not necessarily so for another. For example, not every institution will require childcare services. However, institutions that target mature students and have a large number of part-time students may find the provision of childcare services an important inducement. It is reassuring for a parent to know that his or her child is in a caring and educational environment. The development of childcare services to offer places all year round will be an attraction to an institution's staff. Outreach by the service to the community will strengthen community links, and may well bring in some much needed revenue for childcare facilities. The increasing move to modularization and the opportunities that are afforded by credit accumulation transfer schemes and accreditation of prior experience and learning may also attract students who require flexible childcare facilities.

Institutions that attract large numbers of mature students will find that it is very important that such students have budgeted appropriately for the duration of their courses. Mature students will have financial commitments, which include mortgages, house up-keep costs, childcare costs, travel costs and costs of services. The abolition of the mature students' allowance will exacerbate their situation, while students who were on benefit need to be aware that they are no longer eligible.

With institutions relying upon funding based on student numbers and the increasing attention being paid to student retention rates, it is important that students are able to complete their studies and avoid wastage both of their own time and abilities and of scarce institutional revenue.

These two examples of childcare facilities and financial advice illustrate how student support services can support the institution in its objectives, and they also illustrate how managers of student support services need to have an astute awareness of the environmental influences within which their institutions operate, as illustrated in Figure 12.1.

Models of student support service delivery

Since HEIs are managed as business organizations, with all the complexities created by diversity, another important task for the manager of student support services is to develop a system of student support that enables the services to integrate into all the parts of the institution. The delivery model will differ from one institution to another, according to the structure of the institution.

Model 1

In this model the student support services function alongside the rest of the institution. Users of the services can refer themselves or can be referred by staff. It is largely a reactive model, within which there is probably little interaction between the student support services and the rest of the institution (see Figure 12.2).

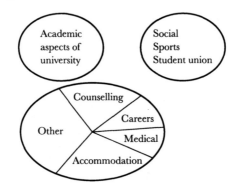

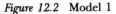

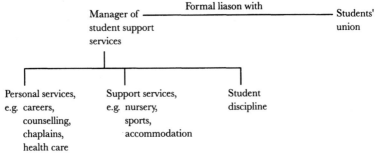

Figure 12.2   Model 1

Figure 12.3   Model 2

Model 2

The second model allows for student support services to be more interactive with the institution, mainly because of the range of functions performed, especially the liaison with the students' union and with student discipline, which reflects the strong influence of the pastoral care model in higher education (see Figure 12.3). Again, however, there is no formal linking into the institution's main activity of teaching and facilitating learning and the advancement of knowledge.

Model 3

The third model is an attempt to make student support services more proactive and to address the issues of a vastly expanded system, the increase in the numbers of modular courses with a consequent loss of the sense of belonging, the learners' sense of isolation in a complex system and the provision of adequate tutorial support by academics. To address this last point it is necessary to take a wider view of student support services, in that to provide support to students it is vital to provide support for

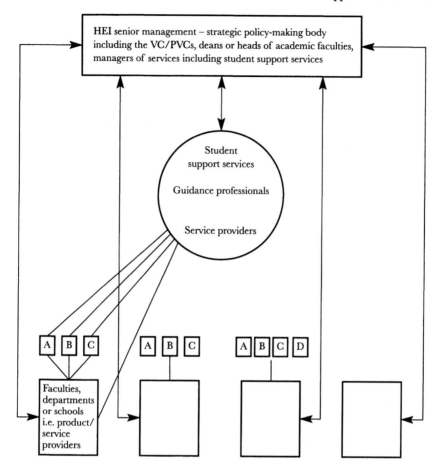

Figure 12.4 Model 3

academic colleagues, both in a consultancy role and by providing skills training workshops.

This model would involve student support services being embedded within the organizational strategy and structure of the institution (see Figure 12.4). The professionals within the service would be influencing strategy by facilitating staff and students to address issues such as:

- engaging the student with the HEI (induction);
- pre-arrival information;
- planning for life in higher education;
- studying and learning in higher education;
- coping with the transition to higher education;
- equal opportunities;
- drug and alcohol misuse;
- living in student accommodation.

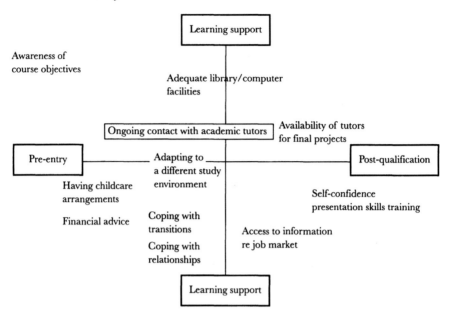

Figure 12.5   Model 4

In presenting these models of student support services organization, I fully recognize that there are other models; for example, I have not taken into consideration the role of student peer support services, such as 'night-line' or supplemental instruction. Readers may also be aware of the initiative supported by the National Union of Students for the training of students to be more active members of HEI committees. This training develops those transferable skills to which I referred earlier, and can lead to the acquisition of useful additional NVQ level 3 qualifications.

Model 4: The proactive model

There is a fourth model, which defies graphical representation. This is the 'amoeba' model, which may be a more appropriate system in an organization that responds to the environment in which it exists, constantly adapting to requirements and allowing students to access a range of support from pre-entry to post-exit, as shown in Figure 12.5. This support enables students to understand how they learn, so that they can genuinely take responsibility for their own learning.

The need for such a flexible and adaptive model arises from the expectations being placed upon HE, as a result of the shift to 'massification' over the last decade. The effect of these changes is to create a change in the culture within HE, to what has been described as the 'new collegialism', characteristics of which include a focus on the total student learning experience and a focus on the process and the outcomes of higher education. The new collegialism is outward looking and responsive (Harvey, 1995).

In this environment, student support services would become more student-centred by being more issues-focused, thereby changing from being a reactive service to a proactive service, in that it actively addresses the issues that users (students, employers, the community) identify. This customer service model could use a variety of feedback systems, such as student satisfaction surveys, to identify aspects of the student experience to which the skills and expertise of the student support services personnel can be applied. This requires the application of a soft systems methodology, which helps to identify what are usually awkward and unstructured problems. This approach to problem-solving relates closely to the process proposed by Checkland (1973 and 1981). (Editors' note: see also Clemson (1984) on cybernetics as a management tool.)

An application of the proactive model

Let me take an example, the introduction of guidance and learner support programmes in HE. Guidance and learner support might be described as the modern equivalent of the pastoral care model, though there are differences in that it is a learner-centred experience, which is an entitlement students can access from pre-entry to post-exit. It is impartial and accessed with equal opportunity, while recognizing that students have obligations and responsibilities within the learning environment (Higher Education Quality Council, 1995).

The demand for guidance and learner support comes directly from the environment within which the HEI operates and includes the needs of employers for graduates with transferable skills, and those of students who require support in an HE system that is changing from a teaching environment to a learning environment. From within the economy, the thrust appears to be coming from a number of sources, including employers' forums such as the Confederation of British Industry (CBI). Its expectations of HE were advanced in the publication *Thinking Ahead* (1994). The spear-carrier for guidance and learner support, which enables students to acquire the skills of life-long learning, would appear to be the Department for Trade and Industry (DTI), initially through the Training, Enterprise and Education Directorate (TEED), which sponsored the Enterprise in Higher Education Initiative from 1987. The Department of Employment was responsible for encouraging the advancement of these ideas, largely through the Higher Education Projects Fund, the most recent of which focuses on 'career management skills', whose outcomes will include the 'ability of graduates to manage their lifelong careers' and the ability of careers staff to 'work with academic colleagues and other partners within and outside the institution to develop career management skills in students.' Another element of the project is Using Graduate Skills, aimed at 'assisting employers to make effective use of the skills, knowledge and net-works which graduates can bring' (Department of Employment, 1995a). The purpose behind these is to encourage higher education, the Training Enterprise Councils and local employers to work more closely together.

The recent amalgamation of the Department for Education and Department of Employment is not surprising, for it emphasizes the government's views that education should be responsive to the needs of the economy. As far as HE is concerned, its graduates need to be equipped with life-long learning skills, and the increased involvement of the Department of Employment in higher education over the past ten years is aimed at ensuring that students do have access to guidance that helps people to make well informed choices about how to develop and use their individual talents, to integrate learning and working and to become autonomous life-long learners (Department of Employment, 1995b). To help achieve that goal there are currently five projects sponsored by the DfEE, within a guidance and learner autonomy network (GALA). They are: at the University of Northumbria at Newcastle, the design and development of a comprehensive and accessible guidance service; at the University of North London and Oxford Brooks University, the development of a university-wide education guidance system; at the University of Central Lancashire, 'careers education'; at Nene College, the development of a whole-institution policy and implementation strategy in respect of learner guidance and support; and at the University of Greenwich, the transition to higher education – a framework for guidance.

The problem of introducing a programme for guidance and learner support is a complex one, which can be made more manageable by the application of a systems model such as that shown in Figure 12.6. The application of this model leads to the realization that student support services is just one of the sub-systems that exist within the organization. Furthermore, it illustrates that within student support services there are sub-systems, the implication of which is that student support services professionals need to view themselves in a more holistic way, accepting that they have a range of generic skills that can be applied to 'client' issues.

Managerial skills

In Models 3 and 4 there is an assumption that managers of student support services have the skills necessary to build a team of staff with adaptable and flexible attitudes to the utilization of their skills. These skills centre on the ability to interact with people and include the skills of reflection and analysis, presentation, advancement, advocacy and decision-making. Again, these relate closely to the previously described transferable or life-long learning skills.

In the current economic and political climate, when HEIs are run as business organizations, it is important for their senior managers to be able to 'read' the environment, to be able to identify opportunities and to assess

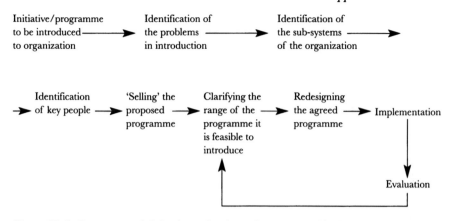

Figure 12.6 Systems model for introduction of a programme for guidance and learner support

threats. Similarly, managers of student support services must be able to identify opportunities and assess threats that relate to their part of the organization.

To illustrate this point, let me take the application of the previously mentioned Department of Employment project Using Graduates' Skills, which underlines the general recognition that life-long careers no longer exist and that the previously large recruiters of graduates no longer have sufficient vacancies. Therefore, new outlets for graduate employment must be found (for example, in small and medium-sized enterprises (SMEs)), for not only do careers services have a role in helping the student to develop his or her skills, they also have a role in finding new employers of graduates and showing them the benefits of employing graduates. In such an environment graduates will not have the benefit of a graduate training programme: they must be productive from day one. Therefore, they must leave the HEI with all the personal transferable skills that enable them to manage their life-long careers and are so valuable to employers.

For this environment, graduates will need to be adequately prepared. They will need the opportunity to address their own self-esteem, build up their self-confidence, learn to be assertive, so as to develop their personal presentation skills. They will also require leadership skills and need to know how to be a valuable member of a team. As managers they must also know how to work on their own and to 'time-manage', and, of course they will need to know how to access information and extend their knowledge. Before graduates obtain a position, they will require job search skills and have to be able to write a curriculum vitae. The delivery of training for the acquisition of these skills will come from a variety of sources: their academic tutors, careers advisors, counsellors, mentors and, of course, their peers. I would argue that the application of a soft systems methodology enables managers to conceptualize the whole of the problem within its total environment.

The need for quality

A major criticism of the pastoral care model of student support is that it applied to HE at a time of relative certainty. Issues such as lack of finances, increasing student drop outs or the need for academic tutoring during the 1960s and 1970s are well documented (Raaheim *et al.*, 1991) and are therefore not new. What is new is the more rapidly changing times in which we live, creating uncertainty. This emphasizes the need for students to be able to access competent, well informed guidance and advice as part of the total student learning experience.

That this is so is reinforced by the approach of both the HEQC and the funding councils in their assessments of quality. The HEQC has published *A Quality Assurance Framework for Guidance and Learner Support in Higher Education: the Guidelines*, which is 'intended to assist with approaches to – quality assurance, policy development – service development – staff development – curriculum development' (HEQC, 1995: 3). The HEFCE (1995c) has similarly published guidelines, the key features of which address the overall strategy for support and guidance, admissions and induction arrangements, academic tutorial support, pastoral and welfare support, careers information and guidance.

Central to an institution having high-quality guidance and learner support systems is the delivery of high-quality student support services. Therefore, it is incumbent upon managers of services to ensure that they have a quality framework in existence, which I would suggest should include:

1. An agreed statement of purpose.
2. The means of monitoring the needs of users.
3. Procedures to evaluate the effectiveness, efficiency and economy of the service.
4. Evidence of involvement in initiatives leading to the development of transferable skills in students.
5. A staff development programme as part of a human resource strategy.

Final thoughts

I commenced this chapter by stating that HE in the UK had a tradition of providing student support that addressed the whole person. I hope I have shown that the tradition continues and has to be addressed in a manner that suits the needs of the time, the institution and its students. I would suggest that the evidence I have presented shows that there has never been a greater need for high-quality, competent, well informed advice, provided by appropriately skilled professionals. Therefore, the organization and management of support services should be such as to make them an integral part of the institution's total provision for students. (Editors' note: see Roberts and Higgins (1992) and Haselgrove (1994) concerning 'The Student Experience'.)

13

External Relations

Frank Albrighton and Julia Thomas

Editors' introduction

This chapter's style showcases the strengths of professional external relations staff. The portfolio of external relations managers varies from HEI to HEI and the role described in this chapter is the 'pure' form, which does not deal in depth with income generation. This is a major topic in its own right, and interested readers might wish to refer to the Open University Press publication *The Income Generation Handbook* (Warner and Leonard, 1992).

Introduction

We all want to be liked and admired. That is just as true for institutions as it is for individuals. But is it sufficient reason for all the energy and money that HEIs put into external relations? Only if you accept the premise that teaching and research will benefit from a climate of good opinion. Like it or not, it is not enough to be doing a good job unsung and unrecognized. HEIs are subject to decisions made by many people who need information on which to base their judgements. External relations is concerned with making sure that those people have *accurate* information about the institution, so that in exercising discretion they will be well informed and, you hope, favourably disposed.

External relations in HEIs is not about image-making. An undeserved reputation will do as much damage as a bad one, and it will ultimately be found out. The purpose of external relations is to encourage and maintain the best reputation an institution deserves with its key external constituencies.

The problem with that kind of general statement is that it leads to people saying: 'I think we ought to do this; it will be very good public relations.' They mean that it is something they want to happen, something whose effect cannot be measured and something they expect someone else to pay for. External relations is by no means an exact science, but it is important to be as systematic as possible and to measure performance as far as you can.

Begin with the mission

This first thing is to identify the key audiences on whose good opinion the institution depends. This can turn out to be a very long list. It will include: potential students, their parents and their teachers; funding councils; research councils; the professions; employers; industry and commerce; former students; the local community; staff in other institutions; politicians; taxpayers; and the media. We have deliberately placed the media at the end of that list because there is sometimes a presumption that external relations equals media relations.

The list of key audiences for particular institutions could be much longer than this. The first task is to prioritize them. For an HEI that is research-based and wants to recruit good postgraduate students, final-year undergraduates in other institutions might well be one of its target groups. Another institution with a large number of part-time, home-based mature students will place the local community high on its list of important groups. The planning of an external relations strategy has to be linked to the mission and strategic objectives of the HEI itself. There is no separate external relations agenda. Nothing should be done simply because it is good public relations, or even because it will raise the standing of the institution in the eyes of a particular group. It is only justified if it supports the overall aims of the institution and can be demonstrated to do so. External relations is not about creating warm feelings opportunistically with anyone you happen to come across.

In fact, it is not about creating warm feelings at all. It should be based on a systematic strategy to create in the minds of the key audiences the opinion you want them to hold. This is where the mission statement comes in. That will describe the institution as it wishes to be and, therefore, as it wishes to be perceived. If all your external audiences already hold that view about the HEI then there is no need to go any further. But, of course, they do not. They will not believe, for example, that every HEI in the UK is a centre of excellence dedicated to high quality in all its activities, and achieving international recognition across a broad range of disciplines. But that is the kind of statement that practically every HEI makes about itself. If that is all the mission statement says, then the external relations department has a problem, because you need rather more than that to latch on to. You need a sharply focused and *distinctive* profile that will separate your institution from others and enable you to project an image that is recognizable.

Who do they think you are?

We now know whom we want to influence and what we want them to think of us. The next stage is to decide how we are going to encourage them to arrive at the right conclusion. That can only be done if we know the distance they have to travel and the direction from which they are coming. The starting point for any external relations work has to be systematic and reliable opinion research. This does not mean running around wildly in response to such sayings as 'My visitor said that his taxi driver had never heard of the university', or 'Why is it that no one has heard of my research group, which is doing work at least as important as that at Imperial College?', or even 'My daughter is 17 and she says that our prospectus is the worst in the system.' In fact, staff and their families, who appear to hold strong views on everything from a corporate identity policy to what should be in the student recruitment video, are almost certainly the least reliable sample. How can they possibly be unbiased? Even staff professionally involved in external relations activities may be prone to the unsubstantiated assertion. Resist all preconceived notions.

Opinion research must be done systematically, rigorously and objectively. The money spent on market research will be tiny in relation to the expenditure on prospectuses, annual reports, videos, etc. Years ago, HEIs used to recoil from spending money on graphic design, because they thought it was an unnecessary cosmetic in a context where the written word, unadorned with pictures and other devices, would surely suffice. It is no good nowadays for a publication to be beautifully written and beautifully designed, if it is saying the wrong things addressed to the wrong people. Proper opinion research can provide invaluable guidance, and a proper foundation for the huge investment.

For each of the audiences you identify, opinion research is able to tell you two important things. The first is their opinion of your institution. The information you gather can be as detailed as you want. You will almost certainly want to know where your institution stands in some kind of pecking order. But you can break that down from the general public to such groups as teachers, sixth-formers, parents, research directors in industry and so on. You can compare it with the whole HE sector or just with those institutions with which you are directly comparable. You can find out whether your reputation depends on the life-saving work done in your medical school, or on the fact that you have many thousands of satisfied customers from your diploma courses. Your reputation is not static and unpredictable. If something happens in your institution (as it did in ours) which you think may have had a damaging effect on your reputation, you may be pleasantly surprised (as we were) to find that it had the opposite effect.

The second important information will be about the sources they turn to in order to form that opinion. Is it, for example, newspapers, your own publications, friends, parents, teachers, alumni?

Some of the answers will not be surprising, but will provide reassurance that your work and expenditure are justified. Prospectuses, for example, will almost certainly turn out to be a very important means of communicating with potential students. But what about videos? What about recruitment fairs in the UK and overseas? What about new electronic means of communication? Everyone, of course, is subject to information coming from a variety of sources, but the research will enable you to measure their relative influence. Still thinking about potential applicants, what is the relative importance of advice received from friends, present students, teachers, careers officers, parents and so on? And where do they, in turn, get their information from?

At the end of this exercise, in addition to a better understanding of your reputation, you will also have identified the factors that contribute to that reputation, and from what sources people gain their information in making their judgements. This leads very directly to an external relations strategy, which tells you what you should be saying and through which media.

Straight talking

Which media? The market research gives you some clues on which means of communication are most important and powerful for each audience, and it will almost certainly have indicated that a mix of activities will be required.

The more direct the means of communication, the more effective it is likely to be. Talking one-to-one to an individual is more likely to inculcate understanding than pinning up a notice and hoping he or she will stop and read it. In some cases, external relations will consist literally of face-to-face contact, like a vice-chancellor briefing a local Member of Parliament. But normally a shortage of time and resources means that methods have to be used which target large numbers of people in a way that is seen to be cost-effective. HEIs exist on reading and writing, and it is not surprising that publications perform such an important role in external communications. Our external audiences can safely be assumed to be literate and prepared to devote some attention at least to absorbing information and ideas.

Put it in writing

The culture of many HEIs, where the publication of research papers is seen as the apogee of literary achievement, does not always lend itself to the type of publication that the external relations professional needs to produce. This is why it is important that all publications should be professionally managed. Communication is the objective, and the needs and interests of the reader should be paramount. It is all too easy when producing a brochure or a prospectus to write something designed to impress colleagues or superiors, which may leave the real reader confused or unmoved. Publications are a tool to communicate strategic messages. The text should be written with this in mind and edited rigorously to excise anything that is irrelevant, obscure or self-indulgent. The same applies to design, photography and illustration. These are not cosmetics larded on by authors in an attempt to attract a young and fickle readership of, say, an undergraduate prospectus. Nor are they optional extras to the serious message of the words, to be dispensed with in favour of that vital additional paragraph. They are an essential and integral part of the medium and should be used professionally, skilfully and with restraint, in a way that enhances and reinforces what the publication is trying to say.

For every publication the editor should have certain points very clearly in mind. Who will read this? In what circumstances, or at what stage in their relationship with the HEI, will they read it? And what do I hope they will do or think when they have read it?

All too often, publications disregard the reader and are preoccupied with self-justification and pompous self-importance. Ask yourself, are the 16-year-old readers of a prospectus really interested in the age of the institution or the distinction of the head of the department? If you think they are, because that conveys the fact that you are a well established institution and that their teachers will be of high quality, then say so overtly.

The vice-chancellor requests the pleasure

The same objective approach should be applied to the organization of events, which are another way in which you can influence people very directly. But beware of the trap of thinking that the event is an end in itself. It is very easy to convince yourself that bringing together important external contacts of the institution and senior members of the academic staff will be a very good way of influencing external opinion. It may be, but not if the food is awful, and the home team spends the whole evening talking to each other. You must have some defined objectives. What messages are you trying to communicate during the course of the evening? Who will speak to identified individuals, and how will you follow up afterwards? Providing other members of the HEI with a good dinner and leaving your guests wondering why on earth they have been invited will not advance your cause.

The problem with direct communications is that they are open to the charge of 'Well, they would say that, wouldn't they?' Your readers, listeners and guests will know that you have written those words and that you have controlled that message. That doesn't mean that it is not worth doing. Direct communications are effective on even the most critical and intellectually sharp minds. There is, however, added value if the praise about your organization comes not from yourself, but from a disinterested third party.

What the papers say

Third parties can be foes as well as friends, and this is where the media come in. Some people who have had little or no experience of dealing with the media find the prospect very worrying. Others, who have some experience, try to represent the process as mysterious and unfathomable. In fact, there are some very simple rules. One of these is that if you do something bad you will get bad publicity. Happily, if you do something that is very good, you may, if you are lucky, get some good publicity. But for most of the time HEIs are trying to convince editors and reporters that what they have done, which is probably only fairly good and only fairly interesting, is worth reporting to a wider readership.

The effect of the media is curious. At one level they are utterly ephemeral. One evening, after you have watched the television news, just try to anticipate the list of stories when the news reader says 'And here are the main points again.' Quite often something that was a major story will come as a complete surprise only 25 minutes after you have been told about it. On the other hand, the media create stereotypes, which can be indelible and last for many years after they have been conclusively proved to be entirely wrong. Working with the media is a rough and ready and largely unpredictable business. All you can hope for is to know something of the rules of the game and try not to lose through scoring an own goal.

One of the first things to remember is that the media will report matters on their own terms. They will decide what interests their readers or viewers, and no amount of insistence on your part that the setting up of this new laboratory or the signing of a link with a university in Japan is a major development in the history of the world will have any effect if you do not meet certain criteria. Topicality is often important. How does your news connect with a recent important event? Superlatives catch the eye: best, first, worst, biggest. Stories should almost always have some kind of human interest. Reporters have to be able to say why this is important for someone, whether it is the whole of humanity or the people who live in your town.

So when you are preparing information with a view to trying to interest a journalist, the key is to look at it from the reporter's or, better still, the reader's point of view. News editors are used to receiving mountains of news releases about topics that they know are of no interest to anyone other than the author, and it will not aid your credibility to be included in this category too many times. Be as rigorous as you can in looking at the story and asking what will interest someone whose every instinct is to disregard it, throw it away and forget all about it. If you cannot answer the question convincingly, then you probably have not got a good story. Try to decide whether it would interest you if it were about some other institution.

When you present the story, whether it is in a telephone conversation or in a written summary, keep your mind focused on the reader's interests. This will lead you to present the conclusions first. This is the very opposite of writing a report or an academic paper, but you will see that this is how news reports themselves are written. The first paragraph has to contain all the relevant information briefly and directly. In subsequent paragraphs you can support what you have said with an increasing amount of detail. But do not go on too long. You must be brief and to the point. There are two reasons for writing in this way. The first is simply that you need to capture the reader's interest and cannot rely on him or her following a reasoned argument to your conclusion. The second is that if your news release is to find its way more or less intact into a publication, sub-editors will always shorten an article from the bottom upwards. You will need to be sure that if everything but your first paragraph is cut and it appears as a brief item, perhaps in a diary column, the main essence of your story will have survived.

If you find it difficult to write this way, a good exercise is to put down exactly what you would say if you met the reporter and he or she said: 'OK, I've got five minutes, what's this all about?'

Working with the media can be a tricky business, especially on controversial items, but beware of trying to be too subtle about it. A simple rule is that you should not say something unless you are happy for it to be printed on the front page of every national newspaper. This means that you should avoid any sentences beginning 'Don't quote me on this but . . .' or 'I shouldn't really tell you this but . . .' unless this is just a way, and it is a good way, of drawing the reporter's attention to the point you are about to make.

Media relations is a craft in its own right and can be discussed at great length. But for most people, most of the time, the simple guidelines are: be realistic about what will interest the media; don't say anything unless you want it to appear; don't try to be clever; and, if it gets complicated, bring in a professional. This is particularly important during a media crisis. Then, *everything* said by *anyone* must be managed by the external relations office.

For old times' sake

Another external relations technique that has blossomed in recent years is the cultivation of alumni, although Oxbridge colleges have been holding their Gaudies, or alumni (old members) annual reunion dinners, for many decades, if not centuries. There is no doubt that this has been driven by an observation of fund-raising techniques commonly used in North America. The first maxim in good fund-raising practice is 'friend-raising before fund-raising', and whether or not it is your plan to ask alumni directly for financial contributions, they are a great potential benefit in terms of developing your reputation and acquiring influence in areas that are important to you.

In this sense, you are asking alumni to do you a favour. You are asking them to speak and act on your behalf in circumstances when they don't have to, and if you want someone to treat you as special the best way to go about it is to treat him or her as special. Alumni have to believe that their relationship with the institution does not end on graduation, that you continue to take an interest in them and that you regard them as permanent members of the institution. If they feel themselves to be part of the family, to belong to the institution, then they are much more likely to be sympathetic towards it and interested in its continued well-being.

How are you to bring this about? As so often in external relations, realism is important. You need to apply realism at a number of points. The first point is on the day of graduation. Although much is made of the feelings of euphoria felt by graduates and their families on that day of days, there is a marked decline in the days that follow. Not surprisingly, new graduates are interested in their careers, or lack of them, they are interested in starting a new phase of their life and, as the years go by, they become interested in career advancement, families, mortgages and all the rest. In those early years of their twenties and thirties only a small proportion of graduates will feel moved to maintain a strong and active commitment to their former HEI. What they almost certainly do feel, however, is a sense of commitment and friendship towards people who were students with them. Those strong ties formed at the institution, many of them in the first week of the first year in the corridor of a hall of residence, are destined to be life-long friendships, stronger than many other relationships formed in their lives. In a sense, they enter a perpetual state of alumni reunion. There will be keen ones, of course, like former officers of the students' union who have had a taste of institutional life and want to remain in overt and active contact, but for the vast majority of former students their interest in the institution will be superficial and probably perfunctory. Try not to lose them, try to get them to tell you changes of address and make sure that your database has a good record of their parental homes as a back-up way of reaching them. If you want them to tell you about their house moves and their career moves, then they have to believe that that is worthwhile. Alumni will only bother to do it if they think that effort brings some benefit. The minimum you should offer is some kind of annual communication, typically a magazine that they find sufficiently interesting and rewarding to want to send in a form to receive it. For the vast majority of alumni, not only the young ones but all of them, this is the only direct contact they are likely to want to have with the institution over the years.

Remember that a publication is one of the most powerful means of direct communication. You can use the magazine to give alumni messages and general guidance on the current role of the institution – what it is that you want them to think about it and how they can help it. All the market research, design and writing techniques you have brought to bear on a prospectus should be used in the production of the alumni publication. Ask the alumni themselves what they want to read about in a magazine. Top of the list will probably be news about other alumni – especially their contemporaries – and about their old departments. So try to be even-handed in the magazine, and achieve a balance of disciplines and people. Report on the famous names, but don't forget the individual who gave it all up to become a sheep farmer in the Outer Hebrides. The circle of close friends most people make at their HEI is not that great and the number with whom they want to maintain contact afterwards is even smaller. So your database of perhaps tens of thousands of alumni conceals a myriad of interlocking relationships, each network containing, at most, perhaps a few tens of people. The magazine can foster relationships by giving people news of reunions and groups of alumni in their regions, or attached to their former departments or halls of residence, sports club and so on.

This variety of groups gives another clue to the nature of alumni relations. We talk about the institution and its alumni and there is a sense in which you should assert the HEI's ownership of alumni. They are not the property of a single department, because, for example, a graduate of your business school may be more useful to your medical school if he or she has become a director in a pharmaceuticals company. But it is also important to remember that the loyalties of the individual are almost never to the institution itself. They will probably feel the strongest links with the smallest units to which they can relate. In academic terms, this will be the department before the faculty, and the faculty before the institution. In social terms it might be their house-mates or the people along the corridor in the hall of residence. It is remembering those connections and those activities that will bring the warmest glow to your alumni, rather than a lofty assertion that the HEI is proudly fulfilling its research mission. So it is important that you work closely with academic colleagues and support their activities.

Alumni activities are designed to sustain this loyalty and friendship and to encourage action on the institutions's behalf. You cannot achieve an intense supportive relationship with all your alumni, and it will be important to identify the groups that are most important to you. They might include, for example, teachers in secondary schools, captains of industry or local politicians. You can use all the well established alumni activities, ranging from selling souvenirs to arranging reunions. But it is well to remember the words of the late Roland Hurst, when he was information officer at the University of Kent, that 'A reunion is a gathering of people who have never met each other before.'

A sense of identity

Much of what we have written in this chapter has been about an HEI's corporate identity policy. Yet we have managed to discuss it without using the word 'logo' once. In some HEIs, the words 'corporate identity' have ousted those long-running favourites 'car parking' as the words most likely to arouse strong feelings among members. They are equated with a bureaucratic infringement of that most important of academic freedoms, the right to design one's own letter paper.

An effective corporate identity policy is essential to effective external relations activities, but matters of graphic design, typography and logos are only the visual expression of what should be a much more fundamental policy. That policy is the one we have been discussing throughout this chapter: the expression of a clear and unambiguous statement about the institution. If that message is to be coherent and readily understood in all contexts, then its expression too should be carefully managed. This is why the visual identity is so important. Some people will say that it does not matter what your logo is or what your typeface is as long as they are consistent. To a certain degree that is true, because it will at least enable you to achieve the minimum objectives of a visual identity policy: the activities of the various parts of the institution will be seen to benefit from and to contribute to the reputation of the whole institution, and vice versa.

You can, though, expect much more than that. The proper design of a logo, the selection of a typeface and the tone of a design can themselves help to state your messages. One design will appear to be classic, elegant, long-lasting, perhaps even aloof. Another will be modern, lively, friendly and approachable. Words such as these will appear in the subtext to your mission, if not in the formal expression of it. The visual identity is just one of the ways in which the corporate identity is expressed. The others will include the way in which you describe your institution in your various publications, the photographs you choose to illustrate activities, the types of success stories you offer to the media and even the way in which you organize formal and informal occasions. All these will be saying something about your institution and will be leaving an impression on your audiences.

The difference with the visual identity is that it impinges on so many members of the HEI. They may not care too much how you write the opening paragraphs of the prospectus, but they will care very much if you dictate how their letters are to appear, how their departmental brochures are to be written and the colour of the new departmental van.

If any external relations professional can engender widespread support for a corporate identity policy, particularly the visual identity expression of it, then he or she will have achieved a great deal. Everything else will flow from this commitment, and all your activities will be seen in that context and make sense both to the members of the institution and to the outside world whose views you are trying to influence.

A new corporate identity policy cannot be introduced without the wholehearted and sustained support of the vice-chancellor and other senior managers. If there are political or organizational tensions within the institution, the introduction of a visual identity policy will certainly expose them. The policy may be used as a safe battleground for arguments about who runs the institution: 'If I am spending my money why can't I decide how it should be spent?', 'The customers of this department have a special relationship with us, which is quite distinct from the relationship with the HEI as a whole.' The visual identity policy may be seen as a soft target that members of the institution can attack with relative impunity, weakening the authority of the higher management without, in their view, losing anything themselves. This is deep political water, and you should enter it with great care. A corporate identity policy is not an optional add-on that the professional can introduce without wholehearted institutional support, because it is about the very identity and essence of the institution itself. This may sound melodramatic, but it is such a fundamental part of achieving a good reputation for your university that if you cannot embark upon it in this unequivocal way, then it would be a better idea not to attempt it at all. You may have to content yourself with a more modest plan of action, working away at different projects and activities aiming to achieve high quality, but without expecting thoroughgoing consistency through them all.

Identity begins at home

These political issues are a good reminder that internal communications are an essential part of external relations. If members of staff are ill-informed about the institution's strategies, you cannot expect them to present your messages clearly. If each department is working to a local set of priorities, which do not derive from the institution's, you will never convince anyone that you are well organized and integrated. In implementing an internal communications policy, you will need the confidence of many levels of management and the cooperation of very many colleagues. Use all the techniques you would apply to an external audience. Again, a publication is likely to be your main means of communication: make your newsletter interesting and not merely safe, but do not kid yourself that you are not an agent of the bosses.

Is it working?

However ambitious your plans and activities, you need to measure how effective they have been. This is not a measure of output. Publication does not equal communication. Column inches are not the same as good publicity, and holding a dinner party does not always mean you are making friends. What you are trying to achieve is a change in attitudes, and the only way you can measure that is to check the opinions of your key audiences over a period of time. You started by using research to find out what the current attitudes to your institution were. This research should be conducted repeatedly, measuring the effect of particular individual activities and the general reputation of the institution against your defined objectives and in the context of the money you have had to spend. Even though you should operate as a self-confident professional, you should not be drawn into regarding the achievement of high standards in your public relations activities as your main goal. The purpose is to create a climate of opinion in which the principal teaching and research activities of the university can flourish. Which is where we came in. (Editors' note: for further reading see Keen and Greenall, *Public Relations Management* and Keen and Warner, *Visual and Corporate Identity*, plus related volumes, Keen and Higgins, *Young People's Knowledge of Higher Education*, Robert and Higgins, *Higher Education: The Student Experience*, and Haselgrove, *The Student Experience*.)

14

Academic Support Services

Colin Harrison

Editors' introduction

In this chapter, which covers the key academic support services of learning methods, libraries, media services and computer services, the author has indirectly raised what the editors believe to be potentially one of the most important issues in the future of HE management. The author argues strongly for the integration, merger or convergence of the portfolio of academic support services, against the traditional model of separate and independent services. Nevertheless, he urges that a head of the combined services should come from one of the areas involved; that is, he or she would be 'someone having high levels of knowledge in at least one of the subject areas, who can develop detailed understanding of the other areas and has good managerial and leadership qualities'. However, the person concerned should not remain as head of the service from which he or she comes, as this 'can lead to distrust and jealousy within the merged services – it is better to make a clean break'. At this point in the history of HE management, the editors merely question why the first quality required by the author is essential and why the second is not necessary *and* sufficient.

Introduction

The role, purpose and place of the academic support services are under debate at all times within higher education. This is inevitable, since collectively they are one of the largest spenders of 'non-staff' monies. In recent years, given the changes to the funding of HEIs and the positive steps being taken to diversify learning styles, they have been under even greater scrutiny than ever before. These services are moving into more positive and direct learning development and support roles for both students and staff. In most HEIs, and more particularly in the statutory universities, changes in learning styles, increased staff : student ratios and pressures on space have all come together to provide an opportunity for the academic support services to take a leading role in the change process alongside their teaching colleagues.

This has been expressed forcefully by John Cowan when he says,

> Too long has the phrase 'teaching and learning' been used glibly, when the speakers or writers meant merely 'teaching' – and instruction at that. Our challenge is to be involved effectively with all aspects of the teaching and learning relationship, and to see teaching – dare I suggest it – as the purposeful creation of situations from which motivated learners should not be able to escape without significantly learning or developing as a result of our efforts. That definition covers instruction – aye *and* facilitation and student support in all forms and places, *including libraries and information centres.*
>
> (Cowan, 1994: 16)

The achievement of this requires a firm management steer that affects not only the departments concerned directly but also, and equally importantly, the whole of the HEI.

So what constitutes the academic support services? This is a moving target, and there is no genuine consensus across the sector. However, some elements are common: the library services and the computer services will feature in every list, while learning methods and media (teaching aids, graphic design, printing, etc.) will feature in more than a few. On a small number of lists will be telephone services, wide-area networks as well as local-area networks, staff development services; the list could go on. A good definition would be 'those services that work directly into the learning process through immediate contact with the students (library and computer staff) or contact with the students via the teachers (media and learning methods staff).' The examples are not, like the services within a particular HEI, fixed; for example, it is quite common for a media service to 'teach' students directly when working with them on the creation of assessment packages that are media based.

Aims and objectives

The role and purpose, and the way they deliver the broader strategy of the HEI, can be discovered by reflecting upon a specimen set of 'aims and objectives' for these services. The ones that are set out below are not universal examples, and many HEIs will have very different sets, but they provide a good case study. It is also possible to spot the opportunities for 'convergence' that are apparent within them. This issue will be addressed later, since it forms a major management issue at present.

Learning methods

The core purpose is to provide a staff and educational development service for the HEI itself and for other post-school institutions in association. The main aims are to provide or undertake:

1. A series of award-bearing courses for teachers and trainers in the post-compulsory education (PCE) sector, such as:
   - the certificate in education (PCE), for HE and FE teachers;
   - the postgraduate certificate in education (PGCE), for graduate teachers in HE and FE;
   - BA(Ed)(PCE), for FE teachers wishing to gain a first degree;
   - MA (teaching and learning in HE and FE), for FE and HE teachers wishing to reflect on the practice of teaching.
2. Staff development short courses and workshops both in-house and for external clients, such as:
   - an induction course for new HEI staff;
   - an annual staff development workshop programme.
3. An educational development consultancy service:
   - teaching and learning development;
   - course design and evaluation;
   - staff appraisal and departmental/institutional review.
4. Initial management training for the post-compulsory education sector:
   - short courses for the HEI's staff in course leadership and other management skills;
   - short courses and workshops for public and private clients on specific management issues, such as appraisal or training.
5. Research projects in educational development:
   - externally funded projects on developments in teaching and learning;
   - small-scale research in organizational and managerial change;
   - international developments in post-compulsory education and training.

Operating philosophy

The operating philosophy may be summarized as:

1. A strong belief in the value of partnership between the department and its clients and their sponsors in:
   - analysing needs for training and development;
   - designing appropriate programmes of education and training;
   - implementing the programmes;
   - evaluating the worth and effectiveness of all short courses, workshops, conferences and training programmes provided by the centre.
2. An active student- or client-centred approach to learning and teaching.
3. A commitment to improving the quality of all training and educational programmes provided by the centre.

4. A strong interest in educational development and research.
5. An intention to view staff and educational development within regional, national and international perspectives.
6. A willingness to forge links with other centres and departments interested in educational development.

Library

The strategic aims are:

1. To establish a learning environment that is stimulating, motivating and academically and culturally enriching.
2. To create an outward-looking, user-centred range of services and to liaise with faculties and their sub-structures, staff, students and management to maintain a close understanding of their needs.
3. To promote the use of libraries as a learning and research tool.
4. To identify and provide access to all forms of information and literature for staff and students of the university.
5. To identify the resources required to support the above within a framework of cost-effectiveness and accessibility.

The objectives are:

1. To establish a learning environment that is stimulating, motivating and academically and culturally enriching by:
   - fostering a user-centred approach to service delivery;
   - reflecting the changing pattern of learning and teaching in the breadth and depth of the collection;
   - providing a mixed environment that attracts students from all disciplines and is sympathetic to a range of study modes;
   - making the service as efficient and economical of user time as possible.
2. To create an outward-looking, user-centred range of services and to liaise with faculties and their sub-structures, staff, students and management to maintain a close understanding of their needs by:
   - seeking to appoint and develop high-calibre, highly motivated staff, who are up to date with changing educational methods, information sources and the associated body of professional knowledge;
   - appointing named staff to liaise with and provide 'total' care to individual faculties;
   - membership of and participation in the work of academic, faculty, course boards and other appropriate committees;
   - developing and monitoring an agreed set of performance indicators.
3. To promote the use of libraries as a learning and research tool by:
   - teaching information retrieval and handling skills on all courses across all sites;
   - developing workshops in conjunction with other parts of the learning

support services, to allow staff to see and use new materials and technologies that may help in their teaching and research;
- promoting services and access to materials by appropriate courses, publications and guides;
- undertaking such research, consultancy services and income generation as appropriate and consistent with providing a full range of services to users.

4. To identify and provide access to all forms of information and literature for staff and students of the HEI by:
   - establishing effective communication with all users, present and potential;
   - creating appropriate collections to meet the needs of all users;
   - seeking to develop services on all sites to a comparable standard, indicated by agreed performance indicators.

5. To identify the resources required to support the above within the framework of cost-effectiveness and accessibility by:
   - feeding information from annual user surveys, reports from standards committee and other formal and informal sources into the total planning process;
   - developing and monitoring performance indicators and quality control;
   - expressing user needs and demands to the management and deans, so that they are fully aware of user requirements;
   - developing computerized and other systems to underpin service delivery and to monitor service performance.

Media services

The central purpose is to provide a complete audio-visual media and reprographics service for the HEI. The principal functions are:

1. To support teaching and learning through the provision of audio-visual materials and equipment.
2. To produce teaching and learning materials in collaboration with teaching staff.
3. To run the HEI's printing and reprographics services.
4. To provide a graphic design service for the production of learning materials, publication and inward and outward publicity.
5. To collaborate with learning methods in offering appropriate in-service training in the use of audio-visual resources, and with the library in supplying learning materials, particularly stored on video and photographic media, to staff and students.
6. To teach a wide range of media skills on award-bearing and other courses.
7. To engage in income-generating activity.
8. To further the application and development of educational media through secondment of academic staff from the faculties to the unit.

Computer services

The objectives of the services are:

1. Central computer services. To manage and develop a reliable central computer service for the HEI, which takes account of the time-critical nature of some applications, and to ensure that adequate levels of personnel support are provided.
2. Networks. (a) To manage and develop the university's electronic data communication networks in cooperation with such other internal and external agencies as may from time to time be appointed, and to facilitate ease of access to them. (b) To provide guidelines for all aspects of networking and communications within the HEI and to oversee their implementation.
3. Evaluation and standardization. (a) To evaluate hardware and software and to determine standards with a view to advising and assisting staff and students of the HEI on their information technology needs, requirements and problems, on a proactive as well as a reactive basis. (b) To advise and assist staff and students of the HEI on problems as they arise.
4. Procurement support. (a) To offer its services as advisor to staff and students, when appropriate, in the procurement of appropriate goods and services. (b) To assist throughout the HEI where requested in support of faculty computer facilities.
5. Staff development. (a) To encourage and facilitate the engagement of the staff of the unit in research activities, consultancy and participation in external professional activities, in accordance with such guidelines as may be laid down from time to time. (b) To maintain an adequate level of staff awareness by encouraging staff to develop their own professional knowledge through approved visits to formal training courses, conferences and shows.
6. Training and learning. (a) To provide a range of staff development courses with the objective of improving the general standard of individual computer competence among the staff of the HEI. (b) To promote and support the application of information technology in the teaching and learning situation through the provision of documentation, resources and open access areas.
7. Academic support. (a) To provide teaching support for faculties as requested from time to time, subject to the availability of staff and materials. (b) To work closely and sympathetically with boards of study and other committees that may be appointed from time to time within the HEI and to which staff of the division are appointed or co-opted.
8. External activity. To generate income for the HEI, either through one of the methods outlined in item 5 above, or through the provision of fee-paying short courses for members of the public.
9. General. (a) To provide as much as possible of the above within the budgetary constraints laid down by the institution's senior management.

(b) To review and update the above objectives in the light of current needs, practices and experience.

The first thing to note is that each of these departments or units has created its own aims to reflect the realities of its own professional skills and abilities, but in each case they are firmly founded upon delivering the wider HEI strategy. This is an essential in the management of any service, but particularly in that of the academic support services. What is delivered from each provider must underpin and support the teaching faculties and provide 'added value' for the students.

Integration or separation?

A first requisite for the management of groups of staff involved in these services is the recognition of their individual professional abilities, not regarding all academic support services as being made 'from one cloth'. Their backgrounds and professional qualifications give them specialist positions, and this aspect is neglected at the cost of good leadership and management. They add as much variety to the life of the HEI as does any range of subject areas.

In the same way that the teaching areas need to be organized and led, so do the academic support services. It has not been uncommon for the two larger departments (libraries and computer services) to report directly to the vice-chancellor. In recent years a different pattern has become more common and this has developed from a recognition that while the services retain their individuality there are a number of common factors acting as change agents upon them all.

These agents come from the outside world, and are not unique to the world of academia. The advent of electronic information sources, and the network that has developed to link them, commonly called the 'information superhighway', the need for students, and staff, to have integrated information access for both research and teaching development, and the impact of computer-based systems and software upon graphic design, libraries and computer services have all hit the academic support services in much the same way. This has created a position where either each service employs specialist staff to handle the technology of change, risking a variety of expensive solutions between each department, or some common development pathway is managed.

A variety of names have been used as labels for the technology-driven convergence. They range from the simple 'converged' services through 'integrated' services to 'merged' services. The effects have been widely different across the sector. In some instances, merger has been seen as a total management integration of all staff. Often this has been based upon the precept that all can be multi-skilled and become interchangeable across the services. At the other end of the spectrum, the convergence has been recognized by the appointment of one of the heads of the services to be the overall manager of the totality, but retaining the role of individual departments. The promoted person has usually been selected from the library or computer services fields and there is no clear pattern as to a particular preference.

In 1986, Carnegie Mellon University in the USA was early into this convergence pattern, and took the decision to merge its libraries with the central computing group into a single division of the university. Arms (1988: 161) writes of this convergence:

> The main reasons for bringing libraries and computers into the same organisation were long-term reasons, a belief that both worlds are changing and that in future the areas of overlap will increase. This belief appears to be working out in practice. The Academic Services Division has been able to contribute a university perspective in numerous areas of rapid change. The existence of a single organisation has, undoubtedly, helped in engendering an easy flow of ideas. Here are some examples. Planning, the division has developed a single combined planning process whereby the departments work together on an outline five-year plan . . . numerous joint projects have come out of this interaction.
>
> The Oakland Consortium, the three major libraries in the Oakland neighbourhood of Pittsburgh have formed a consortium to share resources . . . The Academic Services Division has been able to contribute expertise and resources in non-library areas such as computing and communications.

In 1989, my own college took a similar step, but one that was based upon experience gained from convergence of the services within one of the two colleges that merged to form the then Anglia Polytechnic. Later, as university status was granted, the services were given the rank of faculty, alongside the four 'teaching' faculties of the university. Anglia Polytechnic University (1991) described its convergence as follows:

> The Faculty was created to bring together the chief elements in the University's support for changing and improving the learning and teaching environment.
>
> Anglia Polytechnic University's Strategic Plan states the University's overall mission as developing 'a University of national standing which places emphasis on excellence in teaching, applied research and consultancy relevant primarily to the economic, social and cultural requirements of East Anglia'. The Faculty has therefore adopted four broad aims in the planning and delivery of its services in support of the University's mission statement.
>
> 1. Excellent learning and research facilities – especially through its libraries, media production and computer services divisions.
> 2. Excellent teaching support facilities – through its support and design of the teaching environment, its involvement in course design and

assessment, the production of teaching materials (by all its divisions) and its knowledge of the applications of modern teaching equipment.
3. Excellent production facilities – through its media production division and the associated educational technologists and the development of computer based teaching and learning packages through its computer services.
4. Excellent staff and educational development services – from its Centre for Educational Development for individual teachers and departments within the University and the associated colleges. The staff of all divisions are involved in a planned programme of development workshops covering all aspects of the Faculty's provision.

The structure of the divisions of the Faculty and the management integration have been designed to focus outward to user needs and demands as well as to play a leading role in changing the learning/teaching environment of the University.

Its staff attend all major course development meetings and represent the whole Faculty in so doing. From this information the Faculty can put together short life working parties to respond quickly to particular demands or needs. This same principle is adopted in its general service to the University community – the University will seek a solution by bringing together its full range of expertise.

This is slightly different from the first example at Carnegie Mellon, in that at Anglia the wider view was taken, that the role of these departments in the whole field of changing and improving the learning experience was directed at students as well as the organization. The commonality of their services allows for some joint representation across the wider university. This has been called 'one stop shopping'. A single person can represent all the services in an information-gathering and communication setting and then ensure that specialized colleagues are sent to deliver the exact response that is required. Where the services can be physically brought together in a single building, the 'one stop shopping' concept can be extended to the delivery of services – they all appear as a single offering to the user.

What does all this mean for the structure and management of these areas? Pack and Pack (1988: 140) wrote interestingly on this issue and, in part, said that their immediate reflections upon taking such a job were

an immediate awareness of the 'difference' on accepting the post without fully appreciating what these differences were. It is easy to be wise in retrospect but those were pioneering days and one learnt by experience, often by one's mistakes!
The need to have a strategy for dealing with the fact that you were responsible for areas of college activity where you have staff with different qualifications and experience.

The need to deal with the various levels of academic management in the college.

The ability to delegate and . . . not to hold on to the job you were doing as well as tackling the new one.

How are these decisions reached and on what basis? Looking across the sector, it seems to me that most of the appointments have been made, at least initially, on an internal basis from among the existing heads. The selection would seem to be based upon the concept, long around in management terms, of the best person to be converted into an hybrid manager.

Literature is readily available on a definition of what constitutes such a person, but in the terms of higher education and academic support services it would appear that a helpful description would be: someone having high levels of knowledge in at least one of the subject areas, who can develop detailed understanding of the other areas and has good managerial and leadership qualities, so as to lead their conjoint development and represent them in a positive fashion within the HEI. This is different in nature from having the heads report to the same senior manager. It gives them direct professional subject as well as managerial leadership. An essential ingredient in this structure is for the new manager to be a senior manager of the HEI.

As in industry generally, the role of the hybrid manager is to present the case and services of those whom he or she manages and to represent to the services the needs of the users more widely. It is often made easier, since the public face of the hybrid manager is not directly tied to the promotion of one particular service, and he or she can offer solutions based upon a more rounded picture than, perhaps, a single head could have done. We often hear the statement 'Well, they would say that . . .', usually when librarians or computer people extol their own area of operation. The hybrid can blend the skills and knowledge and present a less technically complicated case, upon which decisions can be made. The role almost has the position of 'universal translator' built into it; that is, taking the jargon of specialist staff and re-presenting the core concepts to non-specialists who have to take the decisions.

Pack and Pack (1988) indicated that there is a danger of such a person either not being allowed, or not being willing, to step aside from his or her personal specialism, and where this happens the full benefit outlined above is weakened. It is not uncommon for promoted heads to retain the post of 'head' of the service from which they came. This can lead to distrust and jealousy within the merged services – it is better to make a clean break as indicated by Pack and Pack.

In June 1995, Allan Foster at Keele University undertook a survey, via the closed conference group 'lis-merge-com', of how these mergers or convergencies had settled down. In his summary of the replies he noted (at present only available on e-mail):

You will observe that most of the messages are quite positive. The one consistent theme is the difference of cultures between computer people and librarians, and it would appear that it is the library culture that is most resistant to integration into a common framework – which genuinely surprised me.

Foster's findings reflect the impression gained at conferences over the past few years. In the main, convergence has worked well and provided a plus for the users of services. The 'two cultures' also come as no surprise, and it is an important aspect of the role of the hybrid manager to attend to this division.

Performance indicators and service level agreements

In the management of these services it is usual to develop and use both performance indicators and what have been called service level agreements, to ensure that the service delivers at least an approximation of that requested by users.

The two approaches are different, in that performance indicators (see HEFCE, 1995b, for a good example) are almost always a retrospective of the delivered service, and the service level agreement predicts the services to be provided for the resources allocated. These services are different from the generality of the learning support offered by an HEI, since they are very much an unrestricted and open door provision. This makes the staffing levels, support areas, etc. difficult to match closely with user demand. A good example of this is the comparison with how many teaching departments are staffed. It is quite common for a staff : student ratio to be set for a subject area. It may vary from subject to subject, with technological subjects having lower ratios than, say, humanities. This, to some extent, protects the teaching staff and is a measure of their workload. In the academic support services no such load setting is possible. The computer centre has a maximum number of machines, but even when they are all in use the students still come in and demand staff time. Fault call-outs cannot be stopped once an agreed number have been received. The libraries cannot shut when they have issued their target number of items for the day! So pressures are in a very real sense uncontrolled by the university or the local management. Queues get longer, students stand behind each other waiting for the use of a computer, printing services take longer to deliver copies; the list goes on and on. In the event of sickness or sudden meetings, it is not uncommon for classes to be cancelled at short notice and the load transferred to the learning support services – almost always without warning. These are real pressures for the staff involved and for their managers.

Because of these facts, the management of such services requires a number of approaches to ensure that some quality is delivered. Decision-making powers need to be devolved to a very local level, with the local manager having the ability to call upon a pool of staff to deal with these unpredictable pressures. Managers need to monitor service demand overtime so that staff lists can be planed to have 'best guess' staffing levels available to meet expected demands. All this has to be set against the long opening hours of the services and the need for the staff to have reasonable conditions of service. In many HEIs it is common to have so-called 'core' hours of provision, say 08:30 to 18:00 hours. During this time, professional support, expert systems people, graphic designers, technicians, etc. are on duty and available to help users. Outside these hours, a lower level of service is often provided, with student helpers, part-time staff and a few full-time staff keeping the service running. This meets some requirements, such as keeping staff costs down while keeping opening hours up as high as possible, but it fails to provide a stable quality of service across all opening hours. In particular, part-time students often get a poorer service since they often use services in the evenings and at weekends and so may never get the full 'core' provision. This must be a matter of concern for quality assurance audits.

Quality and final thoughts

In a recent article (Harrison 1994: 212), I outlined some issues relating to the management of quality in academic support services and, in part, said:

Four factors need to be in place at the centre if each part of the organisation is to deliver quality:

1.1 focus on human resources and staff development;
1.2 a review process for the delivery of an information service;
1.3 a feedback system;
1.4 an integrating, broad, view of reviewing service delivery and information systems, with the assistance of a quality development specialist.

The process of developing and reviewing standards of quality can be presented graphically as in Figure 14.1.

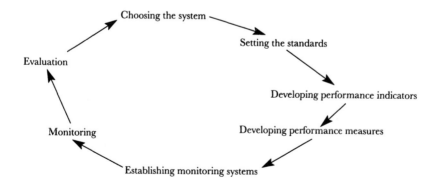

Figure 14.1 Developing and reviewing standards of quality

Elements involved in the choice of system could include:

1. Improving user experience
   - development of charters, codes of practice;
   - statements of user entitlement;
   - feedback from users on the service;
   - setting up complaints procedure.
2. Accountability to users and others
   - reliable data for funders;
   - defined target groups;
   - services delivered and outcomes defined;
   - demonstration of cost-effectiveness.
3. Improved market share
   - descriptions of service quality levels;
   - identification of new services;
   - prioritization of resources.

Quality can be said to come from four elements. First, there is the description of the process that provides the basis for all that follows.

Second, there is the management structure for both the service and the way the service is allowed to interface with the wider institution. Is the structure appropriate to deliver the agreed objectives or to assess what those objectives should be?

Third, there is the quality of staff and materials. Good quality staff can often cover for less than generous financial allocations for materials. However, examples of stock sitting on the shelves for over a year without being used could be considered as an indicator that quality selection was not being employed. This may not be the fault of the service department, but might indicate lack of understanding between teaching departments and service departments. (A figure of 20 per cent of library stock falling into the not used within 12 months of purchase category was the last research I saw from academic libraries, but that was several years ago.)

Fourth, there is the resource allocation that allows the service departments to deliver good quality. It must be closely tuned to the needs of students and staff, so that reasonable quantities of materials can be supplied. Often we can provoke expectations and then not meet them, this gives the users the feeling that quality is missing.

We must recognize that some aspects of quality are very hard to measure reliably, and that quality means different things to different people. There will always be a tension between being client-centred and the pressures applied from the funders of the service. The whole cycle will follow the survey, evaluate, review and change model used for the quality assurance of all university activities.

These, to me, represent the key factors that all who manage academic support services must return to on a regular basis. They provide the *raison d'être* of our work and we neglect them at a cost to our students.

15

Managing Student Learning

Diana Eastcott and Bob Farmer

Editors' introduction

This book is primarily intended for non-academic managers: those members of HEI staff who until very recently would have commonly been called 'administrators'. The editors, therefore, felt it to be very important that the last chapter should remind us all that one major element of the core business of an HEI is effective student learning. It is so easy for managers to become removed from students, but their success is one key indicator of our own.

In the context of this book, it is interesting (and gratifying) to note that the authors have chosen to use 'Managing student learning' as their chapter title: 'managing' is indeed 'bringing about' in the context of facilitating and of configuring scarce resources so as to enable people to give of their best and to achieve their best (whether staff or students).

Introduction

This chapter examines some of the issues that students and staff in HE are facing in the mid-1990s from the perspective of teaching and learning. Our starting point is that promoting effective student learning is a major element of the core business of HE.

We believe that 'managing student learning' is an appropriate title for the chapter, as it indicates the involvement of all staff working in HE in the process of helping students to learn. We use the term 'management' particularly in the sense of 'to bring about'.

Many of the initiatives in teaching and learning in HE over the past decade have emphasized interdependence and interdisciplinarity: interdependence in the sense of students working together in teams and lecturers working with employers; interdisciplinarity implying the blurring of boundaries between disciplines and between professional groups. For example, a major initiative in the Faculty of the Built Environment at the University of Central England in Birmingham is based on architecture students, construction and surveying students, and those from all disciplines in the built environment working together from the outset of their degree to gain deeper understanding of the range of professional groups in their field (see Rance, 1995).

In the same way that these professional groups are working together on courses, staff in HE need to explore more fully how they can best work towards interdependence and interdisciplinarity themselves in order to manage student learning effectively. The *Investing in People* report (Fender, 1987) emphasized the need for a constructive environment in which all staff work together. These ideas are developed further in *Promoting People* (Fender, 1993), in which the significance of collaborative performance in teams is stressed. The reports use the experience and practice of other large organizations from the public and private sectors and also build on the concepts of total quality management (TQM), and in particular the team working aspects of this approach. The concept that emerges from these reports and is potentially exciting for staff is that of HEIs becoming 'learning organizations'. The core business is learning, both 'student' learning and 'staff' learning – the term 'staff' to include management, lecturers, librarians, outside advisors and employers. The 'learning company' concept has been extensively researched in the private sector (see Pedler *et al*, 1991). There is an irony here for HE: 'learning', isn't that what *we* are all about? (See also Duke, 1991 and Schuller, 1991 and 1995.)

The structure of this chapter is as follow. The first section is on contextual issues, which include UK government policy and changing circumstances at work and in society. It will provide an outline focus for the chapter and, therefore, does not explore these issues in depth. The second section looks at student-centred approaches and student choice as a basis for exploring ways of supporting student learning. This is followed by a section on research into improving student learning, linked to the professionalization of teaching in HE, which is discussed in the next section. We conclude by relating back to our introductory section and to the importance of the concept of the learning community and the crucial tasks of managers in supporting student learning.

Some contextual issues

In referring to HEIs in the 1990s, we are referring to a variety of establishments and a wide range of staff and students. The concept of studying in HE is now diversified, as it includes a variety of types of activities and study patterns and a wide range of qualifications as the outcome. HE in the UK is moving towards a mass system, providing access opportunities through links with local colleges and the community and encouraging returning to learning. According to a recent article by Richard Hoggart, a third of all school leavers now go on to HE, compared with about 5 per cent only a few decades ago (Hoggart, 1995). The 'learner' in HE is now a member of an increasingly heterogeneous group, often with a customer orientation.

It is not the purpose of this chapter to explore the background to the recent changes in higher education in any depth (Editors' note: see Scott, 1995b and Schuller, 1995). However, we will develop two themes briefly, with a particular emphasis on the implications for teaching and learning.

UK government policy and larger classes

In the 1970s and 1980s, both Labour and Conservative governments had a policy of expansion in HE at lower unit costs. Conservative governments since 1979 have changed the funding mechanisms, so that institutions have often enrolled more students without increasing the number of staff. The increase in staff : student ratios and mergers of some institutions have put pressure on both staff and students. In North America and parts of Europe, large classes are the norm for much undergraduate work. Gibbs and Jenkins (1992) argue that radical changes in teaching and assessment methods are necessary if we are to maintain quality in learning in HE. With the help of funding from the Polytechnics and Colleges Funding Council, a team of consultants working with Professor Graham Gibbs at the Oxford Centre for Staff Development developed a range of materials on teaching large classes and ran workshops at HEIs throughout the UK. Eighty-eight workshops were delivered between April 1992 and January 1993. The significance of these workshops was two-fold. Not only did they support lecturers facing increased student numbers and larger classes, they also contributed to putting the process of teaching and learning more firmly on the agenda for many institutions. The task of teaching became a topic for discussion – the importance of helping students to learn in a particular discipline was considered along with the subject matter being taught.

Changing circumstances at work and in society

It is unlikely that the students of today will do the same job for the rest of their working lives – the emphasis is on developing life-long learning competence, the ability to be flexible, to train and retrain, to learn how to learn, to work with other people and learn from experience. Learning is not something that ends after a three-year degree. The Department of Employment initiative Enterprise in Higher Education and the Higher Education for Capability initiative of the Royal Society of Arts have stimulated developments in student autonomy in learning and acquiring the skills and competences valued by employers. The relationship between teaching and learning and the employer or professional body is now a much closer one; likewise the relationship between theory and practice in the curriculum. Both the Enterprise in Higher Education and Higher Education for Capability initiatives have provided incentives and a context to raise the profile of student learning in our HEIs. These initiatives have also contributed to additions to the vocabulary of student learning: 'Learning to learn, transferable skills, problem solving skills, skills in handling information technology and learning from experience now take their place in the vocabulary of higher education' (Barnett, 1992: 9).

Cooperation and social interaction in negotiating understanding and meaning are now of more significance in the process of learning. This represents a shift from the lecturer dispensing knowledge and other students providing competition but being marginal in the process of learning. Another important implication of the Enterprise in Higher Education and the Higher Education for Capability movements is that they have tended to encourage a shift from compartmentalized, discipline-based approaches to interdisciplinary, cross-curricular initiatives where it is recognized that those working in different disciplines can learn from each other.

Student-centred approaches and student choice

There are both educational and logistical reasons for the movements towards more independent learning for students in HE. The educational reasons are not unique to teaching and learning in the 1990s. Ramsden (1992: 19) quotes from an essay first published in 1929, in which the main theme is that 'the proper function of a University is the imaginative acquisition of knowledge' (Whitehead, 1929).

Ramsden goes on to quote from the Hale report (Hale, 1964), which asserted that 'an implication of higher education is to encourage students to think for themselves.' The so-called 'current' movement towards a more student-centred view of higher education has long been foreshadowed by statements such as these. 'The aim of teaching is simple: it is to make student learning possible' (Ramsden, 1992: 5).

Student choice

Large complex courses, including modular courses, have in part been a response to the wider needs of students entering HE, and aim to provide links with outside groups so that there is a more flexible response to need. The standardized units that a modular course provides are designed to be interchangeable between faculties of an institution and between institutions. This trend towards more student choice also points up different ways of organizing knowledge, where interdisciplinarity and multi-disciplinarity are on the increase. It has the consequence of raising the profile of the educational processes necessary to enable students to make these connections.

Resource-based learning

Conventional lecturing, seminars and tutorials have been put under a lot of pressure as teaching methods as student numbers in HE in the UK have expanded. One response to this pressure is resource-based learning (RBL). There has been considerable investment in the production of resources such as open and distance learning materials, and also the production of computer courseware through teaching and learning technology projects. Many of these materials have remained on the bookshelves or in the filing cabinets of lecturers, and have not contributed to students learning more effectively under increasing pressure of numbers.

The Course Design for Resource Based Learning Project, funded by the HEFCE through the Effective Teaching and Assessment Programme (ETAP) (Gibbs *et al.*, 1994), focused on the course design issues that are crucial in making RBL work. These course design issues include generating appropriate assessment and learning activities, using class contact time differently, developing staff's and students' independent learning skills and providing social glue – a framework in which students and staff can interact with one another. The project focused on identifying best practice in nine subject areas in order to identify course designs that used new learning resources effectively. The focus was on students learning on campus more independently than on conventional courses through the use of print-based learning materials.

The significant points to emerge that are relevant to this chapter are the importance of coordination and teamwork for RBL to be successful. The course team, which includes both teaching staff and managers, can be a strange notion where teaching has been characteristically individualistic, but would not be so unusual in Open University experience. However, the cooperation and blurring of boundaries that this approach suggests are essential in order to maintain the quality of student learning. All staff, including lecturers, library staff and managers, need to understand what RBL is and to develop new roles in this context.

Supporting students

On large courses in particular the tasks involved in coordinating the students and their assessed work are very demanding. The job of teaching in this context involves more than knowing the subject, giving the students the information in a stimulating way and assessing their work. Now it often involves the management of large groups of heterogeneous students on a range of courses. Studies of modular courses have shown how important these management issues are: dealing with change of modules, arrangements for seminar groups, distributing lecture materials, providing coordination and a sense of focus for students. Again, lecturers and administrators working in teams seems to be the effective way forward to support student learning.

Two further examples of this approach are as follows. Some large courses appoint one course administrator per year of the course and that administrator stays with a cohort of students throughout their entire course. Second, a student resource Centre for Business Students at the University of Auckland is described in the publication *Supporting More Students* as follows:

> The University of Auckland School of Commerce, Economics and Business and the Graduate School of Business has set up a student resource centre to deal with the enormous administrative burden associated with their 3000 students. It includes a reception area with an office and 'shop'. All coursework assignments are handed in and handed back here with an ID and receipt system. There are pigeon-holes for courses and an assignment distribution system for markers. All information about course choice and planning, timetabling, location of classes and so on is also available from special staff who can provide advice or refer students to a 'duty dean' for academic advice if necessary. Four remedial tutoring clinics also run from the centre. All administrative forms about such matters as enrolment and course choice are distributed from and returned to this centre. All course materials and handouts are also stored in and distributed or sold from this centre. Support staff, previously in a faculty office near to lecturers, are located next to this centre.
>
> (Bochner *et al.*, 1995: 69)

Improving student learning: research and teaching

One of the key influences that has raised the profile of teaching and learning is the impact that research on student learning is starting to have on the way in which lecturers approach the job of teaching. Other influences have been briefly examined in the section on contextual issues. The public accountability of HE in terms of quality audit and appraisal of teaching has contributed to the professionalization of teaching in HE, and these factors form part of the substance of the next section.

To return to the main theme of this section: research into student learning is not new, it is well established and much has been published regarding its outcomes. What *is* new, however, is evidence that lecturers in higher education are using research frameworks and research tools to make sense of their own teaching and their own courses: 'Until recently higher education was not notable for its examination of learning. Driven, quite legitimately by a dominant interest in knowledge, issues of learning occupied a marginal place in the academic community' (Barnett, 1992: 4).

The relationship between research into learning and the process of teaching is at last being recognized as being of mutual benefit – the two processes can overlap and exchange with each other instead of being separate activities.

This is another example of the theme of interdependence discussed at the beginning of the chapter.

There is now a well developed research framework which shows that when students are studying on courses in higher education they approach learning in a variety of ways. This very often involves a difference in intention. They are trying to achieve different things: 'Students understand what learning itself is, what knowledge is and what they are doing when learning in profoundly different ways' (Gibbs, 1994: 2). Similarly, lecturers in HE have a range of assumptions about what learning is, how it takes place and what the purpose of teaching is.

Students' approaches to learning

Work by Marton and Säljö (Marton and Säljö, 1976, 1984) identified two extreme intentions, which are known as a deep approach – learning as an intention to make sense of the material – and a surface approach – learning as reproducing the subject matter. Further work by Säljö (1979) distinguishes five categories of answer to the question of what students mean by learning:

1. *Learning as an increase in knowledge.* Students see learning as something that is done to them by lecturers rather than something they do for themselves. It implies a passive accumulation of facts.
2. *Learning as memorizing.* Memorizing information is an active process, but the information being memorized is not transformed, made sense of or changed in any way by the learner. This can be described as a rote learning process.
3. *Learning as acquiring facts or procedures that are to be used.* Learning includes skills or, for example, formulae that can be used or applied at a later date, but as in the previous category there is no transformation of what is learnt by the learner.
4. *Learning as making sense.* Here the student makes active attempts to abstract meaning in the process of learning. It involves trying to understand ideas and concepts so that they can be explained in the learner's own words or applied in the learner's particular context.
5. *Learning as understanding reality.* This is learning that enables the student to perceive the world differently, in a way that has some personal meaning or significance.

Study of this developmental scheme, which is based on a substantial number of interviews in which students were asked what they meant by learning, reveals that stages 4 and 5 are qualitatively different from stages 1 to 3. At levels 1 to 3 students typically adopt a surface approach and have problems understanding what a deep approach is. A range of research studies, 'which have spanned small specialist courses and large undergraduate degree programmes containing over forty disciplines and over 2000 students have demonstrated that a surface approach has a disastrous impact on the quality of student learning outcomes' (Gibbs, 1992: 4). Students who adopt a surface approach will be unlikely to have a full understanding of a concept or to recognize the key ideas in a lecture, and their learning outcomes will take the form of unstructured and undigested detail. A familiar example on book-based courses is the essay in which the student thinks up everything he or she can that is vaguely related to the topic(s) being considered, and then lists them as they come to mind. A 'deep' approach to the subject is demonstrated by comparisons, conclusions and evidence of relating the topic being considered to other areas of knowledge; in other words, the ability of students to make sense of things for themselves.

One of the crucial points here is that the approach that students take to learning is not necessarily related to their 'intelligence', a concept that itself is open to many interpretations. Research studies have demonstrated the importance of students' perceptions of what learning is, the influence this has on how they approach their studies and their subsequent success.

What about the students at levels 4 and 5 of the developmental framework outlined by Säljö (1979)? These students have the facility to take either a deep or a surface approach, depending on their perceptions of the learning task. Students taking a deep approach are able to integrate and structure ideas and demonstrate an ability to go beyond the immediate topic to apply ideas to a related area.

Students' perceptions of teaching

What counts as good teaching for students? Another important factor in the complex relationship between teaching and learning is that of students' notions of good and bad teaching. Research evidence demonstrates the wide variation in students' understanding of what good teaching is. Work by Van Rossom and Taylor (1987) and Entwistle and Tait (1990) has produced evidence that students who take a deep approach to learning have different ideas as to what good teaching consists of from those students who take a surface approach. Van Rossom and Taylor defined two conceptions of teaching: an 'open' conception in which the learner has responsibility for directing his or her own learning within a framework set by the teacher; and a 'closed' conception of learning, where the teacher selects the content, presents it to the student and tests to see if it has been memorized. Hardly surprisingly, the closed conception of teaching was found to be held almost exclusively by students who have the conceptions of learning identified at Säljö's levels 1, 2 or 3, while the open conception is that of students who have conceptions of learning at levels 4 or 5.

Studies by Gibbs *et al.* (1984) have shown developments in the students' orientation to learning, from reproducing towards a more meaning-oriented approach, which are directly related to the underlying model of teaching, learning and assessment that is used by the lecturer. Gibbs (1994) argues that students who have a reproductive or surface conception are strongly affected by their experience of closed teaching.

Lecturers' perceptions of teaching

What about the lecturer in this process? Research into lecturers' conceptions of teaching has shown that there are fundamental differences in what lecturers think the job of teaching in higher education consists of. Some of these differences relate to differences in academic discipline, while others relate to the underlying and often implicit model of teaching and learning that lecturers hold. It is only by getting to the heart of such models that we can begin to understand the part of the lecturer in the complex picture of improving the quality of student learning. Northedge (1976) explored contrasting analogies for the learning process, based on 'building' and 'gardening', and demonstrated how apparently rational decisions about the design and delivery of courses could be related to these implicit notions. Such analogies are often founded on deeply held values. These values may be based, for example, on how the lecturer was taught and learnt, the nature of the subject matter, notions of power and authority, external factors, such as the influence of professional bodies, and many more factors. Gibbs tells the anecdote about a staff development workshop on teaching large classes in politics. He had been demonstrating techniques that involved students discussing topics in small tutorless groups within a larger class: 'The professor had been looking increasingly perplexed and disengaged and he eventually brought proceedings to a halt with the statement, "I can't see what students could possibly gain from talking with each other"' (Gibbs, 1995: 22). Such a statement is based on underlying perceptions as to how students learn and the purpose of lecturing in HE.

Improving the quality of student learning

A surface approach to learning can be seen to contribute to poorer quality student learning outcomes, such as limited understanding and short-term recall of information, and, furthermore, in an assessment system that rewards the outcomes of a deep approach those students who adopt a surface approach will tend to get low marks and poor degrees.

What can be done to improve the quality of student learning? As the research has shown, student learning takes place in the context of students' perceptions of learning and teaching and lecturers' values and assumptions. Gibbs, in the Improving the Quality of Student Learning project funded by CNAA, made use of the research on surface and deep approaches to learning to support lecturers to study changes in their courses, which were designed to increase the extent to which students took deep approaches in their learning. The outcomes of this work were disseminated through leaflets to 30,000 people and through two national conferences, a book and more than thirty workshops. Many of the innovations that took place as part of the project made use of studies that have identified that appropriate course design, teaching methods and assessment can foster a deep approach. An additional factor is teaching that involves the learner in constructive learning activities. Typically these activities involve, according to Biggs (1989):

- a positive motivational context, where the student has a need to know, and experiences some degree of ownership of their learning;
- a high degree of learner activity, related both to tasks and to planning and reflection;
- interaction with others, negotiating meaning and manipulating ideas with others through discussion for learning, which can take place in many different forms;
- a well structured knowledge base, which provides both breadth and depth through well structured and integrated subject matter (ideas and concepts are related rather than learnt in isolation; for example, through interdisciplinary approaches).

The 'professionalization' of teaching in higher education

Students' or lecturers' perceptions of what learning and teaching are can become an implicit 'theory in use' (Argyris, 1976), and thus direct the students' learning or the teachers' teaching. Argyris makes a distinction between espoused theory, this being the 'official' theory one holds, and the 'theory-in-use', the implicitly held theory that drives action. Biggs argues that 'the process of professionalisation of teaching involves matching the two, that is where the espoused theory becomes the theory in use' (Biggs, 1994: 2).

Most HEIs in the UK now run some form of programme that aims to train and develop lecturers in their teaching role. In some institutions, including our own, such programmes include experienced staff, thus providing a balance and an opportunity for lecturers to learn from each other. In other institutions, programmes are run solely for new lecturers. Some such programmes are run on an open learning basis, with participants coming together occasionally in learning groups. Others, such as at UCE and the University of Brighton, are run on an action learning model, so that participants have the opportunity to try out theories learnt on the course and reflect in groups and through diaries on the impact of their actions.

The Staff and Educational Development Association (SEDA) accredits a number of these programmes in the UK. They are based on a model whereby research and theories about students' learning, teaching and assessment inform the practice of lecturers, and practical strategies and ideas used in the lecture theatre or laboratory can feed back into the theory. Our own certificate in education programme at UCE is based on this concept and draws from the ideas of Schon (1987) regarding problem-based professional education and the notion of the reflective practitioner. We work with new and experienced lecturers from a wide range of subject disciplines: interior design, accountancy, music, speech therapy, health promotion, engineering, drama; all together in one group. We start from the notion that teaching is essentially a problematic activity: what counts for 'good' teaching in interior design will not be the same as in accountancy. We do not believe that we can give these lecturers a set formula that can be applied whatever the context. One evaluation from a participant summed up our 'espoused' theory on our behalf, by commenting that we are not *taught* how to teach, we *learn* how to teach in our own context. We do believe that accountants can learn from interior designers and vice versa, and similarly speech therapists from engineers. There have been many sessions on the course when lecturers have been sharing their 'classroom' experience and a fresh perspective from another discipline has provided real insight. Likewise, we would claim that as course tutors we have provided some insights based on research into student learning, course design and assessment. For lecturers in the first year, survival in the classroom is of paramount importance. The immediate reality consists of preparing lecture notes and teaching materials, managing the awkward students in the back of the lecture theatre and coping with vast quantities of assessment. At this stage, the process is very teacher-centred and some new lecturers believe that reflection on the effects of teaching on student learning is 'only' educational theory, to be sharply contrasted with reality. One of the criteria for the assessment of participants' work on the certificate in education at UCE is that where it is appropriate the focus of concern should shift from teaching to effective student learning. The lecturer who is referred to by Ramsden (1992) as 'the expert teacher' looks at teaching from the point of view of the learner, not the teacher.

Ramsden has written that the 'best' of the courses for lecturers in the UK and Australia are based on a 'unified' model, where ' "classroom strategies" and "theory" are in constant dependence with each other, each taking meaning from the other' (Ramsden, 1994: 23).

The SEDA Teacher Accreditation Scheme recognizes programmes of training for teachers in HE. Teachers who successfully complete recognized courses are accredited by the scheme. The overall aim of the scheme 'is to assure a common and appropriate standard of performance of teachers in HE who complete recognised programmes of training' (SEDA, 1995). The scheme now has 16 recognized programmes, and a further 18 where training has been completed are still in the process of recognition. This includes a mixture of chartered universities, statutory universities and other HEIs. It is expected that the first overseas programme will be accredited in 1995 in Singapore.

The SEDA Teacher Accreditation Scheme does not prescribe one model of training for teachers in HE. It identifies the underpinning principles and values, and the objectives and outcomes, that any course or programme must demonstrate that it assesses. It allows flexibility within the scheme for institutions to focus on their own priorities.

The increasing demand for accountability in HE has influenced institutional priorities. One of the implications of quality audit and quality assessment has been that these processes have contributed to putting discussions about teaching and learning on the public agenda of our institutions. Appraisal of teaching has likewise had considerable impact on the process of 'professionalization' of teaching in HE. If these processes are handled constructively, our students should benefit.

Concluding observations

Our starting point in writing this chapter is that promoting effective student learning is a major element of the core business of HE. We have reviewed some of the changes and developments in HE from the perspective of teaching and learning. In order to work with these changes, staff in HE need to learn and develop. Historically there has been a hierarchical structure, and division between the categories of lecturing staff and non-academic management staff. We have argued throughout this chapter that just as team work and interdisciplinarity are important in our students' education, so we need to build on the existing cooperation in course management and student guidance, which is beginning to break down the traditional boundaries between 'academic' and 'non-academic' work. (Editors' note: see Roberts and Higgins (1992) and Haselgrove (1994) on 'The Student Experience'; also, Caul (1993) on 'Value-Added'; Bocock and Watson (1994), Brown and Atkins (1990), Committee of Scottish University Principals (1992), Earwaker (1992), Loder (1990) on HE teaching; and finally, Piper (1994) on 'Are Professors Professional?'.)

Notes on the Legal Framework within which HEIs Operate

The editors regret that space constraints have precluded a chapter on HEIs and the law. Readers are, however, referred to D. J. Farrington's authoritative *The Law of Higher Education* (Butterworths, 1994) and to *Universities and the Law*, edited by Farrington and Mattison (CUA, 1990). For a USA perspective, see Kaplin (1985).

In terms of employing staff, maintaining safe premises, complying with food hygiene regulations and respecting relevant legislation on data protection, building regulations, copyright and patents, HEIs are, generally, in the same position as any other UK company or public sector organization. Hence readers are referred, via Farrington, to the standard legal texts on these matters, as also on such areas as contract law, trust law, land law, planning law, the law of intellectual property, and insurance law.

The legal status of HEIs is, usually, as exempt, incorporated, charitable, chartered or statutory institutions or (in a few cases) companies, all as discussed in Farrington. For wider discussion of trust law and charity law as applicable to the governance of HEIs as exempt charities, see standard texts such as P. H. Pettit, *Equity and the Law of Trusts* (Butterworths, 1993), and H. Picarda, *The Law and Practice Relating to Charities* (Butterworths, 1995). It could be that a greater awareness of the role of the council or board of governors in terms of being charity trustees would be helpful in the context of the collegiality–managerialism debate (discussed elsewhere in this book), and in relation to the power of chief executive, vice chancellor or principal (see Farrington, Chapter 4). See also relevant guides for governors and Members of Council produced by HEFCE and by similar bodies (for example, the Colleges' Employers' Forum 'A Model Code of Conduct for Corporation Members', June 1995; and the Committee of University Chairmen 'Guide for Members of Governing Bodies of Universities and Colleges in England and Wales', June 1995, available from HEFCE). Palfreyman (1996) provides a summary of the duties of Charity Trustees.

Picarda (Chapter 41) and Farrington (pp. 43–53) detail the potentially important (and growing?) role of the Visitor for resolving, relatively quickly and cheaply, disputes between a student and a chartered university (see also Sir Michael Davies's report as Visitor on his investigation of a dispute at Swansea: *The Davies Report: the 'Great Battle' in Swansea*. Thoemmes Press, 1994). For statutory HEIs the equivalent is judicial review (Farrington, pp. 53–8; Wade and Forsyth, 1994).

The 'student contract' is worthy of special mention and care, especially in an era of increasing consumerism, marketization and 'charterism' within HE in the UK. The medieval concept of the student as a 'junior member' of the *studium generale* (a relationship governed by the internal domestic law of the institution, subject to Visitor appeal and operating within a general framework of charity law) has largely and only recently given way to a commercial reality of the student as a customer purchasing a service under a contract. Farrington discusses all this in his Chapter 7 ('Students: scholars, clients and customers'), and draws the distinction between 'the contract of admission' (the offer of a place) and 'the contract of matriculation' that it turns into (the taking up of that place), i.e. the applicant to enrolled student process. There is a *separate* contract for the delivery of accommodation services for students 'living in', and care is needed not to assume wrongly that the penalties available under the matriculation contract are *automatically* available where the student breaches the accommodation contract (for example, failing to pay rent during a 'rent strike').

It should also be noted that the students' union operates within a legal framework set by detailed regulations under the various Education Acts of recent years *and* in the general context of trust and charity law (again see Farrington, pp. 184–99, for a full analysis, and Picarda, p. 56, for a warning about political activity endangering the fiscal advantage of charitable status).

For detailed discussion of the powers and duties of charity trustees in relation to the investment of the charity/HEI endowment capital (if any!), or even of short-term cash surpluses ('treasury management'), see Palfreyman (1996), M. Harbottle, *Investing Charity Funds*, 1995 and N. Richens and M. Fletcher, *Charity Land and Premises*, 1996.

Finally, managers especially need to be aware of 'the law of meetings' – notice, quorum, minuting, voting, chairing, etc. – as set out in the Institution's Statutes, Ordinance and Regulations, *and* as governed by the general rules and case law concerning proper procedures and formal accountability, especially since the former may be silent on some details. See Farrington, pp. 209–17.

Notes on Further Reading

For wide-ranging surveys of UK university and college management, see Bosworth (1986), Bland (1990) and, especially, Lockwood and Davies (1985). For older texts on university management, now of somewhat limited use, see Fielden and Lockwood (1973), Livingstone (1974), Moodie and Eustace (1974) and Page (1975).

For *initial* follow-up reading in relation to each chapter in this book, we suggest, as a starting point, and in this order, the relevant sections in Bland, Bosworth, and Lockwood and Davies, as referred to above, plus any references given in the relevant chapter.

For a historical perspective, we recommend Flexner (1930), Truscot (1943, 1945), Kerr (1963), Perkin (1969, 1989), Thompson (1971), Engel (1983), Kogan and Kogan (1983), Anderson (1992), Halsey (1992), Tapper and Salter (1992), Salter and Tapper (1994) and Shattock (1994). For political analysis of the fate of the universities during the 1980s decade of Thatcher change, see Kavanagh and Seldon (1989, Chapter 15: 'Higher Education'); Annan (1991, Chapter 23: 'The dons learn bitter realities'); Paxman (1991, Chapter 7: 'Money by degrees'); Letwin (1992, pp. 264–76: 'Taming the universities'); and Jenkins (1995, Chapter 7: 'Taming shrews').

For those interested in thinking about how UK higher education *might* evolve, we draw attention to Keller (1983), OECD (1987, 1991), Kedourie (1989), Hague (1991, 1993), Schuller (1991, 1995), Duke (1992), IPPR (1992), Russell (1993), World Bank (1993, 1994), Ainley (1994), Brown and Scase (1994), Scott (1995a, b), Shattock (1995).

For wider reading on management, we suggest Belbin (1981), Peters and Waterman (1982), Kanter (1983), Mintzberg (1983, 1994), Drucker (1985), Jay (1987), Minkes (1987), Deal and Kennedy (1988), Harvey-Jones (1988), Kakabadse (1988), Pollitt (1990), Twiss (1992), Fraser and Neville (1993), Handy (1993, 1994) and Kay (1993).

For an interesting US perspective (especially on the philosophy of higher education), see Kerr (1963), Bok (1982, 1990), Keller (1983), Bloom (1987), Birnbaum (1988), Giamatti (1988), Oakeshott (1989), Rosovsky (1990), Barzun (1992), Berquist (1992), Getman (1992), Pelikan (1992), Oakley (1993) and Sommer (1996).

In recent years there has been a spate of books critical of higher education and its, allegedly, weak management, poor value-for-money, and fawning 'trendiness': notably Hague (1991, 1993) in the UK, but many more in the USA, ranging from

Bloom (1987), through Sykes (1988, 1990), Bartley (1990), Smith (1990), Anderson (1992) and Bromwich (1992), Gross and Levitt (1994) to Sommer (1995). Herron (1988) and Oakley (1993) defend 'the liberal arts tradition' of American universities.

On the use of performance indicators (PIs) within HE, a topic not especially focused upon in this text, we refer readers to Cave *et al.* (1991) and Johnes and Taylor (1990).

For 'fun' reading (especially 'the university novel'), we suggest Cornford (1908), Snow (1951), Amis (1954), Proctor (1957), Dundonald (1962), Bradbury (1975, 1987), Sharpe (1976, 1995), Lodge (1978, 1985, 1989), Jacobson (1984), Davies (1986, 1988), Parkin (1986), Becher (1989), Carter (1990), Evans (1993) and Ellis (1994).

The bibliography that follows is lengthy and, we hope, reasonably comprehensive. It is meant as a long-term resource. We welcome our attention being drawn to gaps in its coverage of areas or to important texts that we may have overlooked.

Bibliography

ABRC (1982) *Report of the Working Party on Postgraduate Education*. London: ABRC.
ABRC (1994) *Report of the Working Group on Postgraduate Support*. London: ABRC.
Adelman, H. (1973) *The Holiversity*. Toronto: New Press.
Ainley, P. (1994) *Degrees of Difference: Higher Education in the 1990s*. London: Lawrence and Wishart.
Allen, M. (1988) *The Goals of Universities*. Milton Keynes: SRHE/Open University Press.
Amis, K. (1954) *Lucky Jim*. London: Gollancz.
Anderson, M. (1992) *Imposters in the Temple*. New York: Simon and Schuster.
Anderson, R. D. (1982) *Universities and Elites in Britain since 1800*. London: Macmillan.
Annan, N. (1991) *Our Age*. London: Fontana.
Anglia Polytechnic University (1991) *Faculty Aims and Objectives*. Cambridge APU.
Argyris, C. (1976) Theories of action that inhibit individual learning, *American Psychologist*, 31, 638–54.
Arms, Y. with Michalak, T. J. (1988) The merger of libraries with computing at Carnegie Mellon University, *British Journal of Academic Librarianship*, 3 (3), 153–64.
Bagehot, W. (1867) *The English Constitution*. London.
Barnett, C. (1986) *The Audit of War*. London: Papermac.
Barnett, C. (1995) *The Lost Victory: British Dreams, British Realities 1945–1950*. London: Macmillan.
Barnett, R. (1990) *The Idea of Higher Education*. Milton Keynes: SRHE/Open University Press.
Barnett, R. (1992) What effects? What outcomes? In R. Barnett (ed.) *Learning to Effect*. Buckingham: SRHE/Open University Press.
Bartley, W. W. (1990) *Unfathomed Knowledge*. La Salle, IL: Open Court.
Barzun, J. (1991) *Begin Here: the Forgotten Conditions of Teaching and Learning*. Chicago: University of Chicago Press.
Becher, T. (1989) *Academic Tribes and Territories*. Buckingham: SRHE/Open University Press.
Becher, T. and Kogan, M. (1992) *Process and Structure in Higher Education*. London: Routledge.
Beck, R. (1985) Personnel management. In G. Lockwood and J. Davies (eds) *Universities: the Management Challenge*. Windsor: SRHE AND NFER-Nelson.
Belbin, R. M. (1981) *Management Teams*. London: Heinemann.

Bensimon, E. M. (1993) New presidents' initial actions: transactional and transformational leadership, *Journal for Higher Education Management,* 8(2).

Berquist, W. H. (1992) *The Four Cultures of the Academy.* San Francisco: Jossey-Bass.

Biggs, J. (1989) *Does Learning about Learning Help Teachers with Teaching? Psychology and the Tertiary Teacher.* Supplement to *The Gazette,* 26(1).

Biggs, J. (1994) Student learning research and theory: where do we currently stand. In G. Gibbs (ed.) *Improving Student Learning: Theory and Practice.* Oxford: Oxford Centre for Staff Development.

Birnbaum, R. (1988) *How Colleges Work.* San Francisco: Jossey-Bass.

Bland, D. E. (1990) *Managing Higher Education.* London: Cassell.

Bloom, A. (1987) *The Closing of the American Mind: How Higher Education Has Failed Democracy and Impoverished the Souls of Today's Students.* Harmondsworth: Penguin.

Blume, S. and Amsterdamsk, O. (1987) *Postgraduate Education in the 1980s.* Paris: OECD.

Bochner, D., Gibbs, G. and Wisker, G. (1995) *Teaching More Students – Supporting More Students.* Oxford: Oxford Centre for Staff Development.

Bocock, J. and Watson, D. (1994) *Managing the University Curriculum.* Buckingham: SRHE/Open University Press.

Bok, D. (1982) *Beyond the Ivory Tower.* Cambridge, MA: Harvard University Press.

Bok, D. (1990) *Universities and the Future of America.* North Carolina: Duke University Press.

Bradbury, M. (1975) *The History Man.* London: Secker and Warburg.

Bradbury, M. (1987) *Cuts.* London: Hutchinson.

Bromwich, D. (1992) *Politics by Other Means.* New Haven: Yale.

Brown, G. and Atkins, A. (1990) *Effective Teaching in Higher Education.* London: Routledge.

Brown, P. and Scase, R. (1994) *Higher Education and Corporate Realities.* London: UCL Press.

Bruton, M. J. (1987) University planning and management in conditions of complexity and uncertainty, *Higher Education Quarterly,* 41(4), 373–89.

Burgess, R. G. (ed.) (1994) *Postgraduate Education and Training in the Social Sciences: Processes and Products.* London: Jessica Kingsley Publications.

Burgess, R. G. *et al.* (1993) *Postgraduate Research Training in the United Kingdom.* A Report for the OECD. Coventry: CEDAR, University of Warwick.

Butterworth, R. and Tarling, N. (1994) *A Shake-up Anyway: government and the universities in New Zealand in a decade of reform.* Auckland: Oxford University Press/ Auckland University Press.

Cameron, J. M. (1978) *On the Idea of a University.* Toronto: University of Toronto Press.

Carswell, J. (1985) *Government and the Universities in Britain.* Oxford: Oxford University Press.

Carter, I. (1990) *Ancient Cultures of Conceit: British University Fiction in the Post-war Years.* London: Routledge.

Caul, B. (1993) *Value-added: the Personal Development of Students in Higher Education.* Belfast: December Press.

Cave, M., Hanney, S. and Kogan, M. (1991) *The Use of Performance Indicators in Higher Education.* London: Jessica Kingsley.

Chartered Institute of Public Finance and Accountancy (1994a) *Treasury Management in Higher Education.* London: CIPFA.

Chartered Institute of Public Finance and Accountancy (1994b) *Higher Education Finance.* London: CIPFA.

Checkland, P. B. (1973) *Towards a Systems-based Methodology for Real-world Problem Solving.* Lancaster: Department of Systems Engineering, University of Lancaster.

Checkland, P. B. (1981) *Systems Thinking, Systems Practice.* Chichester: John Wiley.

Clark, B. R. (1983) *The Higher Education System.* Berkeley: University of California Press.

Clark, B. R. (ed.) (1984) *Perspectives on Higher Education.* Berkeley: University of California Press.

Clark, B. R. (ed.) (1993) *The Research Foundations of Graduate Education: Germany, Britain, France, United States and Japan.* Berkeley: University of California Press.

Clark, B. R. (ed.) (1996) *Places of Inquiry: Research and Advanced Education in Modern Universities.* Berkeley: University of California Press.

Clemson, B. (1984) *Cybernetics: A New Management Tool.* Tonbridge Wells: Abacus Press.

Cobban, A. (1988) *The Medieval Universities: Oxford and Cambridge to c.1500.* Aldershot: Scolar Press.

Cohen, M. D. and March, J. G. (1974) *Leadership and Ambiguity: the American College President.* New York: McGraw-Hill.

Committee on Higher Education (1963) *Higher Education: a Report.* Cmnd 2154. London: HMSO (the Robbins Report).

Committee of Public Accounts (1994) *University Purchasing in England.* London: HMSO.

Committee of Scottish University Principals (CSUP) (1992) *Teaching and Learning in an expanding Higher Education System.* London: CSUP.

Committee of University Chairmen (1995) *Guide for Members of Governing Bodies.* London: CUC.

Confederation of British Industry (1994) *Thinking Ahead: Ensuring the Expansion of Higher Education into the Twenty-first Century.* London: CBI.

Connock, S. and Johns, T. (1995) *Ethical Leadership.* London: Institute of Personnel and Development.

Cornford, F. M. (1908) *Microsmogaphica Academica: Being a Guide for the Young Academic Politician.* Cambridge: MainSail Press (1993 edn).

Council for Graduate Schools (1990) *Organization and Administration of Graduate Education. A Policy Statement.* Washington, DC: CGS.

Cowan, J. (1994) The student and the learning process. In M. Adams and R. McElroy (eds) *Colleges, Libraries and Access to Learning.* London: Library Association Publishing.

CUA (1986) *Beyond the Limelight.* Reading: CUA.

CUA (1989) *Strategic Choice: Corporate Strategies for Change in Higher Education.* Manchester: CUA/Touche Ross.

CUA (1990) *Universities and the Law.* Reading: CUA.

CUA (1992) *Universities in the Marketplace.* Manchester: CUA/Touche Ross.

Customs and Excise (1994) *VAT (Education) Order.* London: HMSO.

CVCP (various years) *News.* London: CVCP.

CVCP (1986, 1987, 1988, 1989) *Academic Standards in Universities.* London: CVCP.

CVCP (1988) *The Costing of Research Projects in Universities.* London: CVCP.

CVCP (1992) *Sponsored University Research: Recommendations and Guidance on Contract Issues.* London: CVCP.

CVCP (1994) *Higher Education Statistics, Autumn 1994.* London: CVCP.

CVCP (1995) *Guidelines on Town and Country Planning.* London: CVCP.

Cyert, R. M. (1975) *The Management of Non-profit Organizations – with Emphasis on Universities.* New York: Levington Books.

Daalder, H. and Shils, E. (1982) *Universities, Politicians and Bureaucrats.* Cambridge: Cambridge University Press.

Davies, A. (1986) *A Very Peculiar Practice.* London: Coronet.

Davies, A. (1988) *A Very Peculiar Practice: The New Frontier.* London: Methuen.

Davies, J. L. (1984) The entreprenurial and adaptive university, *International Journal of Institutional Management in Higher Education,* 2(1).

Davies, J. L. (1985) Policy formation. In G. Lockwood and J. L. Davies (eds) *Universities: the Management Challenge.* Windsor: SRHE and NFER-Nelson.

Davies, Sir M. (1994) *The Davies Report: The 'Great Battle' in Swansea.* London: Thoemmes Press.

Deal, T. and Kennedy A. (1988) *Corporate Cultures: the Rites and Rituals of Corporate Life.* London: Penguin Business.

Department for Education (1993) *Charter for Higher Education.* London: HMSO.

Dearlove, J. (1995a) Collegiality, managerialism and leadership in English universities, *Journal of Tertiary Education and Management,* 1(2), 161–9.

Dearlove, J. (1995b) *Governance, Leadership, and Change in Universities.* Paris: UNESCO (IIEP).

Department of Employment (1995a) *Using Graduate Skills.* London: HMSO.

Department of Employment (1995b) *Higher Education Projects Prospectus 1996–98.* Sheffield: HMSO.

DES (1985) *The Development of Higher Education into the 1990s.* Cmnd 9524. London: HMSO.

Donaldson, L. (1987) Strategy and structural adjustment to regain fit and performance in defence of contingency theory, *Journal of Management Studies,* 24, 1–24.

Drucker, P. F. (1985) *Innovation and Entrepreneurship.* London: Heinemann.

D'Souza, D. (1991) *Illiberal Education.* New York: The Free Press.

Duke, C. (1992) *The Learning University.* Buckingham: SRHE/Open University Press.

Dundonald, J. (1962) *Letters to a Vice-chancellor.* London: Edward Arnold.

Earwaker, J. (1992) *Helping and Supporting Students.* Buckingham: SRHE/Open University Press.

Economic and Social Research Council (1991) *Postgraduate Training Guidelines on the Provision of Training for Postgraduate Students in the Social Sciences.* Swindon: ESRC.

Ellis, R. (1993) *Quality Assurance for University Teaching.* Buckingham: SRHE/Open University Press.

Ellis, W. (1994) *The Oxbridge Conspiracy.* London: Michael Joseph.

Enderud, H. G. (1977) *Four Faces of Leadership in the Academic Organisation.* Oslo: Nyt Nordisk Forlag.

Engel, A. J. (1983) *From Clergyman to Don: the Rise of the Academic Profession in Nineteenth-century Oxford.* Oxford: Oxford University Press.

Entwistle, N. J. and Tait, H. (1990) Approaches to learning, evaluations of teaching and preferences for contrasting academic environments, *Higher Education,* 19, 169–94.

European Commission (1990) *Workplace Regulations and Health and Safety (Display Screen) Regulations.* Brussels: EC.

European Commission (1991) *Memorandum on Higher Education.* Brussels: EC.

Evans, C. (1993) *English People: the Experience of Teaching and Learning English in British Universities.* Buckingham: SRHE/Open University Press.

Farrington, D. J. (1994) *The Law of Higher Education.* London: Butterworths.

Fender, B. (1987) *Investing in People.* Report prepared for Universities' Committee for Non-teaching Staff. London: Centurian Press.

Fender, B. (1993) *Promoting People: a Strategic Framework for the Management and Development of Staff in UK Universities.* London: CVCP.

Fielden, J. (1975) The decline of the professor and the rise of the registrar. In G. F. Page (ed.) *Power and Authority in Higher Education.* Guildford: SRHE.

Fielden, J. (1993) Delegated management and budgets. Unpublished consultancy paper, 12 October.

Fielden, J. and Lockwood, G. (1973) *Planning and Management in Universities*. London: Chatto & Windus.

Finger, P. and Ford, J. F. (1989) New structure in postgraduate research training in the Netherlands, *Higher Education Management*, 1, 20–35.

Flexner, A. (1930) *Universities: American, English, German*. Oxford: Oxford University Press.

Franks Report (1966) *University of Oxford: Report of Commission of Inquiry*, 2 vols. Oxford: Oxford University Press.

Fraser, A. and Neville, S. (1993) *Teambuilding*. London: The Industrial Society.

Getman, J. (1992) *In the Company of Scholars: the Real World for the Soul of Higher Education*. Austin: University of Texas Press.

Giamatti, A. B. (1988) *A Free and Ordered Space: the Real World of the University*. New York: W. W. Norton.

Gibbs, G. (1992) *Improving the Quality of Student Learning*. Based on the Improving Student Learning Project funded by the Council for National Academic Awards. Bristol: Technical and Educational Services Ltd.

Gibbs, G. (1994) Preface. In G. Gibbs (ed.) *Improving Student Learning: Theory and Practice*. Oxford: Oxford Centre for Staff Development.

Gibbs, G. (1995) Changing lecturers' conceptions of teaching and learning through Action Research. In A. Brew (ed.) *Directions in Staff Development*. Buckingham: SRHE/Open University Press.

Gibbs, G. and Jenkins, A. (1992) An introduction to the context of changes in class size. In G. Gibbs and A. Jenkins (eds) *Teaching Large Classes in Higher Education: How to Maintain Quality with Reduced Resources*. London: Kogan Page.

Gibbs, G., Morgan, A. and Taylor, E. (1984) The world of the learner. In F. Martin, D. Hounsell and N. J. Entwistle (eds) *The Experience of Learning*. Edinburgh: Scottish Academic Press.

Gibbs, G., Pollard, N. and Farrell, J. (1994) *Institutional Support for Resource Based Learning*. Oxford: Oxford Centre for Staff Development.

Gray, J. (1993) *Beyond the New Right*. London: Routledge.

Gross, P. R. and Levitt, N. (1994) *Higher Superstition: The Academic Left and Its Quarrels with Science*. Baltimore: The Johns Hopkins University Press.

Gross, R. (1994) Accommodation of research students, *Journal of Graduate Education*, 1, 21–4.

Hague, Sir D. (1991) *Beyond Universities: a New Republic of the Intellect*. London: IEA Hobart Paper.

Hague, Sir D. (1993) *Transforming the Dinosaurs*. London: DEMOS.

Hale, E. (1964) *Report of the Committee on University Teaching Methods*. London: HMSO.

Halsey, A. H. (1992) *Decline of Donnish Dominion*. Oxford: Clarendon Press.

Halsey, A. H. and Trow, M. (1971) *The British Academics*. London: Faber.

Handy, C. B. (1983) The organizations of consent. In O. Boyd-Barrett *et al.* (ed.) *Approaches to Post-school Management*. London: Harper & Row.

Handy, C. B. (1993) *Understanding Organisations*, 4th Edition. Harmondsworth: Penguin.

Handy, C. B. (1994) *The Empty Raincoat*. London: Hutchinson.

Harbottle, M. (1995) *Investing Charity Funds*. Bristol: Jordans.

Harris, M. B. (1991a) Crisis deepens on Britain's campuses, *Observer*, 10 November.

Harris, M. B. (1991b) Cost-effectiveness and efficiency in universities: a British perspective. A paper to Conference of Executive Heads, the Association of Commonwealth Universities, New Delhi, India, 14–18 January.

Harrison, C. (1994) Quality in learning support services, *The Law Librarian*, 25(4), 212–15.

Harvey, L. (1995) *Quality in Higher Education Project: TQM and the New Collegialism.* Birmingham: University of Central England.

Harvey, L. and Green, D. (1994) *Quality in Higher Education Project: Employer Satisfaction.* Birmingham: University of Central England.

Harvey-Jones, Sir J. (1988) *Making It Happen.* London: Collins.

Haselgrove, S. (ed.) (1994) *The Student Experience.* Buckingham: SRHE/Open University Press.

Hazeu, C. A. (1991) Research policy and the shaping of research schools in the Netherlands, *Higher Education Management*, 1, 20–35.

HEFCE (1993a) *Model Financial Memorandum between the HEFCE and Institutions.* Circular 25/93. Bristol: HEFCE.

HEFCE (1993b) *Audit Code of Practice.* Circular 29/93. Bristol: HEFCE.

HEFCE (1993c) *Good Management of Purchasing.* Bristol: HEFCE.

HEFCE (1993d) *Strategic Estate Management.* Brisol: HEFCE.

HEFCE (1994) *Value for Money Studies in the Higher Education Sector.* Bristol: HEFCE.

HEFCE (1994b) *Private Sector Funding in Higher Education.* The Bain Report. Bristol: HEFCE.

HEFCE (1995a) *The Effective Academic Library: a Framework for Evaluating the Performances of UK Academic Libraries.* Bristol: HEFCE.

HEFCE (1995b) *A Guide to Finding Higher Education in England: How the HEFCE Allocates Its Funds.* Bristol: HEFCE.

HEFCE (1995c) *Review of Higher Education: Submission by Higher Education Funding Council for England.* Bristol: HEFCE.

HEFCE (various editions) *News.* Bristol: HEFCE.

Herron, J. (1988) *Universities and the Myth of Cultural Decline.* Detroit: Wayne State University Press.

Higher Education Business Enterprises Limited (HEBE) (1994a) *Postgraduate Taught Courses 1995/96.* London: HEBE.

Higher Education Business Enterprises Limited (HEBE) (1994b) *Research Opportunities 1995/96.* London: HEBE.

Higher Education Information Services Trust (1994/5) *Taught Postgraduate Education: the Student Experience.* Leeds: HEIST.

Higher Education Quality Council (1994) *Choosing to Change.* The Report of the HEQC, CAT Development Project. London: HEQC.

Higher Education Quality Council (1995) *A Quality Assurance Framework for Guidance and Learner Support in Higher Education: the Guidelines.* London: HEQC.

Higher Education Statistics Agency (1995) *Higher Education Statistics for the United Kingdom 1992/3.* Cheltenham: HESA.

HMSO (1987) *Civil Research and Development.* Cmd 185. London: HMSO.

HMSO (1991) *Higher Education: a New Framework.* London: HMSO.

Hogan, J. V. (1992) Graduate education in the USA, *Journal of Education Policy*, 7, 501–9.

Hogan, J. V. (1994) *Graduate Schools: the Organisation of Graduate Education.* Coventry: CEDAR. University of Warwick.

Hoggart, R. (1995) The degree explosion, *Independent Magazine*, 24 June, 9–14.

Holmes, G. (1993) Quality assurance in further and higher education – a sacrificial lamb on the altar of managerialism. *Quality Assurance in Higher Education*, 1, 1.

IPPR (1992) *Higher Education: Expansion and Reform.* London: IPPR.

Jacobson, H. (1984) *Coming from Behind.* London: Black Swan.

Jarratt Report (1985) *Report of the Steering Committee for Efficiency Studies in Universities.* London: CVCP.

Jaspers, K. (1946) *The Idea of the University.* London: Macmillan.

Jay, A. (1987) *Management and Machievelli.* London: Hutchison.

Jenkins, S. (1995) *Accountable to None.* London: Hamish Hamilton.

Johnes, J. and Taylor, J. (1990) *Performance Indicators in Higher Education.* Buckingham: SRHE/Open University Press.

Johnson, G. (1990) Managing strategic changes: the role of symbolic action, *British Journal of Management,* 1(1), 183–200.

Johnson, G. and Grundy, T. (1993) Managers' perspectives on making major investment decisions. The problem of linking strategic and financial appraisal, *British Journal of Management,* 4(4), 253–67.

Johnston, R. J. (1993) Funding research: an exploration of inter-discipline variations, *Higher Education Quarterly,* 47(4), 357–72.

Joint Performance Indicators Working Group (1994) *Report on the Conversion of the Data Submitted to the 1992 Research Assessment Exercise into Performance Indicators* (established by the Higher Education Funding Councils). Bristol: HEFCE.

Joseph, Sir K. (1982) Letter from the Secretary of State to the Chairman of the UGC, 14 July.

Joseph, Sir K. (1983) Letter from the Secretary of State to the Chairman of the UGC, 1 September.

Kakabadse, A. (1988) *Working in Organisations.* London: Penguin Business.

Kanter, R. M. (1983) *The Change Masters: Corporate Entrepreneurs at Work.* London: Counterpoint/Union.

Kaplin, W. A. (1985) *The Law of Higher Education.* New York: Jossey-Bass.

Kavanagh, D. and Seldon, A. (1989) *The Thatcher Effect.* Oxford: OUP.

Kay, J. (1993) *Foundations of Corporate Success.* Oxford: Oxford University Press.

Kedourie, E. (1989) *Perestroika in the Universities.* London: IEA.

Keen, C. and Greenall, J. (1987) *Public Relations Management.* Banbury: HEIST.

Keen, C. and Warner, D. (1989) *Visual and Corporate Identity.* Banbury: HEIST.

Keen C. and Higgins, T. (1991) *Young People's Knowledge of Higher Education.* Banbury: HEIST.

Keep, E. and Mayhew, K. (1996) Economic demand for higher education – a sound foundation for further expansion?, *Higher Education Quarterly,* 50(20) 89–109.

Keep, E. and Sisson, K. (1992) Owning the problem: personnel issues in higher education policy-making in the 1990s, *Oxford Review of Economic Policy,* 8(2), 67–78.

Keller, G. (1983) *Academic Strategy: the Management Revolution in American Higher Education.* Baltimore, MD: Johns Hopkins University.

Kerr, C. (1963) *The Uses of the University.* Cambridge, MA: Harvard University Press.

Kogan, M. with Kogan, D. (1983) *The Attack on Higher Education.* London: Kogan Page.

Latham, M. (1994) *Constructing the Team* (Final Report of the Government/Industry Review of Procurement and Contractural Industry). London: HMSO.

Lawrence, P. R. and Lorsch, J. W. (1967) *Organization and Environment: Managing Differentiation and Integration.* Cambridge, MA: Harvard Graduate School of Business Administration.

Leavis, F. R. (1943) *Education and the University.* Cambridge: Cambridge University Press.

Leavitt, H. J. (1965) Applied organizational change in industry: structural, technological and humanistic approaches. In J. G. March (ed.) *Handbook of Organizations.* Chicago: Rand McNally.

Letwin, S. R. (1992) *The Anatomy of Thatcherism.* London: Fontana.

Livingstone, H. (1974) *The University: an Organisational Analysis.* London: Blackie.

Lockwood, G. and Davies, J. (1985) *Universities: the Management Challenge.* Windsor: SRHE and NFER-Nelson.

Loder, C. P. J. (1990) *Quality Assurance and Accountability in Higher Education.* London: Kogan Page.

Lodge, D. (1978) *Changing Places.* London: Penguin.

Lodge, D. (1985) *Small World.* London: Penguin.

Lodge, D. (1989) *Nice Work.* London: Penguin.

Mackie, R. (1990) Personnel's role on the campus, *Personnel Management,* May, 54–9.

McNay, I. (1995a) Universities in a competitive market: a balance sheet. *ETH Bulletin.*

McNay, I. (1995b) Universities going international: choices, cautions and conditions. In P. Blok (ed.) *Policy and Policy Implementation in Internationalisation of Higher Education.* Amsterdam: EAIE.

McNay, I. (1995c) From collegial academy to corporate enterprise: the changing cultures of universities. In T. Schuller (ed.) *The Changing University.* Buckingham: SRHE/Open University Press.

Marton, F. and Säljö, R. (1976) On qualitative differences in learning II – outcome as a function of the learner's conception of the task, *Bristol Journal of Educational Psychology,* 46, 115–27.

Marton, F. and Säljö, R. (1984) Approaches to learning. In F. Martin, D. Hounsell and N. Entwistle (eds) *The Experience of Learning.* Edinburgh: Scottish Academic Press.

Middlehurst, R. (1993) *Leading Academics.* Buckingham: SRHE/Open University Press.

Middleton, G. (1985) Entrepreneurism – the concept and some of its management implications for Leicester Polytechnic. MBA Dissertation, Leicester Polytechnic (unpublished).

Miller, H. D. R. (1994) *The Management of Change in Universities.* Buckingham: SRHE/Open University Press.

Minkes, A. L. (1987) *The Entrepreneurial Manager.* London: Penguin Business.

Minogue, K. (1973) *The Concept of a University.* London: Weidenfeld.

Mintzberg, H. (1983) *Structure in Fives.* Englewood Cliffs, NJ: Prentice Hall.

Mintzberg, H. (1994) *The Rise and Fall of Strategic Planning.* Englewood Cliffs, NJ: Prentice Hall.

Moberley, W. H. (1949) *The Crisis of the University.* London: SCM Press.

Moberley, W. H. (1951) *Cultural Leadership.* Oxford: Oxford University Press.

Moodie, G. C. and Eustace, R. (1974) *Power and Authority in British Universities.* London: Unwin.

Morrell, D. (1992) Universities: responsibility and motivation. In I. McNay (ed.) *Visions of Post-compulsory Education.* Buckingham: SRHE/Open University Press.

Mynors, C. (1995) *Listed Buildings and Conservation Areas.* London: FT Law and Tax.

National Audit Office (1994) *The Financial Health of Higher Education Institutions in England.* London: HMSO.

National Commission on Education (1994) *Universities in the Twenty-first Century.* London: NCE.

National Postgraduate Committee (NPC) (1995) *Guidelines for Accommodation Facilities for Research Students.* Troon: NPC.

Neave, G. and Van Vaught, F. A. (eds) (1991) *Prometheus Bound: the Changing Relationship between Government and Higher Education in Western Europe.* Oxford: Pergamon Press.

Newman, J. (1852) *The Idea of a University*. London: Dent (1965 edition).

Niblett, W. R. (1962) *The Expanding University*. London: Faber.

Northedge, A. (1976) Examining our explicit analogies for learning processes, *Programmed Learning and Educational Technology*, 13(4), 67–78.

Oakeshott, M. (1989) *The Voice of Liberal Learning*. New Haven, CT: Yale University Press.

Oakley, F. (1993) *Community of Learning*. Oxford: Oxford University Press.

OECD (1987) *Universities under Scrutiny*. Paris: OECD.

OECD (1991) *Alternatives to Universities*. Paris: OECD.

Pack, J. and Pack, F. M. (1988) *Colleges, Learning and Libraries: the Future*. London: Clive Bingley.

Page, G. F. (ed.) (1975) *Power and Authority in Higher Education*. Guildford: SRHE.

Palfreyman, D. (1989) The Warwick way: a case study of innovation and entrepreneurship within a university context, *Journal of Entrepreneurship and Regional Development*, 1(2), 207–19.

Palfreyman, D. (1996) Oxbridge Fellows as Charity Trustees, *The Charity Law and Practice Review*, 3(3), 187–202.

Parkin, F. (1986) *The Mind and Body Shop*. London: Fontana.

Partington, P. (1994) Human resources management and development in higher education. Paper to the Quinquennial Conference of the Conference of European Rectors, Budapest.

Paxman, J. (1991) *Friends in High Places: Who Runs Britain?* London: Penguin.

Pearce Report (1992) *Capital Funding and Estate Management in Higher Education*. Bristol: UFC/PCFC.

Pedler, M., Burgoyne, J. and Boydell, T. (1991) *The Learning Company: a Strategy for Sustainable Development*. London: McGraw-Hill.

Pelikan, J. (1992) *The Idea of the University: a Re-examination*. New Haven, CT: Yale University Press.

Perkin, H. (1969) *Key Profession: The History of the Association of University Teachers*. London: Routledge.

Perkin, H. (1989) *The Rise of the Professional Society*. London: Routledge.

Perlman, B. (1988) *The Academic Intrapreneur*. New York: Praeger.

Peters, T. J. and Waterman, R. J. (1982) *In Search of Excellence*. London: Harper & Row.

Pettit, P. H. (1993) *Equity and the Law of Trusts*. London: Butterworths.

Picarda, H. (1995) *The Law and Practice Relating to Charities*. London: Butterworths.

Piper, D. W. (1994) *Are Professors Professional?: The Organization of University Examinations*. London: Jessica Kingsley.

Piper, D. W. and Glatter, R. (1977) *The Changing University*. Windsor: NFER.

Policy Studies Institute (1994) *Postgraduate Study Following a First Degree: a Survey of Graduates' Choices*. London: PSI.

Pollitt, C. (1990) *Managerialism and the Public Services: the Anglo-American Experience*. Oxford: Blackwell.

Pratt, J. and Silverman, S. (1988) *Responding to Constraint*. Milton Keynes: SRHE/Open University Press.

Proctor, M. (1957) *The English University Novel*. Berkeley: University of California Press.

Raaheim, K., Wandkowski, J. and Radford, J. (1991) *Helping Students to Learn: Teaching, Counselling, Research*, 2nd edn. Milton Keynes: SRHE/Open University Press.

Raelin, J. A. (1985) *The Clash of Cultures: Managers Managing Professionals*. Boston: Harvard Business School Press.

Ramsden, P. (1992) *Learning to Teach in Higher Education*. London: Routledge.

Ramsden, P. (1994) Using research on student learning to enhance educational quality. In G. Gibbs (ed.) *Improving Student Learning: Theory and Practice.* Oxford: Oxford Centre for Staff Development.

Rance, B. (1995) Professionalism in the built environment. In T. Muir and B. Rance (eds) *Collaborative Practice in the Built Environment.* London: E. and F. N. Spon.

Ranson, S. and Stewart, J. (1994) *Management for the Public Domain: Enabling the Learning Society.* Basingstoke: Macmillan.

Richens, N. and Fletcher, M. (1996) *Charity Land and Premises.* Bristol: Jordans.

Richmond, Sir M. (1991) *Support of Science and Engineering in the UK.* Text of speech delivered by Sir Mark Richmond, made available by the CVCP.

Roberts, D. and Higgins, T. (1992) *Higher Education: The Student Experience.* Leeds: HEIST.

Robinson, E. E. (1968) *The New Polytechnics.* Harmondsworth: Penguin.

Rosovsky, H. (1990) *The University: an Owner's Manual.* New York: W. W. Norton.

Rourke, F. E. and Brooks, G. E. (1968) *The Managerial Revolution in Higher Education.* Baltimore, MD: Johns Hopkins University Press.

Rubenstein, W. D. (1993) *Capitalism, Culture and Decline in Britain.* London: Routledge.

Rudd, E. (1975) *The Highest Education.* London: Routledge.

Russell, C. (1993) *Academic Freedom.* London: Routledge.

Ryder, A. (1996) Reform and UK higher education in the enterprise era, *Higher Education Quarterly,* 50(1), 54–70.

Säljö, R. (1979) *Learning in the Learner's Perspective. Some Commonsense Conceptions.* Reports from the Institute of Education, University of Gothenburg, 76.

Salter, B. and Tapper, T. (1994) *The State and Higher Education.* Ilford: Woburn Press.

Schön, D. (1987) *Educating the Reflective Practitioner.* San Francisco: Jossey-Bass.

Schuller, T. (ed.) (1991) *The Future of Higher Education.* Milton Keynes: SRHE/Open University Press.

Schuller, T. (1992) The exploding community? The university idea and the smashing of the academic atom. In I. McNay (ed.) *Visions of Post-compulsory Education.* Buckingham: SRHE/Open University Press.

Schuller, T. (ed.) (1995) *The Changing University?* Buckingham: SRHE/Open University Press.

Scott, P. (1984) *The Crisis of the University.* London: Croom Helm.

Scott, P. (1990) *Knowledge and Nation.* Edinburgh: Edinburgh University Press.

Scott, P. (1995a) University–state relations in Britain: paradigm of autonomy. In J. E. Mauch and P. L. W. Sabloff (eds) *Reform and Change in Higher Education: International Perspectives.* New York: Garland.

Scott, P. (1995b) *The Meanings of Mass Higher Education.* Buckingham: SRHE/Open University Press.

Scott Morton, M. S. (1992) The effects of information technology on management and organizations. In T. A. Kochan and M. Useem (eds) *Transforming Organizations.* New York: Oxford University Press.

Sharpe, T. (1976) *Porterhouse Blue.* London: Pan.

Sharpe, T. (1995) *Grantchester Grind.* London: André Deutsch/Secker and Warburg.

Shattock, M. L. (1994) *The UGC and the Management of British Universities.* Buckingham: SRHE/Open University Press.

Shattock, M. L. and Rigby, F. G. (1983) *Resource Allocation in British Universities.* London: SRHE.

Shattock, M. L. (1995) The university of the future, *Higher Education Management,* 7(2), 57–64.

Sheffield, G. (1990) A manufactory of echoes: a comparative case study of innovation, entrepreneurship and the management of change in two West Midlands universities (Birmingham and Warwick). MBA dissertation, University of Aston (unpublished).

Shilling, R. (1995) Issues of good practice in relation to student appeals against academic decisions. MSc education management dissertation, Anglia Polytechnic University (unpublished).

Shinn, C. (1986) *Paying the Piper: the Development of the University Grants Committee, 1919–1946.* Lewes: Falmer Press.

Simon, H. A. (1961) *Administrative Behaviour.* New York: Macmillan.

Sizer, L. (1982) Assessing institutional performance and progress. In L. Wagner (ed.) *Agenda for Institutional Change in Higher Education.* Guildford: SRHE.

Smith, P. (1991) *Killing the Spirit: Higher Education in America.* Harmondsworth: Penguin.

Snow, C. P. (1951) *The Masters.* London: Macmillan.

Sommer, J. W. (ed.) (1995) *The Academy in Crisis.* New York: The Independent Institute.

Sparrow, J. (1967) *Pattison and the Idea of a University.* Cambridge: Cambridge University Press.

Stacey, R. D. (1993) *Strategic Management and Organisational Dynamics.* London: Pitman.

Staff and Educational Development Association (1995) *The Accreditation of Teachers in Higher Education.* Birmingham: SEDA.

Stankiewicw, R. (1986) *Academics and Entrepreneurs.* London: Pinter.

Suddards, R. W. and Hargreaves, J. M. (1996) *Listed Building Consent.* London: Sweet and Maxwell.

Sykes, C. J. (1988) *Profscam.* Washington DC: Regenery Gateway (also St Martin's Press, 1990).

Sykes, C. J. (1990) *The Hollow Men: Politics and Corruption in Higher Education.* Washington DC: Regenery Gateway.

Tapper, T. and Salter, B. (1992) *Oxford, Cambridge and the Changing Idea of the University: the Challenge to Donnish Domination.* Buckingham: SRHE/Open University Press.

Taylor, M. G. (1989) Implications of new organisational patterns of research, *Higher Education Management*, 1, 7–19.

Temporary International Consultative Committee on New Organisational Forms of Graduate Research Training (1991) *Posgraduate Research Training Today: Emerging Structures for a Changing Europe.* The Hague: Netherlands Ministry of Education and Science.

Thomas, H. (1995) Implementing change: a case study of devolved formula-based resource allocation systems in two UK universities. PhD Thesis, Anglia Polytechnic University (unpublished).

Thompson, E. P. (1971) *Warwick University Limited: Industry, Management and the Universities.* Harmondsworth: Penguin.

Torrington, D. and Hall, L. (1987) *Personnel Management: a New Approach.* London: Prentice Hall International.

Trow, M. (1994) *Managerialism and the Academic Profession: Quality and Control.* London: Open University Quality Support Centre.

Truscot, B. (1943) *Redbrick University.* London: Faber.

Truscot, B. (1945) *Redbrick and These Vital Days.* London: Faber.

Twiss, B. C. (1992) *Managing Technological Innovation.* London: Pitman.

UCoSDA (USDTU) (1992) *Higher Education Administration: Strategies for Professional Development.* Green Paper no. 2. London: UCoSDA.

UCoSDA (1994a) *Higher Education Management and Leadership.* Green Paper no. 9. London: UCoSDA.

UCoSDA (1994b) *A Handbook for University Administrators and Managers.* London: CVCP.

UCoSDA (1995) *Training and Development for University Administrators.* Briefing Paper no. 16. London: UCoSDA.

UGC (1986) *Planning for the Late 1980s: Recurrent Grant for 1986/87.* Circular Letter 4/86. London: UGC.

UK Council for Graduate Education (1995) *Graduate Schools.* Durham: UKCGE.

Universities' Statistical Record (various years) *University Statistics.* Cheltenham: USR.

University of Central England in Birmingham Student Union (1995) *Unpublished Report of Senate.* Birmingham: University of Central England In Birmingham.

Van Rossum, E. and Taylor, I. (1987) The relationship between conceptions of learning and good teaching: a scheme for cognitive development. Paper presented to the American Educational Research Association Annual Meeting, Washington, DC.

Wade, H. W. R. and Forsythe, C. F. (1994) *Administrative Law.* Oxford: OUP.

Walford, G. (1987) *Restructuring Universities: Politics and Power in the Management of Change.* Beckenham: Croom Helm.

Warner, D. and Crosthwaite, E. (1992/3) Human resource management in higher education, *Current Business Research*, 1(3), 48–70.

Warner, D. and Crosthwaite, E. (1995) *Human Resource Management in Higher and Further Education.* Buckingham: SRHE/Open University Press.

Warner, D. A. and Kelly, G. (eds) (1993) *Managing Educational Property.* Buckingham: SRHE/Open University Press.

Warner, D. A. and Leonard, C. (1992) *Income Generation Handbook: a Practical Guide for Educational Institutions.* Buckingham: SRHE/Open University Press.

Warnock, M. (1989) *Universities: Knowing Our Minds.* London: Chatto Counter Blasts.

Warren, R. C. (1994) The collegiate ideal and the organisation of the new universities, *Reflections on Higher Education*, 6, 34–55.

Weick, K. E. (1976) Educational organisations as loosely coupled systems, *Administrative Science Quarterly*, 21, 1–19.

Weil, S. (1994) *Introducing Change from the Top in Universities and Colleges: Ten Personal Accounts.* London: Kogan Page.

Weiss, C. H. (1982) Policy research in the context of diffuse decision making, *Journal of Higher Education*, 53(6), 619–39.

Welsh, J. M. (1978) The supervision of postgraduate research students, *Research in Education*, 19, 77–8.

Whiston, T. G. and Geiger, R. L. (eds) (1992) *Research and Higher Education: the United Kingdom and the United States.* Buckingham: Open University Press.

Whitchurch, C. (1992) Planning and funding. In *A Handbook for Administrators in Higher Education.* Sheffield: CVCP Universities' Staff Development and Training Unit.

White Paper, Office of Science and Technology (1993) *Realising our Potential: a Strategy for Science, Engineering and Technology*, Cm 2250. London: HMSO.

Whitehead, A. (1929) *The Aims of Education and Other Essays.* New York: Free Press (1967 edn).

Wiener, M. J. (1985) *English Culture and the Decline of the Industrial Spirit, 1850–1980.* London: Pelican.

Williams, G. (1992) *Changing Patterns of Finance in Higher Education.* Buckingham: SRHE/Open University Press.

Wilson, R. M. S. (1981) Financial management in universities, *Public Finance and Accountancy*, 7(6).

The World Bank (1993) *Higher Education: Issues and Options for Reform.* Washington DC: World Bank.

The World Bank (1994) *Higher Education: The Lessons of Experience.* Washington DC: World Bank.

Index

References in italic indicate figures or tables.

The Society for Research into Higher Education

The Society for Research into Higher Education exists to stimulate and coordinate research into all aspects of higher education. It aims to improve the quality of higher education through the encouragement of debate and publication on issues of policy, on the organization and management of higher education institutions, and on the curriculum and teaching methods.

The Society's income is derived from subscriptions, sales of its books and journals, conference fees and grants. It receives no subsidies, and is wholly independent. Its individual members include teachers, researchers, managers and students. Its corporate members are institutions of higher education, research institutes, professional, industrial and governmental bodies. Members are not only from the UK, but from elsewhere in Europe, from America, Canada and Australasia, and it regards its international work as among its most important activities.

Under the imprint *SRHE & Open University Press*, the Society is a specialist publisher of research, having some 60 titles in print. The Editorial Board of the Society's Imprint seeks authoritative research or study in the above fields. It offers competitive royalties, a highly recognizable format in both hardback and paperback and the worldwide reputation of the Open University Press.

The Society also publishes *Studies in Higher Education* (three times a year), which is mainly concerned with academic issues, *Higher Education Quarterly* (formerly *Universities Quarterly*), mainly concerned with policy issues, *Research into Higher Education Abstracts* (three times a year), and *SRHE News* (four times a year).

The Society holds a major annual conference in December, jointly with an institution of higher education. In 1993, the topic was 'Governments and the Higher Education Curriculum: Evolving Partnerships' at the University of Sussex in Brighton. In 1994, it was 'The Student Experience' at the University of York and in 1995, 'The Changing University' at Heriot-Watt University in Edinburgh. Conferences in 1996 include 'Working in Higher Education' at Cardiff Institute of Higher Education.

The Society's committees, study groups and branches are run by the members. The groups at present include:

Teacher Education Study Group
Continuing Education Group
Staff Development Group
Excellence in Teaching and Learning

Benefits to members

Individual

Individual members receive:

- SRHE: News, the Society's publications list, conference details and other material included in mailings.
- Greatly reduced rates for *Studies in Higher Education* and *Higher Education Quarterly*.
- A 35 per cent discount on all SRHE & Open University Press publications.
- Free copies of the Proceedings – commissioned papers on the theme of the Annual Conference.
- Free copies of *Research into Higher Education Abstracts*.
- Reduced rates for conferences.
- Extensive contacts and scope for facilitating initiatives.
- Reduced reciprocal memberships.
- Free copies of the *Register of Members' Research Interests*.

Corporate

Corporate members receive:

- All benefits of individual members, plus
- Free copies of *Studies in Higher Education.*
- Unlimited copies of the Society's publications at reduced rates.
- Special rates for its members e.g. to the Annual Conference.
- The right to submit application for the Society's research grants.

Membership details: SRHE, 3 Devonshire Street, London WIN 2BA, UK. Tel: 0171 637 2766. Fax: 0171 637 2781
Catalogue: SRHE & Open University Press, Celtic Court, 22 Ballmoor, Buckingham MK18 1XW. Tel: (01280) 823388.

HUMAN RESOURCE MANAGEMENT IN HIGHER AND FURTHER EDUCATION

David Warner and Elaine Crosthwaite (eds)

The major element of the budget of all educational institutions is spent on people. Their management and motivation is a prime concern of educational managers. At a time of unprecedented changes, this book provides the first ever comprehensive coverage of the key aspects of human resource management – central to the success of every educational institution.

Human Resource Management in Higher and Further Education has been written by a team of senior educational managers, academics and external experts. They examine the current major issues and future challenges; reflect and explore the trend toward greater managerialism; and include helpful case studies as well as analytical accounts of the topics covered. This is an essential guide to all the important areas of human resource and personnel management as they relate to further and higher education institutions.

Contents
Setting the scene – Managing change – Developing a human resource strategy – Managing diversity – The learning organization – Effective communication – Managing and rewarding performance – Executive recruitment – Essential employment law – Making educational institutions safer and healthier – Developing managers – Industrial relations strategies and tactics – Managing information – Bibliography – Index.

Contributors
Jo Andrews, David Bright, Elaine Crosthwaite, Emily Crowley, Diana Ellis, David House, Peter Knight, Elizabeth Lanchbery, Patricia Leighton, John McManus, Geoffrey Mead, Rebecca Nestor, Jennifer Tann, Elizabeth Walker, Roger Ward, David Warner, David Watson, Bill Williamson.

224pp   0 335 19377 3 (Paperback)   0 335 19378 1 (Hardback)

CPSIA information can be obtained at www.ICGtesting.com
Printed in the USA
LVOW032112270312

275005LV00013B/45/P